Healing Image
The Great Black One

ཨཱི། ཙི་འདོད་རྒྱར་འཕེབས་མགོན་དཀར་མཆོན་ལྕན་མོ།།

GOM KAR, White Mahakala

Healing Image
The Great Black One

An "International Year of Tibet" presentation

by
William Stablein Ph.D.

SLG Books
Berkeley - Hong Kong

First Published in 1991 by
SLG BOOKS
P.O. Box 9465
Berkeley, CA 94709
Tel. (415) 841-5525

All photographs by William Stablein unless otherwise credited.

All woodblocks by Roger Williams
Cover art & book design by Yuk Wah Lee
Editor: Roger Williams / Karma Tinzin Tinley
Printed in Hong Kong by Snow Lion Graphics
Typography: Mark Weiman / Regent Press

Library of Congress Cataloging-in-Publication Data

Stablein, William, 1943-
    Healing image: the great black one /
    by William Stablein
        p.   cm.
    Includes bibliographic references and index.
    ISBN 0-943389-06-2 (pbk.)
    1. Stablein, William, 1943-
2. Mahakala (Buddhist deity) - cult.
3. Spiritual life. 4. Title
BQ988.T27A3   1991
294.3' 42113--dc20   90-41469
                                                 CIP

*In memory of Sa-Bcu-rin-po-che,
Padma-rgyal-mtshan and Grandfather.*

Acknowledgements

This book has been written in the spirit of homage to those, both East and West, who have passed through my life in pursuit of the constant unknown (what I call <u>Im</u>) and how to express that invisibility or Godhead in a creative and spiritual manner. More than an autobiography I am writing about a set of images that have been stepping stones and guide posts through the plethora of crosscultural grafts and pursuit of hidden things. I will grasp this opportunity to express my grief at the passing away of Professors Balkrsna Gokhale who imparted to me an appreciation of the historical approach to culture, Yoshito Hakeda with whom I extensively read and translated the Mulamadhyamikakarikas (the emptiness school), Anton Sigmund Čerbu who was my mentor in the prajñāpāramitā (perfection of Wisdom school) tradition and Royal Wieler who helped bring to life the ancient Vedas of the Indoeuropeans and hence add to the memories of my grandfather. I remember them with fondness and admiration. During my stay in Nepal, I had the good fortune of assisting the late Dr. Bethel Fleming in the establishment of a crosscultural medical clinic on the premises of the Monkey Temple. I remember with fondness Terry Beck, Joe Reinhart and Rex Jones for their innumerable suggestions and stimulating fellowship. My utmost thanks go to the officials of the Nepalese Government, Santibhavan University and the Nepal National Archives. My mentors and living companions were the members of the Karmarājamahāvihāra (the monkey temple) in Kathmandu as well as the Ladakhi students at Banaras University. Whenever I needed some expertise on the subject of Nepalese culture and Ayurvedic medicine or someone to comment on my own scholarly efforts I called on Manavajra-Vajrācārya: he was the main priest at my marriage ceremony. Thank you Will and Ann for your patience and understanding, considering my lack of psychological support; and for Will, my physical presence for the past two years. Thanks Ellen and Dr. Tom Pautler, the godparents of Will and Ann, for your continual encouragement, advice and rapport with the family. Joe Jauquet, Bob Lyons, Richard and Susan Baldwin, and Stephanie and Richard Volkman, Kenny Mandell and Marilyn Stablein, as a group have been a source of energy for my writing. I hope Jay Hammermiester does not mind me giving away some of his secrets concerning motorcycle care. I would like to thank my sister Junemarie for keeping me informed of her healing treks into the North-West wilderness with my nephew Ron; hence maintaining the nature-worship tradition of Grandfather. I want to thank Roger and Frances Williams at Snow Lion Graphic /SLG Books, for their enthusiasm, professional know-how and willingness to extend themselves for the sake of the publication. Thank you Marge Moench in Sonoma for your Margework supportive meditation group and good friendship. Nancy Barclay, a participant in the meditation sessions, who demonstrated an uncommon interest in Buddhism and the healing traditions graciously copy edited the text in one of its crucial phases. Thank you Shirlee Francis in Sonoma for your fast and accurate typing skills when I was without my computer. A special thanks goes to Nan Perrott and Sean Daily for their special attention. Jill Gruetter offered some last minute suggestions that were very useful. I owe a very special thanks to Thelma Zulch and her son Bill who are always there with love and practical encouragement. I would like to offer a special acknowledgement to all our friends in the various Twelve step programs in Seattle, and Sonoma County.

A Note On Language And Culture

Except for four Chinese phrases Kuan-yin, Tai-chi, Yung-hung-ko and Tien-an-mein, all foreign words that have dashes between the syllables like gzhal-yas-khang are Tibetan. All other foreign words are Sanskrit. When reading the Tibetan terms the reader should be conscious of the fact that when there are adjoining consonants such as the 'mg' in mgon-po or the 'gzh' in gzhal the first consonant, except in some Western Tibetan and ladakhi dialects, is not pronounced. Also, when the syllable ends in a consonant or sibilant it is not pronounced and changes its sound, like in yas, the 's' is dropped in the pronunciation, and the sound 'a' changes to the phoneme 'e' as in ye.

There are an enormous number of Sanskrit words, not only in Tibetan ritual and teachings, but in all languages influenced by Hindu and Mahāyāna Buddhist spiritual culture. Indeed, Mahāyāna and Vajrayāna Buddhism are sometimes called the way of the mantra (Mantrāyāna). This is because translators and practitioners have always felt the need to pass on the original feeling and spiritual empowerment of the Sanskrit word. The Sanskrit alphabet has retained its sense of being the Mother alphabet as noted by the term mātrikā which means Grandmother. There is the expectation among most of the followers of Mahāyāna and Vajrayāna Buddhisim that the Sanskrit letters and sounds plays a significant role in their spiritual practice. There are always Sanskrit syllables and words not only in Tibetan mantras, but in all other languages that use Sanskrit as a sacred ground. In this book all mantras and seed syllables (like *om* or *hūm*) will be in Italics. Mantras and seed syllables are passed on from teacher to student, and in the context of ritual it is purely academic to attempt to standardize their sounds. Musical notations as used in the rites denote a more realistic utterance. In meditation the sounds come from within.

The Sanskrit words throughout the text have the standard

diacritical marks as represented by various dictionaries and grammars. I use the symbol 'sh' instead of the 's'. There is no notation for the nasal anusvara or for the semivowel 'r' as in the word Sanskrit which technically speaking should both have a dot under the 'm' and the 'r'. The usual diacritical mark used in the Tibetan transliteration is the 'h' (with a dot). We did not use these in order to simplify printing.

Among the people of Nepal, the Newars are the predominant linguistic group in Kathmandu Valley – some are Buddhists and others are Hindu. The Buddhist Newars practise the rites of Vajrayāna Buddhism and use the original Tantras, written in Sanskrit, as a source of inspiration. The priests are called Vajracāryas, i.e. Buddhist teachers of the Mahāyāna and Vajrayāna paths. Vajra designates our spiritually and hidden empowered environment. Their colloquial tongue, besides Nepali, is Newari and many Newars speak Tibetan.

Forward

Dr. William Stablein here shares with the reader his adventures in India and Nepal of living with Tibetans and gradually getting within their system. In this sense his account is probably unique for a Fulbright awardee to have stretched out his stay, mostly in Nepal, for a successful embrace of Tibetan religious values, and to have so much to show for it in his personal transformation of consciousness. He asked himself what events and which individuals influenced him in his quest of The Great Black One (Mahakala). His memory is strong, even recalling the F. D. Lessing notebooks on the Great Black One, which I let him examine some twenty years ago when he was finishing his studies at Columbia University. The University awarded him a Ph.D. on academic grounds. In the present work, William does exhibit his scholarly side with some translation of Mahakala evocation literature, and the reader is treated to a portion of his dissertation, going with the reproduction of six tankas. In contrast, most of his discourse is an honest, uncomplicated, depiction of his living conditions there, his feelings, dreams, and spiritual experiences.

The underlying theme is comradeship, and that is why we find pictures of his Tibetan and Ladakhi friends. He also includes photos of the Mgon-po ceremony that were taken by himself at the New Year's ceremony of svayambhunath in 1969, 70, and 71. All together, there are thirty-two pages of pictures. Dr. Stablein demonstrates his ease on moving through images, a topic on which he has insightful remarks.

The production of this book mirrors the author's own frustrations and successes during these years of trials and redemption.

Alex Wayman
Professor of Sanskrit
Columbia University
New York, New York

Table of Contents

List of Illustrations

List of Plates
(Following page 242)

Plate 7A: Adornment of fire and flowers for offering cake.

Plate 8. The divine eyes on the great reliquary (caitya) of Svayambhunath. The four cornered pillar from which the eyes are staring represent the four keys of balance and harmony, i.e. literally, the four domains of Brahma (Brahmavihara) which gives us an idea of how the eyes are seeing (with friendliness, compassion, joy and equanimity).

Plate 9. Nepalese two handed Mahākāla.

Plate 10. The Brahmin Mahākāla.

Plate 11. Priest making offerings.

Plate 12. Sonam.

Plate 13. The spire rising above the eyes. The golden spire (chatrabali) with its thirteen circular canopies (chatra) representing the thirteen realms that a person might pass through on the way to enlightenment and the sacred knowledge of all forms (sarvakarajnatajnana).

Plate 14. Ratnabirsingh.

Plate 15. Outdoor ceremony during Gunla.

Plate 16. Tibetan sacred music at the monkey temple.

Plate 17. Nepalese musicians playing sacred music in the morning time at Svayambhunath.

Plate 18. Mahākāla with the crown of five skullheads representing the five Buddhas.

Plate 19. Mahākāla with his five-colored mansion.

Plate 20. Another perspective of the skull that is filled with black beans indicating the conglomerated and congealed darkness within ourselves about to be fed to The Great-Black-One.

Plate 21. The image staring through the iron gates at the pilgrims.

Plate 22. Image of flayed human skin.

Plate 23. Image of flayed tiger and elephant skin.

Plate 24. Weapons used for torture.

Plate 25. One of the black boxs that contains the effigy.

Plate 26. The priest becomes Mahākāla in order to quell the dark forces with his vajra-dagger.

Plate 27. Eight-handed Mahākāla.

Plate 28. Four-faced twelve-handed Mahākāla.

Plate 29. Karma Bkah-rgyud-pa four-handed Mahākāla with consort Sri Devi and retinue.

Plate 30. Four-handed Mahākāla.

Introduction

The Great-Black-One as part of the title sounds a little ominous, and the image that arises in the reader's mind should not be without interest. The Healing Image, on the other hand may access a different sort of image and feeling. It is curious that for most people these two phrases in our title will usually conjure a variety of sensations which in some way are opposing and often difficult to reconcile. This book is about my own journey that led me to the reconciliation of the dark and wrathful with the peaceful and idealistic.

In Sanskrit, The Great-Black-One is called Mahākāla, which also translates Great-Time. In Buddhist texts, the adjective Great often refers to the extrardinary, the mystical or the archetypal. For example, Great-Man, Mahāpurusā, does not refer just to a hero, to someone who performed a great deed or a wealthy man, but to a cosmic being who controls the movements of the planets and the configuration of the planets themselves: Mahā (for mahat in Sanskrit compounds) refers to a quality of experience difficult or impossible to consistantly describe—a poetic and spiritual condition. To continue our example, more commonly, Great-Man refers to the Buddhist ideal of humaneness, i.e. the Bodhisattva, the individual who gives up the isolation of nirvāna in order to be reborn as a human being for the sake of helping others. Literally, nirvāna means to blow out (vā=blow,nir=out) which designates the blowing out of the fires of lust, envy, greed,

1

hatred and so on. Nirvāna can also be thought of as the transformation or recycling of these malicious forces. The complete
blowing out of the emotions is called parinirvāna, sometimes the
word for death. For the Bodhisattva there is a constant interplay
between removal from the world, and working with the emotions in the world as a way to help others: the latter fulfills the
Bodhisattva vow. Mahākāla, Whose Time is Great, refers to an
extraordinary time—a Great Time within and at the same time
encompassing ordinary time. This is the sense behind the image
of Mahākāla in union with his consort Srī devī which is thought
of in the most sublime sense as The Great-sign or seal,i.e.
Mahāmudrā. A mudrā (sometimes designating a signature or
seal) is an image, gesture or other symbol that sends a message
that is hard to put into words, but usually can be described in a
variety of philosophical and poetic ways. Mahāmudrā designates pure experience in the realm where the transpersonal and
personal unite; where the spiritual and material become
undifferentiated and where relationships are empowered with
excstasy and compassion: These are all qualities (of the Im) that
belong to Mahākāla, The Great-Black-One.

The writing style of this book is from a personal point of view
and is written in the first person, but it is also substantive in that
I am describing how the ideas, symbols and meditations learned
in my exploration changed the life around me, and at the same
time, connected my Asian-Tibetan influences with the culture of
my family of origin represented by my grandfather. I realized
later in life that without my grandfather's childhood tutoring the
spiritual quest would not have been so rich and edifying. The
text is autobiographical, but does not lead the reader through a
linear time sequence. Rather than moving from one point in time
to another, the text takes us from one image to another as related
to my own journey and quest for the mysteries of The Great-
Black-One as discovered in my study, initiations, travels, dialogue with my teachers, musing, meditations, my experiences as
a mentor-counselor and playtime in my Grandfather's Bavarian
forest.

The photographs are meant to reveal the text, those aspects of
my life that place the Asian-Tibetan influences in relief, which
also reflect the shades and light of the ritual meditative practices

of Mahākāla. The religious paintings, thankas, were painted by my friend Mr. Wang-rgyal who resides and teaches in New York. In the sense that I wanted to see the visual representation of the prototypes, these paintings are academic. Yet, because both myself and Mr. Wang-rgyal had been given permission and were empowered to study, practice and paint the images, the paintings which are all blessed by Sa-bcu-rin-po-che, are alive with the spirit of the image—the Im.

The reader is offered an introduction to a form of healing and spiritual growth that is usually relegated to sectarian, academic or religious language. There are popular movies such as Star Wars, a movie inspired by Joseph Campbell's A Hero with a Thousand faces, that have touched, and I think stimulated our curiosity for a deeper look into the images that surround negative forces (that we call dark) and the process of healing: the shadows that lurk in our genetic and familial environment; the poisons and hooks that enmesh us in anguish and distress. There are two scenes in the trilogy of Star Wars that parallel two dominant experiences which are emphasized in Buddhist Tantra: One is the awareness that oneself has the potential for being on the dark side, indeed, that oneself is really no different from the shadow that bears evil, which is what Luke Skywalker saw but did not relize when he confronted an image of Darth Vader, and cut his black helmet head off with the sword called a light saber; and then, to Luke's astonishment saw his own face in the severed helmet as it rolled on the ground. The second episode was when Luke was able to reverse the flow of the dark force to turn against itself. He was able to do this through a deep faith that his father, Darth Vader, despite his having been converted to the dark side, had retained some feelings from the good side of the force. However, the key to Luke Skywalker's success was his ability to utilize his martial-meditative skills learned from the wise Yoda to redirect the energy of his anger into self-control, compassion and self sacrifice. In this final combat with his father, he refuses to give in to the anger to deliver the death blow, which would have converted Luke to the dark force. Luke skywalker's inability to fully grasp the significance of his own propensities toward the dark side in the beginning of the trilogy, in his training period to become a Jedi warrior, portrays the

psychological and moral problem of spiritual practice that re-
volves around the mercurial and trickster nature of the dark
images within oneself. It is the repression and misdirection of
these forces that leads to the sickness of the mind and spirit.

One of the most devastating and common causes of chronic
mental suffering is a distorted identity and self-image. This is
especially the case in a multi-ethnic and quickly changing indus-
trialized society. We are confronted with a plethora of images in
the modern world; to which do we adhere? With which image
do we become possessed? How much of a choice do we have,
and at what period of our lives are we able to make these
choices—if we have them? How many images are drawing us in
various directions at the same time? In an atmosphere of relative
freedom of choice and permissiveness, from what image-complex, does a person draw the energy and commitment to make
decisions for oneself and for others, including the environment?
Often we do not know the image-complex that is affecting our
lives. Many individuals may never know the dominant images
that trigger their particular activities, and I am not saying that
this knowledge is even universally desirable. Yet public interest
in such an awareness is immanent.

A term that I use in my counseling procedure is "Lockup".
That is, we get used to a specific image-complex and it locks us
up. It is a kind of mental Lockup that we unwittingly do ourselves. As long as it works for us everything seems fine, but
then, when life becomes dysfunctional we need to pick the lock
and ease out of the prison. The Buddhists call this psychological
lock picking "skill in means" (upāyakausalya).

We may never clearly see the image-complex that is locking
us up. There are shapes, pictures and a host of architectonic
fragments that are pumped into our psyche from the environment. We translate them and send them back into whatever
culture we find ourselves. All the images in the universe have
the potential to lock us up. When we are totally conditioned we
are locked within the images of that conditioning. If it were not
for the underlying or transpersonal image (what I am calling the
Im) that we never completely see, which is the experience inside
ourselves and hidden within the image; never the apparent, we
would stay locked in a determined world with our pets and

goldfish. It is the force that the image stimulates, the Im, that has the power to heal and also, if misunderstood or left to it's own inner evolution, can also inflict disease and destroy. The images before us are like a complex of magnets beneath which is the magnetism itself.

It is written in Genesis that man is made in the image of God. The way I would translate our biblical phrase for this book is that God is closely related to the underlying Im of man, but so are the images of the dark side and all the invisible spirits of nature. If I were shown a painting that was supposed to depict God I would not visually believe it (at least for myself). I would wonder about the underlying Im—the invisible. Yet the image is important in the sense that it reflects the relative world. Jesus is usually depicted as a gaunt individual with a beard. He is often quite pathetic looking, but I remember in Sunday school that he smiled compassionately upon us from the walls as he carried the helpless lamb. In other pictures he actually looked somewhat robust. And then, there were the paintings that my grandmother had on her walls, like Jesus hanging on the cross with the sadistic Roman soldiers gloating over his torture. The downtrodden and suffering look that has been associated with that special insight into the nature of things has become a kind of fashion. If one looks like they think Jesus looked they feel a close proximity to Jesus and indeed to God. The same can be said for the followers of any religion. What is liberating about the Hindu and Buddhist imagery is its vast and opulent representation. There is the suffering image of Sakyamuni at the end of his renunciation, the peaceful Bodhisattvas, the dreadful image of the wrathful Mahākāla, the peaceful and wrathful deities in union and so on. We would like to think it was not the original intention of the authors of the Great Religions for the coming generations to mimic any particular form or personality type. Those who have come to me for mentoring and counseling, in one way or another, have experienced a phase of active psychic revolution, where the traditional image-usually connected with the parental image—was in some way displaced, wounded and always repressed. The image desperately needed to be revealed and translated in a new way to fit into a new space which include technology, the culture of the third world, the woman's movement and an amalgamation of spiritualities, life styles and health deliveries. My father used to say that there is "nothing new under the sun", but every few years everything seems different to me. Individuals cannot recover and be healed unless they face the dark abnormalities of our age. If it is true "there is nothing new under the sun" we have been distracted by the magic of a great illusion perpetrated by our own knowledge.

I mention my experience as a mentor-counselor not because the tone of the book is intended to be psychologically oriented, but rather, because I was brought into contact with an aspect of the tragic and depressive in others that helped me see myself through another window—a darker stained glass window. The colors of this window are sometimes deceptively pretty and mysterious. I was always curious about the stained glass windows in the churches when I was a small boy. They were beautiful, but also dark at times. For me, the presence of omniscience that seemed to empower these wonderful creations of glass and color was a little frightening. Even now, when I view these windows in a nearby chapel it is the underlying darkness that strikes me as the basis for the transformation of hue and texture that comes about through the sun's rays. The light seems to cast a shadow of images that reminds me of another set of dark forces that kept reappearing in my early life. They were Great-Dark-Ones that seemed to battle with the light—within and without. The windows became reflective of not only the traditional christian imagery, but stimulated the feeling that darkness and the Great-Black-Ones were everywhere—that the sacred was somehow in all things. What is usually thought of as Psychological therapy was not popular in my childhood environment, but as the illusions around me seemed to change, the therapeutic process gradually became a pane in that stained glass window.

Therapy is the pill of our age. It has developed in it's present forms in the context of our social evolution. The image I have of myself is very hybrid and crosscultural. I have been told that it makes me a detached and often effective mentor who has a number of conceptual windows to look through. The counseling process helped me become grounded in the problems of the culture. It helped me decide to write this book which is an account my journey into the healing and contemplative practices of The Great-Black-One.

I believe that I am writing about a wildly ramified shared experience of seeking a vision and truth, but with my own set of traveling bags. The quest for realization and enlightenment has become a common process in modern society; maybe even more so than in the third world cultures that we often emulate, when it comes to spiritual and metaphysical matters. These travelling bags are filled with all the mental tools that are picked up and stored in the quest for vision and knowledge. I learned that these tools may have to be put in storage and eventually recycled and reshaped. This happened as I obtained my own vision in its various pieces and phases.

Cultivating an image is a part of the process of the seeker. The vision is both the image and Im. But when one teaches, the image part becomes very impermanent. The student is interested in image; the teacher is more concerned with Im. The phrase "to find oneself" reflects part of that process. I used the phrase a great deal when I was young. It was of great concern, but there was usually an image attached to the process—even when I did not think there was. I was looking for a self, which always turned out to have a supporting image. The image would appear in sweetness and light; offering an array of gifts. However, the image often evolved to be a dark force—an enemy. The process of finding oneself demonstrates a quirk: It is an image that lurks and follows one on the path. The image is a self that has content, but with no permanent substance. But, then, we are all image makers.

There was a T.V. special on public television that reviewed the life of Ferdinand Marcos and his family. There was one scene in the program where his teenage and adult children were singing "we are the world" while having a lavish party that must have cost thousands of dollars. The party scene made me think how we can sing out for the suffering world, and at the same time be lost in the labyrinth of our own desires. But, it is good that we sing. There are images that evolve mechanically from the rawness of the events and emotions in life, which are constantly arising with a plethora of mixed messages.

Images are siphoned from our imagination and perception;

they are an amalgamation of substance, thought and being, which find their way into our consciousness and dreams. A rock is a rock is a rock, but a rock, in our mind's eye, can be a sponge or a crystal ball. In our mind's eye anything can be anything: that does not mean it will be true, beneficial or ecologically sound. Images are representative of what we project into the world and what the world sends back to us. The demons that follow us on the path are not only there to harass, but, depending on how we see them and ourselves, may clear the cobwebs.

It is difficult to have a self-image without identifying with an image outside oneself. Images are magnetic. They magnetize their environments. They are like certain plants and trees that create a particular ecology by the virtue of their very existence. They are images that come to us in our dreams and passing fancies that exist in close proximity to the rawness of our basic emotions. They are often translations of fragmented thoughts and ideas, which is the reason dream images sometimes seem weird and disjointed. Then, there are images that we just take for granted that hopefully follow us in our everyday effort for survival like the image of eating, intercourse and defecation: these are images related to raw feelings and basic needs. I think of raw structures as the elements and texture of nature. Feelings are raw and at the same time they can be conditioned. There are other raw structures that come alive in nature like storms, forest fires, snow flakes and sunsets. They are the chariots of our dreams on which ride the invisible Im. When we contemplate, do meditation or just focus, we consciously recycle and cook the image, which transforms our relationship to it. It can be an icon, word, person or being, or even an object of study.

I want to place image in nature. I will let it cook under the sun, freeze in the ice and watch to see if it will grow in the fertile ground. I will watch to see if it shudders, burps or gets an erection. Its authenticity at least as an image will then be apparent. Also, image sometimes needs to be isolated in a universe where there is no mentation or the possibility of other images influencing its essence. Image needs to be constantly cleaned and ritually purified. After going through this process many times image will be set up for empowerment, and The Great-Black-Ones will come into play. Then, the arising of the truth behind the image (Im) is possible. As it wells up one can become very calm and sometimes electrified with energy.

When I first began my studies of Mahākāla (The Great-Black-One; also thought of as Great-Time), the image of The Great-Black-One was somewhat abstract; a little bit on the level of the way philosophers talk about self or God or, the manner in which Linguists will discuss the components of a sentence; or, the way historians will plumb historical events and processes for patterns and predictive possibilities. Image came at me in a barrage of words, notecards, grammatical considerations, manuscripts and philosophical musing. During this phase I did not think much about my life with grandfather, but did have dreams and daydreams about The Great-Black-One and his universe.

The turning point, the moment in time when I made the final decision to travel to India, came at Columbia University when my mentor Professor Alex Wayman invited me to spend time in his personal library, which contained the private notes and musings of his mentor the late Professor Ferdinand Lessing. Professor Lessing, who participated in a Scientific Expedition to the Northwestern provinces of China in the late 30's had taken numerous notes on the Mahākāla rite as practiced in the Yung-ho-kung Lamasery in Peking: he bequeathed these notes and papers to his student (my teacher) Professor Alex Wayman who in turn graciously allowed me to study them in his private library for as long as needed. My presence in this minijewel of an archive gave me the focus and inspiration to continue my journey and contemplation. These notes presented to me the information and feelings to make the final decision to pursue The Great-Black-One as a research project. I set my efforts on applying for grants, and I found myself in India.

A little over a decade ago I wrote a doctoral dissertation titled The Mahākāla-Tantra: A Theory of Ritual Blessings and Tantric Medicine: this is an edition of the first four chapters of the Ngor manuscript which I found in Northern India. I call it the Ngor manuscript because it was kept in the Ngor monastery in Eastern Tibet. In reflection, I was lucky to find at least one medieval manuscript (it dates back to the twelfth century): it is a photocopy that a well known Indian scholar, Rāhula Sanskrityāyana, brought back from Tibet in the early nineteen-thirties. He found

it at the Ngor monastery, and donated it to the Bihar Research
Society, which is where I found the manuscript. My dissertation
is also a critical edition of the first eight chapters of the Nepalese
version of the manuscript. The complete manuscript in its
original form was in fifty chapters, but the first eight of the
Nepalese version, and the first four of the manuscript I found in
Bihar, India (the Ngor version) has particular philosophical, ritualistic and meditative appeal. The dissertation contains a technical introduction, including the theory that Buddhist-Tantra is a
system of healing. This is no longer a theory, but an accepted
point of reference.

The completion of the thesis was as much the results of a
dream to attain all those spiritual qualities that one reads and
hears about as it was to fulfill the requirements of an advanced
degree. Also, it was very much a part of the process of resolving
these seeming differences between the Judaic-Christian and Eastern notions of how to think and approach the dark forces of the
universe. A friend has told me, using my own concept, that
despite my interest in the matters of the spirit, I was locked up in
the atmosphere and language of the 60's.

What interested me the most (and still does) were the ideas
and practices that aim to transform the disease process into a
healing and preventative dimension. Since the images that depict this process are not only peaceful and cherubim-like deities,
but also images of the dark and wrathful, I was forced by my
own sense of cultural relativity to come to terms with my early
Christian conditioning regarding darkness, evil and the satanic
dimension. Help came from an unexpected source, the memories and spirit of my grandfather, which the reader will discover
in the following pages.

It has been fifteen years since I completed the final stroke to
my doctoral thesis. The thesis is fairly typical for the kinds of
dissertations that were required, at that time, in university de-
partments which emphasized the classical languages—in my
case that meant the various dialects of Sanskrit and Tibetan.
Students were recommended to locate an original manuscript,
the older the better, and to search out as many manuscripts of the
same kind (and of the same period if possible), which would
then be collated in order to make a critical edition—that is, a

close approximation of an accurate text-grammatically and aesthetically. In the case of The Mahākāla-Tantra, I was able to find eleven manuscripts useful for making the edition.

Editing and collating these old manuscripts is like working on a puzzle. Which ones are the most authentic, and what is one's criterion for authenticity? And how does one collate and make them into an approximation of a correct text? Editing texts brings us closer to a shared experience of image-space. It represents an order of things that has been deemed authentic simply because it is the progeny of a survived tradition that has caught the imaginative, aesthetic and humanitarian sensibilities of people. And, then the Im of the manuscript has the same Im as the icon itself. That is, the manuscript carries the weight of the image beneath the image. Editing texts has always been an important task in the history of the written word. No sooner does a text come close to becoming a classic, that the critical public will want to question its authenticity. For this reason the original handwritten or computer hidden text of a famous author will be in demand. People want to know not only what the author or school of thought intended to say, but the thought process behind the final result.

When a text has multiple translations as the Buddhist Tantras, which were translated not only into Tibetan, Newari and Chinese, but also into central Asian languages such as Mongolian, Tocharian, Khotanese, and Soghdian, we absorb a variety of semantic nuances, and the result is a number of versions. Since it is difficult to categorize any particular version as the absolute original manuscript, we can always be on the lookout for translations that reflect an earlier manuscript than the ones available. In some cases the translations reveal an earlier lost Sanskrit text. Sometimes, as in the case of the Mahākāla-Tantra, the text will be a combination of versions; possibly from two different time periods. In the example of the Ngor manuscript, the first four chapters that I edited, reflect a previously unknown manuscript and system of The Mahākāla cycle of ritual-meditation. Hence, in order to give the reader a previously unknown and possibly deliberately hidden dimension of the practice and philosophy of Mahākāla, I included in my thesis the standard Newari version as well as the Ngor version of the first four chapters.

The image of a manuscript or book has a number of hidden dimensions. Except for the title, the written word is itself invisible until the book is opened. The book has to be of interest, the pages must be turned, and then, one needs to be able to read the contents. One's education and life experiences acts as a set of relay mirrors to bring the new information into one's consciousness. The manuscript is an image and contains the content of a sacred tradition. But every image has the weight of its own content. After the book has been picked up, turned over, read, maybe reread, thought about, discussed and possibly even written about, it's ideas and imagery will soak deeply into the fabric of the reader's being, and bring forth more ideas and imagery. I like to think of this space within the reader as a dimension where the images and ideas flow and amalgamate into new images. It is an alive image space. The manuscript itself is a living image.

I still have an original Nepalese manuscript with its wooden cover on which is smudged red and yellow powders. I can remember the people of Kathmandu Valley rubbing the powders onto the wooden covers (on this very book), and then returning the powders, mixed with a little sacred water from the near by Bagmati river onto their foreheads—a blessing and empowerment: it is the one labeled E in my thesis. Images contain the contents of culture and emotions.

It is this personal-cultural process that has captured the heart of my interest and is the dominant focus of this book. The reader can expect some descriptive accounts of my experiences in the evolution of accommodating the study and practice of The Great-Black-One into the flow of events of which I have found myself.

I have been a practicing mentor-counselor for over ten years in matters of personal growth, relationships and more recently co-dependency and addiction. Counseling has been a way to extend my own work on myself to help others work on their own processes—a new addition to my own personal practice, as well as the manner in which I express myself concerning philosophical and spiritual matters. Having practiced with others in such a way has helped me to detach myself from a number of dogmatic and hence harmful ideas. It has also kept me close to the problems of social change in our society, and finally brought me to the point where I felt the confidence to relate the practices of The

Great-Black-One.

A counselor works with the images of other individuals, which of course stimulate the images within himself: at first, with some exceptions, they are fragmented images. When a person is engaged in a spiritual practice his images are ordered in various degrees by the practice and routine. The individual who seeks counseling, without exception, has a need to express his or her stories as related to these fragmented images; they are self images and images of other people and things. Like a book or a series of paintings, they are a text, at least they become so, as the counseling process continues. Each story is individual and at the same time it will always contain elements with which the counselor himself can identify—with which almost anyone could identify. The images are archetypal. Images associated with the basic emotions such as lust, hatred, envy and confusion can be accessed consciously and profoundly in the counseling process

It takes time for new images to cook in one's consciousness, for them to become integrated into the nomenclature of the machinery of thought and imagination. My main impetus for following the path of Mahākāla was the intuition that here was a treasure of wisdom and practice. To many "following the path" means to go through the steps; to adhere to the rules to one's best ability: And this I have done, but with a compulsion to locate the original manuscript, the prototype, the most workable ritual, the best contemplation and the ultimate spiritual power. "Following the path" came to mean "looking for the path inside the path". And, fortunately Buddhism has opened a very large space for such a seeker.

Now that I am writing and teaching about the way of The Great-Black-Ones, I have won and lost some challenges, and also received some blessings. But in all truthfulness, I cannot say that I have stopped looking for a path within the path. Meanwhile, I will share whatever is useful for others and the environment. During graduate school, I was always practicing something, zen, tai-chi, yoga, being present and all kinds of other things. Yet, it was a leap to begin to think in terms of a definite practice associated with The Great-Black-One as a transformation tool of the negative emotions of ordinary life. It was filling in the Hologram, where all experience eventually became contemplative. This was very much due to the guidance and wisdom of my primary Tibetan teacher Padma-rgyal-mtshan (from now on Petsan), and our shared spiritual guide Sa-bcu-rim-po-che.

How does the image well up? The image seems to liquify and flow, in a sense, into the vats of the senses, where it ferments and takes on the character of the senses themselves, like wine which takes on the flavor of the oak barrels in which it is stored. The image can taste, smell, hear, touch, see and think. It feels depressed or elated as reflected in the host. It can generate terror and extreme happiness or any feeling in between. The image and the host are co-dependant—not always in the pejorative psychological sense. Sometimes the image is the dominant force and sometimes the host, although the host, in the context of his practice, can always negotiate with the image. The practitioner can always create a new kind of relationship with the image. If one eats too much, with help, one can alter their eating habits. There is always the possibility of making a new kind of relationship with the image. The mind is fluid.

The mind-body complex in some way is always at odds with itself and with its images. The image, regardless of its spiritual and archetypal nature, manifests itself as unstable and out of control. When the image feels, it is drawing from one's own feeling-energy supply. When it tastes, it is tasting the host. It is feeding on the hosts psychic innards. When it sees, it influences the host to see a distorted picture and so on. It is difficult for the host to exercise free will—on the other hand, it is equally difficult to realize that one is free in the river of so many images. As soon as one is aware of the influence of image it is not always easy to cultivate conscious thought and intention.

Images are constantly arising for everyone. They arise not only through the colored glasses of the images that one has of oneself, but from the point of view of others; and then, there is also the collective imagery. Images always have a repressed structure. They pop out of their caves and possess one in the manner of spirit possession. As an image takes on both form and content, and is integrated in one's day to day practice it develops a life of its own with anthropomorphic dimensions. The practiced image connects with it's underlying Im: It becomes an ally and one's own rising divinity.

The image can be any gender, but Grandfather thought that all images were by nature female. He thought that mental images were self creative and were intrinsic to the earth, i.e. not just the earth in which we plant the seeds of plants, but the earth within, in which the seeds of images are planted and multiply. Images like words can take either gender according to fancy. The Sanskrit word for divine being or divinity, for example, is a just a matter of changing the last vowel, so, we have deva (masculine) and devā (feminine).

When Im arises and takes the form of image it does so in pairs. Which one is female and male is sometimes difficult to say, often it does not matter. The pairs are not always in opposition like water and fire or earth and iron. They are simply pairs, one of them yin and other yang. The arising polarity may be as fragmentary as an unexpected smell that may come from a long lost memory: As I would walk across the rice paddies on the way to town in Kathmandu Valley, I would catch the smell of the fresh green moss that grew around the stream in my grandfather's Bavarian forest. I can not be sure what it was that stimulated the memory. There are many images that come to us at odd moments. We usually pair off apples with apples and oranges with oranges, but our arising imagery is not restricted to such conventions of logic.

Our image-complexes at their deepest level are not only personal; they are impersonal like the seasons—until we learn to like or dislike them. A repository of images is in space. Grandfather thought that all our thoughts and actions were recorded in space, and with the development of esoteric knowledge one could tap the images therein. It is electronic space—a natural phenomena. We seem to be coming come closer and closer to grandfather's belief. Space is a gigantic image storehouse, and now that we know something about this hidden dimension, we make movies and write books about black holes, cyborgs and machines that tap the imagery in this image-space. It affects our lives to the point where the functions and desires in our life cycle are on the verge of electronic manipulation. Life experiences and electronics are coalescing. An image can move from the thought process to the video screen in no time at all.

We imagine underlying and transpersonal forces as having

many shapes, sometimes tinged with the lamentation and pain of our own creation. Our images come with our desires, our material world, our thoughts and all those ephemeral bodies we cling onto so dearly. It is difficult not to express those underlying powers of nature and self in anything but anthropomorphic symbols. We see the gods and even the concept of an ineffable one-god as having human characteristics—exactly in the way we designate and view material objects such as sexy cars, smart computers, and so on.

What about the underlying ineffable Im, which despite our mental efforts, is difficult to imagine or designate; yet, is able to manifest in the material or the event? Is it always benevolent or enlightening? What I am calling Im is the energy with which the material world can be empowered. What I want to emphasize is that the information space in the universe gives us what we pump it for, and quite a bit more that is unknown.

Because of the experiences connected with the images of darkness that stem from my grandfather and Asia, for me, The Great-Black-One has crossed culture—its form is archetypal and unavoidable. I call it Rudee. I attempt to focus on its underlying Im, and not be seduced and frightened by its shape and inner activity, which can be at times disconcerting. Rudee has helped me understand the nature of the archetype as a synthesis of an uprising in nature and my own mind. Of course Rudee is an illusion in relationship to its transpersonal Im.

In culture the Im comes to a few through traditional ritual and contemplation: it is also channeled through various forms of therapy and innovative spiritual practices. The Im also moves through the arts which can lead one to his or her own artistic expression. Sometimes the Im arises in a hideous and sick form as in sadomasochistic and satanic cults-this is not because of the Im; it is revealed according to the practice and life of each person. The artist, the contemplative and the killer will imagine the Im according their own proclivities. But the form or action in which they find the Im will be a mask.

For me the question has been for a long time, how does the ineffable empower the life around us, the substance, thought and being? How are the dark forces that seem to be buried in our hatred, lust, envy and greed creep into the castles we call

home, into the very fabric we wear next to our skins and into the
food and medicine we share? The Im is always there; it is in the
manner it arises that makes our day. Grandfather and the manner in which I was exposed to Eastern philosophy set me in a
contemplative and therapeutic relationship with the shadowy
and hidden dimensions of our world.

CHAPTER I

Dark Clouds

"But how to imagine a time within a time or a time beyond time?" I once asked my Tibetan mentor Petsan. He replied by asking me to meditate on blackness—pure blackness. Try it! It is almost impossible for any length of time. He then asked me to think about the events or problems in my life that were difficult to think about. He watched me. A few times he interjected "No, not that one" as if he could see the very images I was seeing, and hear the thoughts I was thinking. He asked me to imagine myself to do horrible deeds to the point where I was thinking about the worst possible things and activities imaginable. Finally, I told him that it was almost impossible for me to think of and imagine myself taking part in such terrible, disgusting activities—that I would probably die first. But, then, I was not dead, was I? There was a moment of bright recognition—a flash of light and a peace of mind.

My response to Petsan's exercise concerning my question "How can we imagine a time within a time or a time beyond time?" also answered my other thought as to the nature of Great Blackness: How to imagine pure blackness? What is Great Blackness? Later in another teaching session I mentioned that when I was trying to meditate on pure blackness different colors seeped and streaked through the black space. He then had me do the same exercise with red, green, blue and yellow. Of

course, the same relative phenomena took place. It was hard to
focus on any one color for any length of time. Other colors
tumbled and darted their way through the color screen like a
video space game machine. The Great-Black-One became The
Great-Red-Green-Blue-Yellow or White-One, but it was not easy
to maintain the one color focus or even a balance—an equanimity. I could not help but think, "what color is the self?" That was
the point. Petsan said it would be equally difficult to locate a
permanent self. There were many components in those images:
shape, color, function, cultural value, universal value and imagined values and meanings. I was an image which projected an
image. It seemed like Petsan was in control. It seemed like I was
learning to be in control.

But what about the seeds of images that are not always conscious—especially to children? What about the images that
create images within the hidden dimensions of our mind about
which we know very little? And, then, what about the images
that come out of the collective consciousness that produce unpredictable experiences for the individual. Images that go back
before I was alive concern me. Some people call this cellular
memory related to what Jung called collective unconscious. Images and seeds of images are not always conscious—especially
when we are children. How these images manifest in our own
lives determine the manner in which they can be translated. For
example, The Great-Black-One according to my teacher Petsan,
has been with me for a long time—not only through the teaching
that I was receiving or through the pictures in this book, but
through the qualities of Great-Blackness, the Im that empower
the pictures.

Early one morning about six months before I returned to
America, I took my usual meditation walk to the Monkey Temple.
Opposite from where I sat in my teachers room on a red Tibetan
carpet embroidered with a happy black dragon, a pair of al-
mond-shaped eyes peered at me through the window. These
were the now famous eyes painted on the reliquary that overlooked the Valley of Kathmandu. The room was small with
another window off to my left side, not large enough for an adult
human being to crawl through. I had been told that this window
was purposely built that way for safety reasons. Another win-

dow, next to the head lama's resting place (a bed made from a stack of Tibetan carpets) overlooked the valley where the thin golden tops of pagodas were just breaking above a layer of mist. Occasionally a mischievous monkey careened his way around the parapet on the outside of the building, and stared briefly at our little group—the head lama, the teacher, the senior monk and myself—the four of us drank chai (strong tea with hot milk, sugar and spices; known now in health food restaurants as yogi tea).

That particular morning, after I babbled on about karma, Petsan said, "You don't really understand karma." He explained that I had started my studies many lifetimes ago. Because I did not initiate or was directly involved in an action, does not mean that I was not involved as a support to a particular action itself. As an example he pointed out that centuries ago Tibet had invaded and ruled China, and the Tibetans were reaping the fruits of any malicious action that may have been initiated by the Tibetans at that time. Although I felt that this was self critical to the extreme, Petsan's example did illustrate a point that could be applied or misapplied to any group. As Petsan had considerable information about my life, he could apply his wisdom with some knowledge and skill. I had already told him, for example, about my grandfather, who I thought resembled Petsan.

Petsan reminded me that I had told him about some of my grandfather's personal practices, like building little altars in his Bavarian forest, speaking to the plants, especially the mushrooms, as if they could hear him, and painting deities, some of them black, on his buildings. He believed in a black presence that kept secret in nature, and only revealed itself when the environment was going through turmoil—or at night close to the time of the new moon. If someone surprised this black presence in one of its hiding places, it could be psychologically harmful. Grandfather communicated with this presence at certain auspicious times. Petsan felt that Mahākāla, The Great-Black-One, was at work in our family history. I am sure that grandfather would agree. Like me, he had always dreamed of traveling to the Himlayas. I was fulfilling part of his dream.

Except for my grandfather's influence during my early years, I grew up in a protestant culture: My father converted to Protestantism from Bavarian Catholicism in rebellion against grandfather's paganism and pseudochristianity; he became an ordained minister. Petsan suggested there was some karmic connection between my grandfather's homeland in Bavaria and Tibet; indeed, perhaps either I or my grandfather, at one time in the distant past, had lived in Tibet. For those familiar with the history of Asian scholarship, the karmic connection between the people of the Himalayas and the Northern Europeans is a reoccurring interest that verges on the point of fantasy. But, then, here it was again coming up in my personal life—in Asia. My father's reaction to my grandfather, said Petsan, was not so much a reaction to my grandfather's ideas and behavior, as it was against an even more remote event in his own past life, not necessarily related to grandfather. Likewise, my gravitation to grandfather's presence was due not to reacting against my father but to some events in my own past life. According to Petsan all three of us shared a karmic thread, part of which was left dangling from prehistoric times. The idea was quite appealing and opened a window to a more positive approach to family history and relationships, and stimulated memories which helped me establish a priority of image.

I can look at my life genetically. I can also look through my mind's eye at the structure of the image. The structure will include shape, substance, being and thought. I am amused that I consider seriously the possibility of having lived past lives in different countries and ethnic groups—even on different planets—planets totally out of the range of our most powerful telescopes. To paraphrase a well-known Buddhist paradigm: There are more universes than there are grains of sands on the beaches of the West Coast of America—let alone on the banks of the Ganges.

Imagery seems to flow in sets. There is an inner logic to a particular set of images. Some images are memories of historical events. They can also be dreams or even fantasies. Images can erupt from the unconscious in unpredictable moments of ecstasy, pain or fear. The image sets for each person will have their own individuality and differences.

In therapeutic settings, I sometimes asked the question: What are the thoughts and images that come to mind when you hear, read or think of the phrase "The Great-Black-One"? The ensuing answers and dialogues were always structurally similar. The question always translated into a disclosure process of repressed feelings and images. For me, this was a simple example of how the image of darkness and black can readily shift into clarity and understanding—a kind of enlightenment. Though each client expressed him or herself persc ally, the general themes concerning anxiety, guilt, remorse, repressed desires, hatred, jealously, lust and so on evolved a similar structure as related to the phrase "The Great-Black-One." It is in the therapeutic setting where a person without the direct experience of having practiced the meditation-rituals of Mahākāla can at least experience the archetypal nature and discover a transformational process. With my grandfather's help, I had asked myself this question many years ago.

I have a photograph in my mind's eye of my grandfather kneeling down in one of those dark places in his Bavarian forest communicating with the mushrooms. The spots that he loved were indeed very dark, but also included the element of sunlight which beamed through the foliage at certain times of the day, casting one of nature's common spells and pleasures. Some of these places were very sacred to grandfather. He had a reverence for nature that my father inherited as an uncanny skill for maintaining excellent gardens. Grandfather's "Bavarian forest" was actually one of the last first-growth forests in the Seattle city area, as he was proud to remind us. The forest was very dark and light at the same time—darkness at its best. The Bavarian forest, the woods, no longer exist; only the shadow of a quaint forest that could only survive in meaning and image—an Im that is lodged deep in my unconscious.

There are many kinds of darkness. An acquaintance in grade school was known for torturing animals. He would dare us to do the same and some were afraid of him and his strange power to be able to do evil deeds. He seemed to feel good and powerful about his actions. He indulged in other repulsive acts, such as saving his defecation in his lunch box and eating insects, especially slugs.

"Repugnant and fearful events in your life are there for a purpose," Petsan always said. As an initiate into the Mahākāla cycle, these events would take on a special significance for my practice in the Dharma—for my life. Mahākāla was often depicted as wallowing in vile substances, eating human flesh, drinking blood, wearing garlands of severed heads, and so on. When Petsan asked me to think of some of the worst things I have done or could possibly do, I wanted to back away from my thoughts and fantasies. In a similar way, the first time I read about Mahākāla, part of me receded from the attributes of The Great-Black-One. How could I practice what seemed like the blackest of magic and maintain my sanity?. Nineteenth century scholars often mistook the process of confronting negative emotions for black magic and dubbed the Tantras immoral.

Rising memories, emotions, feelings and dreams come to me in shades of darkness and light—also temperature. The shadows that follow destructive, malicious and ignorant processes are embraced by a light that makes the recycling and transformation of those same negative processes possible. Grandfather's forest of giant firs is now decimated—a mini example of what is happening to our planet. My grandfather was a profound influence—I find myself occasionally talking to plants; in order to realize the light around the dark. Indeed, The Great-Black-One lived in that Bavarian forest.

There is a time and place for my images—especially primal images that sometimes reek of power, greed and lust. What once was a need just to survive on a biological level, became a desire to identify with mass movements and behaviors that verged on the pathalogical. It is quite possible that the terrors and distortions of our Western civilization in the past few hundred years have their cause in the lack of authentic-power-imagery—the lack of identity. The Western world may have lost its own image when the early Christian soldier effectively neutralized the pagan gods. My grandfather in the 1920s and '30s warned his peers of a Hitler appearing in the Germanic west. He thought that the Germanic races were now without a truly spiritual outlet for their energies. They needed a replacement for their lost pagan heroes. He was ethnocentric and claimed that only the Bavarians had been able to retain the authentic-power-images of the nearly forgotten past. He was concerned that those who obsessively cultivated the image of Christ were on the edge of madness, for the Christ image by itself would not be able to transform the destructive urges of man. He said that without a wrathful God of our pagan ancestors, our civilization would be lost. The wrathful did not mean anger or destruction to grandfather. He thought that only an inner wrathful image would be able to confront and dispose the demons channeled to us from our modern environment. Somehow grandfather's Bavarian Catholicism and ancient Teutonic spiritual sensibilities combined to provide him with some very interesting—almost Buddhist insights. I still entertain the thought that he planted his spirit in Petsan in order to maintain the flow of his influence and instruction on me—such an idea is a possibility in Buddhism.

Grandfather, right or wrong, had a time and place for his images. He had a time and place for the Christ image, as well as for his Bavarian forest pantheon with all its dark forces. When I discovered Mahākāla, the Buddhist and Hindu version of The Great-Black-One in graduate school, I recalled my grandfather whose artistic sense of light and shadow seemed to tap the universe for the compressed and hidden energy of darkness. This shifted my perspective from ordinary calendrical time to the time of The Great-Black-One—that is, Great-Time. He taught me to use clock time as a kind of stepping-stone for seasonal time, and seasonal time as a stepping-stone for the time of light and darkness, and the time of light and darkness as a stepping-stone for Great-Time. It is a kind of reality orientation where the anxieties and troubles related to ordinary time can be readjusted in a higher order of things. Petsan supported my grandfather's teachings. He once said that going from one image to another is like crossing a river on slippery stones, and that I had to be very careful—especially when reaching the other side: "there will be another river to cross around the next bend in the path".

Bhairava, "The Terrible One," is a Hindu version of The Great-Black-One, and one of the main protectors of the well-known Gurkha regiment (renowned for their military prowess). The Gurkhas trained only a few hundred feet from the monastery where I stayed—a symbolic reminder of imminent possible disaster. Yet, I felt comfortable with the close proximity of the Buddhist temple, in which I was staying, to the training ground for war. I thought that my Asian war was well behind me-or was it? The nature of war, Petsan always reminded me, was primarily in ourselves, not in the machines of destruction. Petsan had the feeling that the close proximity of the Gurkha training ground to the monastery was karmic; that The Great-Black-One was fond of the training and could keep a watchful eye on the deity Bhairava, on whom Mahākāla stepped in some of the religious paintings. In a similar fashion, Petsan said, I need to process the active and emotional images in my own life in order to slip into Great-Time—an aspect of the practice of The Great-Black-One.

When I was young, part of the excitement of embarking on adventuresome activities or exploring new places was the bravado with which I would step into a new dimension of life—like going on a weekend camping trip with my father in the Canadian Rockies. The area, known as "the land of sky blue waters", and "gold country", stimulated our dreams and expectations of a cache of gold; gold country was known also for mountain lions and grizzlies. I heard a tale from an elderly native-Canadian: The story was how he killed a grizzly with a small knife which he showed me.

I had my Cub Scout hunting knife, as well as a little sack for the gold nuggets I would find. Although not exactly the same, my dream to fill my little bag with gold nuggets, and the dreadful thought that I might have to confront the grizzly were close to the experience of Great-Time. Those types of feelings are experiences of a very personal nature, especially for a young boy.

Feelings of exultation and dread also approach the symbolical and transpersonal. The delight that I felt when I found what I thought to be a piece of gold at the source of the river which my dad and I had been following, combined with the dread and fantasy of confronting a grizzly or some other monster of the wilderness produced images that have led me to a number of challenges in life. Even though the rock was fool's gold and the grizzly was never met, the image formations in my mind were powerful and lasting. I have found and lost some gold and have confronted a number of monsters; some of which have almost took my life and some who have become allies. These images and parallel feelings also have the potential to generate disappointment, anxiety, feelings of failure, lack of self-esteem, and a sense of unreality, which can lead to neurotic complexes and

lifelong mental health problems.
What The Great-Time practice offered was a way of healing.
The image of The Great-Black-One fed on the dark shadows that
I accumulated in my life through negative malicious forces and
self-inflicted punishments—The Great-Black-One ate the devil
for breakfast.
Thoughts of meeting up with a grizzly did put the fear of God
in me, but at the same time gave me a glance into the hero inside
myself.
Another image: I had the opportunity years ago to briefly
work in a silver ore mine in Kellog, Idaho. I remember when I
assisted in the revamping of an old shaft in a mine considered
unsafe, but potentially profitable. My job was to clear out the
loose rock, rebuild the support system and with the use of drills
and dynamite to expand and lengthen the tunnel, with the hope
of reopening some valuable ore veins. The men who worked in
this environment never took anything for granted. We were
fifteen hundred feet under the ground drilling the rock with
huge metal drills. Except for the light provided by my miner's
cap, it was the blackest of black; even the old timers were appre-
hensive. Most of them had experienced an underground acci-
dent of one kind or another. The underground miner was gripped
in a constant apprehension. There is always a part of myself that
fantasizes about facing fear. I hoped my apprehension and fear
could be overcome or transformed into a positive energy. It is
partly this inner quest to overcome or at least be able to cope
with fear that urges me to accept greater challenges in life—
sometimes these challenges take the form of games and sports.
But it is the daily routine of life that sometimes puts me in touch
with my most traumatic fears. Life is fraught with dangers and
anxieties, whether they be occupational hazards or motherhood—
it is the stuff of The Great-Black-One.
When we blasted the darkness fifteen hundred feet under the
ground, the odds and statistics for survival were with us. Yet,
the collective apprehension rose to a peak. The blaster shouted,
"Fire on the line," as we waited crouched behind a protected
turn in the tunnel. There was a moment of absolute silence
before the blaster turned the handle on his electric generator.
Ka-Boom! There was a brief flash of light before the earth

quaked into tiny pieces. I thought that the earth exploded in revenge for ripping the metal from its insides. As I waited for the dust to settle, a crucial moment of contemplation, I feared the reverberation would strike another spot, another tunnel or shaft. This underground experience prepared me for the practice of The Great-Black-One. Curiously, Mahākāla also is associated with extracting wealth from deep, dark places. Some of the Mahākāla practices revealed how to extract wealth from under the ground—not with drills and dynamite, but with the psychic processes of mantra, meditation and ritual which is described in chapter eight of my Doctoral thesis. But let me write briefly about the teachings I received from Petsan about this subject and give you a brief prescription of how to extract wealth from the ground.

When I was studying with Petsan the emphasis was on two meanings operating at the same time: wealth meant both the inner wealth of the spirit and material possessions; ground meant both the apparant structure of the world that we are forced to work through to arrive at the treasure and also the symbol of earth. The key to this practice, as all Tantric practices, was the preliminary meditations of The Four Keys of Balance and Harmony (compassion, friendliness, joy and equanimity). Without a realization of these four, the practice could become distorted and harmful. But then the Four Keys could apply to any work where there is an exchange of material wealth. Even though we had read the chapter called Earth Hole, the eighth chapter of the Mahākāla-Tantra, it was two years before Petsan taught me how to extract wealth from the ground. First of all, he made sure that I was contemplating on a regular basis on the Four Keys, especially equanimity. It was important that I was applying the Four Keys to the world of images. How did the image of Mahākāla reflect compassion and friendliness? How did The Great-Black-One produce, through the act of contemplating his image, joy and equanimity? Before embarking on a practice such as Wealth Extraction the Four Keys had to be in tune. My first task in this practice was to locate a sacred spot, i.e. a place that would be undisturbed by the outside world and any bad vibrations. Preferably it would be a spot that was covered-it could be a tent pitched in a sacred spot. Looking for a sacred spot became a chore that lasted for over a week. I thought that I found a place on the east side of the Monkey Temple on the slopes of Svāyambhunath. I received permission to use a spot that indeed was very special: It turned out to be a favorite resting place of one of the tribes of monkeys that inhabit the area and they not only did not give me permission but confiscated my watch. I was warned not to pick a spot in the monkey area, but I thought my mantra to keep away monkeys would allow me the space I needed. I quickly realized that friendship between me and the monkeys had its limitations. The spot I finally chose near the entrance of the door to my house was near the corner-stone. It had natural protection from the rain, and I enclosed it with a few blankets and a raincoat. This was my spot. I placed a straw mat on the ground and a chair. On the outside I hung the tiger's skin that I borrowed from a friend to keep the monkeys away—A common remedy for removing the immediate presence of monkeys.

After purifying the spot with a mantra that Petsan gave me, in the middle of a no moon night, I offered some buffalo meat, fish, wine, a little blood and some carrots with the appropriate mantras. I knew that some troubling thoughts would arise out of the depths of greed, lust, jealously, confusion and fear. When they arose I began to dig a hole in the ground the shape of a human skull. Petsan had given me the leaf of a sun bush (arkapatra) on which I proceeded to write the mantra, *Om Mahākāla compassionate one confuse, stop, and bind the mouths of all my enemies.* Every time a negative thought or distorted emotion would arise I wrote the mantra with ink that Petsan had helped me make from sulphur of arsenic. Around two o'clock in the morning, I put the leaf into the hole, covered it with dirt and stomped it down with my left foot. I did this every night until the next night of no moon. The effect of this practice was very calming and insightful—the treasure of the inner self. Several days latter I received a check in the mail that I did not expect.

After I quit the mine as a fledgling blaster, I hitchhiked to Indio, California—a hot town situated below sea level. I'd heard that the pay was good in the watermelon fields, but after I arrived I couldn't find any watermelons to pick. Someone had told me that employment in the watermelon fields was easy, but when I arrived in what seemed to me a very strange place, I couldn't find any watermelons to pick. I always had envisioned California as a kind of Shangri-la. At that time in my life, my "on-the-road stage", California had equal status to the Himalayas. However, I was a little disgruntled at being stranded 22 feet below sea level. I hitched further south to Imperial Valley, next to the Mexican border. With only one dollar to my name, and bathed in sweat, I stood alongside Highway 86, and was picked up by two drunken Mexicans in an old Ford pickup with a dragging muffler. They enjoyed making fun of the young gringo and told me that they wanted to take me to the whorehouse. When I declined, they said I had to go with them anyway, because they were in a hurry to get to the whorehouse; they were not going to let me off on the main highway. They turned onto a gravel road that headed straight for the salt flats. I was scared. The men were enjoying themselves until they got into an argument. The location of the whorehouse appeared to be the source of the dispute. There was nothing in sight for miles except a purplish-green horizon and the curling smoke from the city of Indio. An uncontrollable and monstrous emotion infected their speech. Their faces were distorted and there was an dark feeling that momentarily hid their confusion and arising explosion, partly due to their inability to find the whorehouse, and I became the object of their frustration. One of them said, suddenly "Gringo-you die!" the man next to me flashed a knife. Just as suddenly, they dumped me and my bag in the middle of sand next to a salt flat.

Because of their inability to find the whorehouse, I became the object of their frustration. They said they wanted to kill me for distracting them and for being such a typical gringo. I can't ever remember the same quality of fear. I was both humiliated and terrified. After making the decision not to kill me, they quite literally dumped me and my bag in the middle of sand and dirty salt. I was beginning to feel I was unprepared for this "on-the-road" thing.

As I trekked back to the highway around sunset, I smelled the odor of dead flesh. Many dead animals rotted in the ditches and along the roadside. But this odor was abominable. I saw a pair of brown and discolored female legs; they were bruised and swollen with hair showing at the top of the thigh. Her torso was partly visible. The head and breasts were covered with a poncho piled with sticks and rocks. I landed on the very bottom of darkness, and imagined the two drinkers, having decided that I was the cause of all their life problems, returning to sacrifice me to some invisible ogre who dwelled in the ditch. Had they murdered this poor woman? I went into a state of catatonic shock. I was transfixed in misery. I had little redeeming resources—other than to keep walking. A few hours later, headlights beamed at me in the moonless pitch-black darkness. The truck loaded with boulders, was on the way to Indio. The Mexican driver smiled and warned me about traveling alone. His cab was warm and a little blue light was shining from around a small brass statue of the Madonna—like a halo. The huge boulders in the bed of the semi gave me a solid feeling. I imagined that these huge masses, by the virtue of their denseness, restored my energy. The boulders had charisma. I felt content, and made plans to start all over again, but this time not "on the road." I couldn't tell the driver about the corpse until the very end of the trip.

The night of no moon was the night when The Great-Black-One is given special respect. He presided. It was difficult to be present to the fear, hunger and demoniacal image I felt after I saw the female corpse. Only in hindsight can I say that this experience was a preparation for the practice of The Great-Black-One. And only by discovering the kinds of emotions that plagued me on that day would I be able to utilize similar experiences for a. greater understanding. I am especially observant on the night of no moon, a night when many Mahākāla practitioners make offerings, perform rituals and contemplate. Rotting human flesh has an unforgettable odor. The burning human flesh of the Asian wars sears my memories. The Great-Black-One was always there in the midst of the terror and suffering. He frolicked in the offerings of flesh and bones. He lolled in the semen and blood. He hovered over the killing fields of the world, waiting for us to recognize the significance of wanton death and destruction; waiting for a sign to help alleviate the pain in this world.

A few years later, an image began to appear to me in both my night and day dreams, as I worked through the Asian wars. It was a large discolored, disfigured and not quite black image. My image had monstrous characteristics, such as vampire teeth, extra toes, an obscenely large penis in a constant drip: one side of the face smashed in with scar tissue burned with napalm. Welts festered on the back and rump. This image resembled some of the deities in The Great-Black-One's entourage, but I did not understand this resemblance at the time. I discussed the image with my teachers. We agreed it was an aspect of The Great-Black-One. I experienced an archetype.

How thoughts and images arise is a mystery. As a boy I read about the East in books found in my father's library. One passage from The Tibetan Book of the Dead, detailed the phases that the consciousness moved through in evolving towards a new rebirth. At one point, a ferocious dark deity appeared in order to make the final judgment for those who had departed from the earthly realm. He counted out white stones for good karma, and black stones for bad karma. If the wandering soul had an abundance of white stones the rebirth would in turn be auspicious; if black stones prevailed the resulting Karma would indeed, be undesirable to the floating invisible being.

In a nightmare, a strange being played with these stones, flicking them around and sometimes eating them. It roamed the hills and countryside, dropping the white and black stones on corpses—sometimes stuffing them in the orifices—ears, eyes, nose, mouth and anus. This Black-One also fed on the dead carcasses. Sometimes he appeared to sort heads and skulls instead of stones. After mashing these human heads and skulls into a kind of sticky powder he would rub it on his body as if it were an ointment and sometimes ate the mixture. He always sorted things into piles, which he would circumambulate and finally eat.

It was not until I embarked on a study of Buddhism that I was able to make sense of the recurring nightmare. Now that I can zoom in on my not-so-distant past, and bring the phenomena of war-life into focus, I can look at that potentially mentally disruptive cannibalistic figure in my life not as a psychotic occurrence, but as a comic relief to my brushes with death and living with its stench. I named this character "Rudee" from the Vedic prototype of—The-Great-Black-One called Rudra. He does occur in my mind's eye from time to time, and I can call on his image to appear.

Books are power symbols. The written word can massage me into an obsessional state, I hunger for knowledge-especially taboo knowledge; or, knowledge of self and God. I have a friend who wears a pin which says, "I read banned books." Another friend of mine has an erotic literature store—the only one on the West Coast as far as I know. He purchases and sells every piece of erotic literature he can find. Some of my friends have a hunger for knowledge that verges on the risque and the obscene; that borders the socially unacceptable. They live in a darkness that craves the care of an angel of light who can move in the shadows.

My father who was a presbyterian minister was also a craver of knowledge. I remember his somewhat ominous library of theological reference material, which included all the various versions of the Bible, as well as all the sundry dictionaries in Greek, Hebrew, Latin, and Coptic. Amongst these tomes of the Judaic Christian world was a smattering of Eastern wisdom such as T. H. Griffith's translation of The Vedas, Arnold's translation of The Bhagavad Gītā, Kern's Lotus Sutra, and an anthology of Eastern writing, whose author I can't remember, but included the above passage from The Tibetan Book of the Dead.

Most of the books were collected by my father when he was a student at the San Anselmo Seminary, just an hour away from where I live now. He was quite proud that the seminary included courses on Oriental philosophy. Both of my parents were very strong Christians and no doubt this inculcated somewhat of the opposite in myself. I do not know if the Eastern world was more exotic and mysterious to Americans in those days or not, but I remember having a fixation on the comic book series called Terry and the Pirates, and then there was Charlie Chan and the Mr. Moto movies. I do not think that I can give father credit for the Terry and the Pirates influence. The Great-Black-One, however, judging the wandering souls with his black and white stones made quite a dent in my consciousness.

After the Asian wars, my spirit guide, Rudee, receded into my unconscious. He did not show up for a few years. I needed to work out my relationship with the corpses, dusky-libraries, and

Rudee, who became a symbol, a shortcut for expressing the dark and ugly in my life. I began to study with the late Swāmi Vividisānanda of the Rāmakrishna order. He was a delightful, pious Hindu who started me reading the Upanisāds—the more or less philosophical part of the Vedas. I became a vegetarian for about two years, and I still read the Upanisāds. I went regularly to the services at the Vedānta Center in Seattle. Swāmi Vividisānanda conducted a very peaceful ceremony. Most of the American followers of Vedānta, in Seattle, were older woman who were content in living a passive existence. The tea and crumpets setting soon bored me. My personal studies in Sanskrit were not taken seriously. The swāmi was more interested in peace of mind than in learning, and not very interested in combining the two. I couldn't do one without the other.

Swāmi Vividisānanda was not interested in Tantra. But at that time, before the Tibetans came to America, if anyone knew anything about Tantra, they were not supposed to talk about it. If you did not know anything about Tantra, you could pretend that you knew—because it couldn't be talked about anyway. What made it even more complicated and mysterious was the consensus that anything written about such a subject must in some sense be fake. How could you write about a subject that could not be talked about? Despite the discouragement, I sought out the available translations of original texts from Sanskrit and Tibetan as well as accounts of travelers. I am still impressed by the scholarship and curiosity of the explorers and translators of the turn of the century.

How did I go about learning Tantra? Reading the Upanisāds was a good beginning. How does one go about learning anything that is somewhat intuitive and is clouded by a reputation that one cannot learn in the way one usually learns? What I did not know was that I had already accumulated experiences that would not have to be repeated in the learning process. Unbeknown to me at the time something different had formed inside me. Rudee was symbolically representative of this formation. I went many years without putting a value on my own personal experiences—not recognizing that something unusual had formed within me. For the past ten years I have been able to recognize this same process in clients. My personal experiences, especially on the dark side of things, are processed into a practical and spiritual awareness. My significant experiences—I emphasize on the dark side—were different from my teachers' and parent's.

How could my own parents, for example, understand war, let alone an Asian war, when they themselves did not have the experience of combat. I could not relate the dark and negative experiences of my life to either my parents or my teachers, for their pursuits were involved in a different context than my own. I have seen a similar need in the people who come to me for help, the need to find an image that might contain dark experiences, and help translate these experiences into clarity and positive personal growth.

My first teacher of Tantra was Dr. Agheananda Bhārati, author of The Ochre Robe, The Tantric Tradition, Light of the Center, and many articles. He had a unique experience of war and traveled as a Sādhu in India. At the University of Washington under Dr. Bhārati's guidance, who at the time I addressed as Swāmi (he had not become a doctor yet and he is a Swāmi), I was introduced to Oriental languages and the subject of Tantra. He was the first person I met who openly discussed this spiritual art. Not that he was without any hocus-pocus, so to say, but his communications were up front and open to any manner of investigation. I thought about the meaning and significance of the idea of the secret—a buzzword that used to be almost synonymous with Tantra, and started to take a more practical approach to secrets in general. The secret, at least in part, became what you didn't know or haven't experienced. It was also that which others did not want you to know or experience. And then the secret came to denote the mystery of unshared experiences. I came to realize that spirituality, no matter how you looked at it, was a social as well as a personal experience. Dr. Bhārati, the Swāmi, in those days was a mansion of secrets. He probably still is. But he never gave his students the impression that the secrets were unnegotiable, undiscoverable, or impossible. He insisted I learn as much Sanskrit and Tibetan as possible as prerequisite for learning Tantra, which indeed became a dominant focus for me. With the Swāmi, enjoyment and a sense of humor became an important dimension of our lifestyle and relationship. Thinking and enjoying philosophy was not an obstacle to spirituality. I met few, if any, Buddhists or Hindus who could demonstrate a bit of sincere humor or who honestly enjoyed life. Nowadays, with the experiences of Muktānānda, Yogi Bhājan, Mahārishi, Rājneesh and the Tibetan lamas, we not only have a wider experience of the Eastern teachers, but are in the process of accommodating Dharma into the fabric of our culture. The Swāmi gave me a Sanskrit name, Janapriya (who is loved by the people) and also a bit of his wisdom.

The next several years were spent studying South Asian culture, reading Buddhist texts, working part time when necessary, and doing as much spiritual practice as possible. There was ample opportunity at Columbia University in New York to study, practice and have fun—just not enough time. Actually, I hadn't discovered how to put it all in Great-Time.

In graduate school all those undercover books in my father's library came back to me in their original languages. I enjoyed the recycling of my interests in these matters when in my doctoral written exam several years later I found myself translating a small part of the Lotus Sutra as well as The Bhagavad Gītā. Most of my work in graduate school was familiarizing myself with the various forms of classical Indian languages as well as South Asian culture. I also read a great deal of Tibetan, and managed to squeeze three years of Buddhist Chinese into my curriculum. Classical languages are studied according to the genre of written material. For example, the Bible was written in what is called New Testament Greek, which is somewhat different than the Greek of the Iliad and Odyssey. Likewise, there is Pāli the language of the Theravādin Buddhists and Buddhist hybrid Sanskrit the language of many of the Tantras. There is Vedic Sanskrit which is the language of the Rig Veda, and standard classical Sanskrit—the language of the famous Epic, "The Rāmāyana".

For the first two years of my graduate study I did not read any Tantra, except for some brief passages from the Guhya-Samāja Tantra with the late Professor Anton Sigmund Čerbu. I did not have the opportunity to study Tantra seriously at Columbia until Professor Alex Wayman came in my last year of graduate school. Meanwhile I had filled the course requirements for a doctorate. I felt that I had done my father's library justice.

In the practice of The Great-Black-One, a Vajrayāna practice, the rituals and meditations focus in a variety of ways on the image of a deity. Part of the practice is called in Sanskrit bhāvanā, which I translate "cultivate." Literally, bhāvanā means to "bring into being," which is exactly the concern of the practitioner: In an outward sense, it is being able to generate an icon in the mind's eye—a kind of meditative iconography. It is the visualization of the deity. But, what is really important is the relationship that one creates between oneself and the image. The relationship is a network of channels that are developed in one's mind and body that at some point allow the practitioner to become one with the deity.

When I practice ritual-meditation, my mind develops an ability to form pictures of the visualized deity as it is portrayed on thankas or described in ritual-meditation texts. Yet, the ability to imagine or produce the formal shape of the deity and its attributes is not a major goal of the practice—it is just a part of the skill. The image serves as a medium and range of focus for becoming one with its underlying essence, that is, the image that comes very much from my own life and within. Petsan once remarked that a person does not have to do anything special to remember one's father and mother. He said it was the same with the attributes of deities. After you practice for a while, the attributes naturally comes to mind. But to really know one's mother or your teachers is not just remembering their photographic projections. I would need to know the ineffable core of the person, and to understand the other would be to understand myself. My parents, teachers and deities (in this case The Great-Black-One) can truly be known only in the process of intimacy. The Im or the core must be embraced.

I can experience something black inside, but black in the sense of a darkness which contains a myriad of light and color—a hidden black box as the result of bhāvanā, i.e. the results of cultivating a relationship with The Great-Black-One. We can extend the Box metaphor to the image of a computer chip—a black chip that contains all the possible information about The Great-Black-One with all the appropriate graphic, directory-making, joining and restoring capabilities. Everyone who applies themselves with a one-pointed mind cultivates a kind of box or chip that assists the mind-body complex in effortless and compassionate activity. It begins with the thought of enlightenment and rises into the inner mansion of one's being. As it is thought of as one's inner body it parallels the medieval concept of the homunculus—a person within the person that represents the cosmos. Each higher being or deity has its own characteristics. The black box image is my metaphor box that releases the shadows that follow one through life. These are the shadows that make up the dark manifestations of Mahākāla, for he constitutes their many layers as he absorbs and reabsorbs them in the process of living one's life. Each shadowy layer is a coat of informational and experiential impressions of the distorted and repressed areas of life. The Great-Black-One feeds off of our shadows as we offer them. He turns them into a mansion of rainbows.

CHAPTER II

One Image To Another

When I go from one country or culture to another the panorama of images changes. The currency, road signs, gesticulations, expressions, sounds, smells, tastes, concepts and deities look different: to cross culture is to cross images. Following directions, changing money, acquiring the proper transportation and having comfortable living quarters is usually serviced by travel bureaus and guide centers who have decided upon a norm for the translation of images to travelers. The images from the appearance of money to the shape of deities needs explanation and translation.

When a tourist asks what is the meaning of that icon? Who is that (pointing to a statue of Mahākāla for example)? It will be sufficient for the guide to say: "that is Mahākāla one of the emanations of the God Shiva, the protector of Dharma and the household". The guide will point out that almost every old building in Kathmandu has an image of Mahākāla (along with Ganesha the elephant headed deity) inside the doorway. The guide might tell a story about how Mahākāla came to Nepal from Tibet to bring the knowledge of planting rice and so on. He might mention that the spiritual practice concerning this deity is very secret and difficult, and that it is impossible to go very far beyond the present explanation without a proper initiation. In other words, the explanation would need to become an initiation, but in order to make this transition the traveler would have to be motivated in order to entertain this uncommon interest. Even a tourist guide's simple explanation can be a catalyst to a deeper experience. The guide is translating an image. The translation is not complete until the information has been transferred into a form that can be copied or recalled. If our hypothetical traveler decides to leave the tourist group and attempt to become initiated and actually practice the meditations and rituals of Mahākāla, he will seek out a teacher and the explanations of the image will continue, but less and less will be written. He will have started to participate in an oral tradition. As a tourist the explanation was complete when he could recall the ideas of the guide or possibly read an accompanying tourist brochure. But now as a would-be practitioner, the translation is not complete until he can do the practices and convince oneself and the teacher that he is ready for the next step.

There is a difference between recalling an explanation, and following a directive that could change one's behavior or produce a rare experience. When our traveler discovers this, he may decide that explanations are good enough for what he needs to do in life. It is possible that he will decide that his Western religion is good enough, or that a crosscultural experience will add to his spiritual life. He may discover that by practicing the meditations and rituals he is changing his life and behavior in a manner to his liking: that this is exactly what he and the world needs. It's possible that he may quit a drug habit or develop a new skill in the process of his preparing for an initiation and undergoing more practices. Ironic as it may be, it could work the other way around. Almost anything can stimulate an addictive personality to using alcohol and drugs. Spiritual practices are not only enlightening, but very effective tools of denial.

In the case of many artists or scholars who have commitments related to the translation of ideas and images, explanations and lexigraphical definitions are never satisfactory. Unlike the casual vacationer, they have chosen (or have been chosen) the path of knowledge, sometimes above everything else. For these individuals, explanations, at least in their chosen fields, are only a beginning. A translator who offers a transformed image that touches the Im in his own environment is translating culture:

this cultural translation must have taken place when the Tibetan and Chinese translators translated the Buddhist texts and practices into their own sounds and images as reflected by the rituals and meditations. Although elusive, this process is now taking place in America and Europe.

When the Indian scholars and yogis brought Buddhism across the Himalayas into Tibet between the seventh and twelfth centuries, Indian culture was translated into a complex of new images (both icons and words) that reflected those cultures. A word-by-word translation is somewhat awkward and limited, yet it is a beginning. I translated the images of Tantra as applicable to healing. Buddhist Tantra is a combination of meditation, ritual, aesthetics, astrology, art, music, and medicine. The dominant theme and mode of practice is healing oneself and others. Tantra as a way of life is the path of the Bodhisattva.

Even though the Tantras depict the world as a dangerous place fraught with malicious forces, they also indicate that the Buddha-nature is potentially in everything and in all events. In order to realize that even the most ugly and painful can also be a function of the path of enlightenment, the Tantras employ any cultural or emotional image, regardless of how bizarre, that can be used in the transformation of disharmony, confusion and disease. What is fascinating and useful about Tantra is that the very nature of negative emotions can be a healing process—like the venom of a snake can become an antidote. The healing process lies in how the image is received and processed. Within the process of culture change is a healing image.

The process (maybe problem) in shifting from the written word to its possible conscious application in life within one's own culture is reflected by an unconscious fear of losing ones identity in a far away set of images—a place that may or may not be purely imaginative—around the block, or, on the other side of the world. There is a tension between the images of another culture, planet or mind. But there is also a tension between one's presence at the moment and the images that haunt one from the past. Out of anger or simply the desire to change, there is sometimes the attempt to substitute one's conditioned images with the more exotic and stimulating images of another mind set or culture which could also come from around the block or the other side of the world.

Scholars of religion and anthropologists have been trained to treat this fear with some respect. I have had colleagues and teachers for whom the fear of losing their objectivity was a dominating factor in their scholarly lifestyle. They seem to treat their experiences abroad much in the same way as stepping out at night to the other side of the tracks—slumming, so to say. Textual scholars always have a safe refuge behind their manuscripts. I personally have experienced this many times—one's books and intellectual tinkering was sometimes a sanctuary from culture.

In the early part of this century, even up to the time of the second world war, most people who wanted to rid themselves of bourgeois Euroamericanism had to physically leave the country in order to immerse themselves in an other space and time that would help them transcend their own distorted imagery. Expatriatism was common.

Nowadays it is not necessary to leave America to lose myself in another place and time. The other cultures have immigrated here, not only in the form of the people themselves, but in the form of ideas, habits and spiritual practices. Now, one can plunge and immerse oneself into almost any thought form and practice that is known to man. The graft of Asian and Shamanistic spiritualities onto American culture has taken—the fruit is just beginning to ripen. Instead of going to the South Seas as Gaugan did, or, South Asia and the Himalayas as I, one can just run their fingers through the yellow pages or come to California. Also, there is a fairly strong movement toward preindustrial spiritualities. Tattooing, piercing and scarification are becoming more acceptable. The word primitive does not have the same pejorative sense as it did for me ten years ago. I always shuddered when scholarly books used the word primitive when referring to third world peoples, because of the demeaning sense from the nineteenth century. Now, it seems to have the value, not of a paradise lost, but of an ancient wisdom; an ancient wisdom that is ingrained in our images depending on the way in which we utilize them.

I also confront the desire to interpret images when indeed there is nothing to interpret. Sometimes the unknown or the unrevealed makes more sense as an empty space. This presents a difficulty for the mind, because it is always working through imagery. Then, there are one's unconscious assumptions about the world that arise in odd ways when living and working in the midst of not so familiar images. Hidden attitudes, feelings and ideas sometime gnaw away at the new personae that is slowly becoming a part of oneself. These are dark threads that are left hanging by one's history and upbringing. One of these threads is the highly-empowered concept of individuality. It is curious that when we translate the concept of individuality into an image, the image will fall into one category or another-it loses it's individuality. When an image of individuality is not called forth it falls into the realm of pure ego and idiosyncrasy. It is the cult of individuality that makes it difficult to be accommodated into a culture which has its own subcults. They merge and seemingly spontaneously generate new forms and feelings. The cultic aspects that we bring to other cultures prevents us from making the best use of our powers of adaptation, observation and translation. When we constantly translate our experiences through the screen of our own cult personality, we isolate ourselves as an anomaly.

I have difficulty differentiating text from culture—I am always looking for one in the other. Sometimes the imagination supplements the images that the culture does not obviously have; or, supplements images where the culture's images are distasteful and simply do not work. When I discovered Nepalese and Tibetan texts that were directions (or reminders) as to how to conduct rituals, at first the imagery was incomplete, and the mind scanned my own panorama of imagery for an order of things. But, at this stage when I was still in America, the imagery was rejected as being foreign or unauthentic to the text and the Buddhist tradition. In the second stage, in Asia, images indigenous to the text were apparent, but how they might be experienced for one's personal growth came with the practices and living with others who were accomplished in the skill of utilizing the imagery. In this second stage, I was introduced to the rituals, visualizations, meditations and the corresponding imagery became filled with color and meaning. Text and culture began to melt.

In the third stage, back in America, I was forced by circumstances to apply what was absorbed in the above two stages. As a householder and counselor the panorama of images in American culture was transformed into a new challenge. The imagery went through a process of adaptation, and after more that a decade, began to make sense in terms of my own family of origin and culture.

Whenever I read books, I wonder about their imaginative and cultural sources. Where can I go besides my own thoughts and imagery to look for authenticity? It could be just around the corner; in my own mind. It might be on the other side of the ocean. I began to look at other kinds of texts in the same way. I began to wonder about the manner in which we read and perceive the written word. I asked myself the question: Are these prescriptive-type texts, the Buddhist Tantras, only concerned with the proper procedure to do ritual? To what extent are these texts concerned only with ritual and formula? What about the philosophical assumptions underlying the ritual procedure? But, then, I also asked the questions in the opposite direction. How much do philosophical materials assume on the part of the reader a practical knowledge of ceremony and contemplation. For the sake of contrast, what if one asked the question while reading Western philosophy? Maybe the answer to this question lies in the evolution from Existentialism to Existential Psychology. It is interesting to read Heidegger, or any other Western philosopher for that matter, with the idea that there is an underlying rite and meditation—even if there is not. It is common for people who abandoned the traditional Judaic-Christian culture to feel uneasy and a little neurotic with their evolving imagery. It is difficult for them to explain themselves to those who have found a definite way within a traditional religious form. Then, if we feel we connected with the world of learning, we are almost by definition humanists: It is a convenient prop to escape from personal issues of spirituality.

Humanism has the positive value of discovering knowledge through the study of old manuscripts which is the origin of humanism. I personally feel that humanism is a channel to self-discovery. This is in the spirit of its original intention, which was to rediscover our origins and culture. Maybe the discoveries of ritual and meditation such as we have in the Mahākāla cycle will provide one of the missing links to the rediscovery of our past and add to the spiritual tone of culture in general. This is one way it has worked for me.

During the first stage of my search, at the university, I developed an objectivity appropriate to traditional scholarly pursuits. In the second stage, in Asia, there was the lingering fear that this objectivity would be lost as I immersed myself in the culture of Buddhism. In the first stage, there was a repression of images, but in the second the imagery was almost overwhelming, especially since my childhood experiences with grandfather as well as the imagery of the Asian wars were melting in my mind's eye. I always associated scholarly objectivity with my father and felt that losing objectivity was like losing a parental image. Now, in finishing up the third stage, the application stage, I realize that it was the image of my grandfather that maintained for me the integrity of the parental and ancestral imagery as gleamed and stimulated through my Asian connection.

The fear of losing one's objectivity when practicing the religion that is being researched, parallels the fear of losing one's parental image or becoming devoid of a discernible ego. What is lost is an intensity of spirit (the image is blurred); which can be revived, but will never be quite the same. It may be accommodated by another more vibrant image. Sometimes the old image will simply linger on and play a different role in one's consciousness and behavior. The alterego is subject to change.

Dominant and energetic images accommodate older, less functional symbols and images—much in the same way as the Catholic Church incorporated pagan symbols and deities. They just took on different names and were accommodated by different rituals. The Indo-Europeans did the same with the religious deities and symbols of the Indus Valley region which over time they occupied. The Vajrayāna Buddhists also did the same with the Hindu deities, ideas and symbols. These days cross-culture contact flows easily and is so prevalent that what was once a purely evolutionary process is now more conscious and even electronic. An individual can travel to a faraway place with the conscious idea of generating a whole new mind set for him or herself—a self induced, non-drug and mind-altering experience.

When I studied Buddhism in America, imbued with the missing link mentality from my grandfather, I never thought of myself as just being an observer or student of another culture. I was studying myself through the medium of manuscripts, rites, contemplations and how this information system was working for me. I was participating and observing myself in my own culture. But it was not the culture in which I was raised; it was not Christian. It was a culture going through enormous culture changes with a theoretical foundation of humanism. It was ready to explode which it did in the late 1960's when I was in India. I like to entertain the thought that I was studying Buddhism because of being a part of an evolutionary process to heal the planet. But maybe there are creatures on other planets in need of help as well, and now it is clear to many of us that our exchange of information of substance, thought, being and process is a function of interplanetary growth. Objective study of culture even when it is one's own, can turn into an egotistical concept generating the feeling of cultural exploitation, which takes us back to the subject-object problem on a cultural, informational and interplanetary level.

When I approach culture with a camera or a typewriter, my study and interest generates a subject and an object. I have never felt comfortable with the conception of objectifying the life around me (grandfather's influence). Yet when I purchased a manuscript, took a photo and pumped the teachers for answers to questions that had no answer, I was invading a sacred ground. Patience was not one of my virtues. I tried to compensate for the aggressiveness and the guilt. I realized the transpersonal nature of my role as an agent of cultural change—a role assigned to everyone who ventures to add to our understanding of the human condition. Grandfather was such a person. He departed from the norm and dedicated himself, unwittingly, as a seeker of truth. For others he was either an enigma or someone to turn to for advice. But grandfather's advice was not always exactly advice, but rather a comment on some aspect of nature that could be used as a teaching. Sometimes he would talk about the clouds, rain, texture of the earth, the activities of the animal life, the insects, the seasons, the direction of the wind and so on: he would hope the person might see their relevance to the advice being sought. He would also point out the distortions in the historical process as created by man and how they went against nature. It seemed that grandfather predicted all the great calamities of our age. Folks that listened and took him seriously were able to make changes in their lives. He saw himself in the historical process as a medium for others to improve their lot. He knew that people responded to him with the feeling that they could make a difference in their lives. The phrase that knowledge is a dangerous thing means that the expression of knowledge will effect others, but more often than not, we do not know how. That is why grandfather approached knowledge in a sometimes very indirect manner. He taught me to look carefully at historical and natural phenomena. He wanted a clear imagery.

To see oneself in the historical process is to be caught temporarily in a narcissistic stage of reflection. After all, regardless of whether I see myself as good or bad in the historical process it is my own thought that is at the center. It does help to make decisions and accept consequences. Another aspect of history with which the traveler abroad lives is the Judaic-Christian tradition's emphasis on uniqueness and being connected with the only God—not to speak of the shadow of manifest destiny. Throughout time, these ideas have deeply instilled in people the notion of the lack of sacredness of the place and space of others. These are very dark forces that I was happy to hand over to the jaws of Rudee, alias Rudra long before I arrived on the Indian subcontinent.

Having been a practitioner of both the Hindu and Buddhist religions before I went to South Asia provided me a language, an internal image, that allowed me to work on a level where I could share some common images with the people around me. My communication of Buddhist ideas, images and thoughts, though at first awkward, did lessen the impact of culture shock.

I energized myself to be on guard against the distortions of my own past that might seep through the cultural atmosphere in which I breathed and cultivated. Yet being involved with the spiritual calls for a hard-to-define quality of truthfulness. I began slowly to see how these distortions might work for my benefit as well as others. As I emerged from the Asian wars, it was difficult to see how my own cultural distortions could be of benefit—it was somewhat painful. On the Tantric side of things—and I admit the possibility of having overdramatized it in my own mind, there was always an inner sanctum. There was always the fear that the curse of the Tantras to explode the head of anyone not deemed ready for the teachings would fall on me. This fear was partly ameliorated by my initiations and the confidence of intention, but each week it seemed like I was moving closer and closer to the jaws of The Great-Black-One, especially when I was three months in the hospital with a case of the Black fever in Kathmandu. When my Tibetan friends and teachers from the monastery did a Great-Black rite for me, and subsequently brought me some Great-Black medicine in the form of little black pills i.e., pills made from herbs and incantations (the blessings of Mahākāla), I intuited that I would not die in that hospital. I ate the secret pills, unknown to the medical staff, and shortly afterwards began to regain my health.

Cultural distortions take shape in many images that mutate through time—Grandfather provided an old mutation. My grandfather said his ancestors came from Asia—primarily Central Asia en route to Northern India. Since he was eccentric, this idea was ridiculed by the rest of the family. I always thought the Bavarian-Asian connection was a fascinating idea, but discovered in college that it was definitely a figment of grandfather's imagination-or was it? I do not think that grandfather wanted to accept his ancestors as an army of brutes with their, then, modern techniques of horsemanship and swordplay, pouring onto the gangetic plains, looting and slaughtering the indigenous folk of that region who were probably dark-skinned. He had a much more sophisticated theory about his possible ancestors which included their origin from other worlds and the progenitors of culture. It seemed natural for Grandfather to reconcile the opposites, which he seemed to do in his own art and ritual.

For years, up to this day, I have found myself being very critical of my grandfather for having such crazy ideas about his origins. However, it is really difficult to tread through a graduate program in Sanskrit literature without at some point confronting the significance of the occurrence of the term Āryan which occurs many times in the Rig-Veda. My first graduate advisor was the late Professor Royal Weiler, whose specialty was Vedic studies. Whenever a loaded term like Āryan occurred in our readings, he asked the students to do a study of the term and then report to the class their discoveries. I discovered that the name of the country Iran can be construed as the third person plural of the Vedic root ir, which is the same verbal root for Āryan. It was a relief to find out that the word Āryan — whoever those people with blue eyes and long noses might have been — had gone through a transformation of meaning by the time of Sākyamuni-Buddha. It was the historical Sākyamuni-Buddha that made famous the phrase "The Four Āryan Truths," usually translated "The Four Noble Truths." The term "Āryan" is one of those words the Hindus used during Buddha's time to express their superiority. Like other words that served the same function, such as Brahmin (designating the upper caste), ääkyamuni and his followers redefined them in a Buddhist context. The word Āryan in Buddhist literature does not refer to the Indo-Europeans with blue eyes and long noses who stormed onto the Indian plains a few thousands of years before Christ, but to The Four Noble Truths or those who follow them. In the same vein, a true Brahmin is one who has given up the practice of animal sacrifice, practices morality and has compassion for his fellow man and woman. The Buddhist redefinition of Āryan created a new kind of relationship with the Indian tradition, especially with their Vedic past.

When the past is redefined, yesterday's images do not go away; suddenly they activate the collective dream and the future is predicted. After redefinition, the image has a future. Its contents become an oracle. Redefining a word creates motion and thought. It signifies a new creation in the historical process; the willingness to let go of an unworkable or spoiled idea. Attachment to a spoiled and festering idea can lead to psychic and social disaster. Ideas spoil, when the spirit of the idea is lost. The spirit of the idea is lost when its humaneness is drained and replaced only by our animal nature— or worse. This is what Hitler did when he sucked out the humanity from the image of Āryan and formulated his concept of the master-race. It was an odd and tragic mistranslation by the politicians of Nazi Germany. They created a pseudo-caste system based on racial supremacy. Grandfather saw all this coming.

Most readers who have come in contact with the early Vedic tradition have been deeply touched by its thought and imagery, and have skirted the ancient perimeter of The Great-Black-One's space and time. When Sākyamuni redefined the significance of the Vedic canon, he set the stage for a radical transformation of image. The changes would eventually evolve into the imagery of Tantric Buddhism which is a myriad of polar oppositions, symbolized most commonly by the interaction of male and female deities. It is also depicted by the conversion of Hindu deities to Buddhism (that is, in paintings Buddhist deities stand on the bodies of Hindu deities). Many of the Hindu deities are found as underlings to the Buddhist gods. Their images move through a conceptual transformation. In fact, one of The Great-Black-Ones is called the Brahmin-Mahākāla.

At Columbia University I enjoyed a course of study that included linguistics, anthropology, religion and South Asian studies. The curriculum leading up to the study of Buddhist Tantra is about the same, regardless of the sect, time or place (East or West). It will include a study of the sutras, the wisdom texts, the emptiness school, mind-only tradition and the logic-texts—each one of these categories is a major section of almost any Buddhist canon, and considered to be a prerequisite to the study of Tantra. Most of my time was spent reading Buddhist texts. I think of this time, not so much as taking a series of classes, although indeed that was the case, but in completing a series of projects—reading a whole text and bringing it to a completion was for me an exciting and useful project. This happened on several occasions: in Professor Royal Weiler's class, we completed a reading of the first three sermons of the historical Buddha Sākyamuni Buddha with a lot of attention on the first sermon, the Dhammacakkapavatana (Turning the Wheel of the Dharma). I read these in the Pāli language, which is the language in which these texts were first written. With the late Professor Hakeda, a Tantric initiate himself, and the author of the Biography of the reknown eigth century Japanese scholar Kukkai, responsible for the introduction of Chinese culture and Vajrayāna Buddhism, I read the main texts of the consciousness-only school. Also, with Professor Hakeda our class did a complete translation of Nāgārjuna's Mālamādyamikakārikās which is the basic teachings of the emptiness school. At the time, there was no complete translation of this work in English. It was a very satisfying and edifying project. For the Wisdom School, I completely read the book called A Collection of jewels of the Perfection of Wisdom (Ratnagunāsamcayaprajñāpāramitā). I read the text in both Sanskrit and Tibetan. For this section of the canon my mentor was the late Professor Sigmund Cerbu. This text is a very key wisdom text because it is a practical and short version of the perfection of wisdom in eight thousand verses translated by Professor Conze. A few years later I attended a ceremony conducted in a Nepalese household where this same text was read for the welfare of the inhabitants. The final and most influential Project at Columbia, and in a sense the beginning, was the Mahākāla Project under the direction of Professor Alex Wayman. During this last year and a half, I did an intensive study of Buddhist Tantra and translated the Mahākāla Sādhanās in the Sanskrit text called The Garland of Sādhanās (Sādhanāmāla). The reader will find the Sadhanā dedicated to the sixteen-handed Mahākāla in the fifth chapter of this book.

Having completed the course work and preparation to begin my studies in Nepal and India, I began an unexpectedly long journey into Great-Time. I think of it this way because as soon as I landed in India the emphasis of my studies were transformed from book learning into practice. I could no longer spend most of my time reading books. The only access to a deeper knowledge, at this point in my career, was through contemplative reflection, ritual and meditation. Moving from the text to practice and from America to India and Nepal, in turn, brought me closer to Great-Time. On one hand, I knew that my project was beyond what I could accomplish in a year—the time and corresponding funds allotted by the Fulbright-Hays Scholarship Committee. Yet, I had been moved by the force of circumstances and my own desire for a certain kind of experience and knowledge onto a level of activity that demanded more patience than the requirements of academic machinery. At that time, in 1967, I was not aware that the practice of The Great-Black-One was so extensive. My studies became an exploration—an adventure. I made the commitment and left the rest to synchronicity.

Great-Time is not separate from worldly time, but hidden in the substance, being and thought of phenomena itself. I wondered, was this the object of grandfather's communication? I was intent on pursuing the dark images in my life through the medium of Great-Time, as it was now about to be presented to me through another culture. Everyone has a hidden dimension, a kind of ancient Pandora's box, a Karma that does not flow within calendrical structures. The manner in which this hidden dimension was perceived and incorporated the Great-Black image in my life lured me to confronting it in the framework of Buddhism in a faraway place. In the late 60's there were few Tibetans and South-East Asians in America. As I was gravitating to the East there began a migration of refugees from the Asian wars to America. The Great-Black-One has led those in faraway places to confront it here in America—another faraway place. We move from "One Image to Another".

CHAPTER III

The Passage

The first day in a new place often makes indelible imprints. The space between New Delhi's airport and the YMCA was filled with the strange sensation of time lag: a bumper car-like taxi, impressions of bullock carts, half-naked workers, saried women sometimes carrying pots of water on their heads, and a few yogis at the airport, some of them with long needles protruding from various parts of the body. The yogis, it appeared, were staged, and I remembered seeing similar images in books on India and the <u>National Geographic</u>. I thought for a moment that these yogis had also seen the same pictures. It was hot, and in the wake of the time lag it seemed like another planet. I made dozens of obscure mental connections. I kept thinking of the Sanskrit word for bullock cart (goratha), which is very common in Sanskrit literature as a metaphor for spiritual practice. In one of the stories of <u>The Lotus Sutra</u>, the bullock cart represents Mahāyāna Buddhism—as opposed to the other Theravādin practices represented by the goat and the sheep. But now there are cars, trains, airplanes and even rockets. Would the rockets represent the highest vehicle? I imagined running long needles through my body and wondered if I would have to do that as some kind of test. It seemed like I was taking tests a great part of my life. What would The Great-Black-One have in store for me now?

That night I dreamt of Theos Bernard, a renown scholar and

53

adventurer, who also studied at Columbia University. He disappeared in the Himalayas in the mid 1930s. Maybe he was killed by bandits. Maybe the rumor of his death was a hoax, and he really is the rumored Great-White lama, who masterminds a worldwide enlightenment movement from a hidden cave in Tibet. In my dream that night he was still alive, and led me to a shrine deep within a mountain protected by singing serpents. The serpents surrounded us and spoke secretly with Theos Bernard. He reached inside the tummy (always a little protruding) of an image of Mahākāla and pulled out a palm leaf manuscript of the Mahākāla Tantra. I awoke from the dream, at the sound of a drum. It was still early.

I finally fell asleep around midnight, only to be awakened about 45 minutes later by very distant-sounding musical instruments. The sound faded in and out with the movements of my body—sometimes to the opening and closing of the eyelids. There were flutes, cymbals, drums and stringed instruments—probably sarods and sitars. It was difficult to think of the undulating musical passages in terms of any other experience in my life: it blended in with my dream-like time lag mode of consciousness. The music seemed to go on for hours, I faded in and out of sleep, dream and wonderment. I would have similar experiences throughout my stay in Asia. I still have them.

My second day in India, I could not help but remember that the only music I ever heard during the Asian War were the enemies screaming bugles and whistles as their shadowy wall advanced towards our torrent of bullets and artillery shells.

In a conversation with my two new friends, a peace corps volunteer and an anthropologist, I discovered that a three-day Krsna festival was in process. Krishna is the main deity of the Bhagavad gītā (The Song of the Lord in my father's library) who urges the hero warrior Arjuna to carry out his duty (dharma), which is to enter battle against his relatives. Krishna is the lover par excellence of the gopīs—the female caretakers of the cows. He is an incarnation of Vishnu, and maybe the most popular divinity of the Hindus of Northern India and the Himalayas. In Nepal I heard similar sounds with some variation, when Krishna is celebrated for the killing of his evil relative Kamsa; I would remember back to the Asian War.

It took me about two months to move from the YMCA to the Tibetan-speaking community at the Ladakhi guest house and monastery located on the River Yamini in Old Delhi. In those days there was a great deal of political activity that made officials of governments very careful as to the whereabouts and nature of foreigners. In particular they kept a close eye on the hippies. The hippies had many values they could share with both Hindus and Buddhists. When they dressed like sādhus, wandering holy men, they received the respect of sādhus. In a loose sense the hippie movement in South Asia was a kind of self-proclaimed international sādhu trend.

I received exactly what I needed, which was to live in a Tibetan-speaking community where I could establish a foundation to continue my literary pursuits and practice of the Mahākāla meditation. Lama Lobsang had warned me that the living conditions would not be very good, but for someone who had been through an Asian war and graduate school, I felt that it would be a piece of cake. This was not exactly the case; there do not seem to be any pieces of cake in the pursuit of knowledge. I made a number of friends and was introduced to the monastic community. The new social arrangements were so intellectually and culturally stimulating that I neglected my literary pursuits, but the words always took shape in the culture itself. My roommates, Ye-shes-Thondup-rin-po-che (called from now on Yeshes) and bsod-nams (called from now on Sonam) the brother of Dr. Jamspal, were generous with their energy and time. They both ended up being my travel companions on and off for the next three years.

The Ladakhi guest house and monastery is a refuge in more ways than one; actually, the Sanskrit word for refuge is "vihāra," which is the designation for all Buddhist monasteries. The "vihāra" is a reminder of the refuge that one takes as a Buddhist initiate; that is, he or she professes refuge in the Buddha, Dharma, the Sangha and The Four Āryan Truths. It was a refuge into the unknown, into a labyrinth where the discovery was partly the manifestation of my own karma; that is, Petsan appearing as karmicaly connected with grandfather and coming closer to the face of The Great-Black-One. A refuge (vihāra) has not only the aspect of a retreat, but a place where one enters the process of inner discovery—an active process of one's spirit, and an inner adventure and discovery of the manifestations of the Buddha-nature.

In India the concepts of a guest house and monastery (vihāra) are often the same. At times the vihāra seems to reflect more of a family process than a place to meditate. The Ladakhbudhvihāra, housed a number of transient Tibetan refugees. Many of them were quite poor and were very grateful for a space on someone's floor. It became quite apparent that one of the reasons it took so long for me to get permission to stay there was the not-so-complicated reason of overcrowded conditions. There were the burden of thousands of homeless refugees. When I arrived for an interview with Lama Lobsang, I took notice of these conditions. For me, it was a very exquisite setting in which to be introduced to the lifestyle I would be living for the next four years. Yet, it was impossible to overlook the suffering created by the Chinese-Tibet conflict. At the guest house I watched a myriad of pilgrims and refugees come and go. Many of them, including the Ladakhis, were Indian citizens from the Indian side of the sloping Himalayas. They were pilgrims, many of them on their way to Nepal, as well as Lumbini and other places. It is a life ambition for the Tibetan-speaking Buddhist to go to Nepal, the birthplace of Buddha, as well as the spiritual center for the many Buddhist deities. It was here, in this atmosphere of a Nepal pilgrimage, where I absorbed the thrill and magic of being en route to Shangri-la, not just a literary creation, but a stepping stone I could share to an auspicious rebirth.

For many pilgrims, especially the older ones, the mere sight of the great reliquary (caitya) at Bodhnāth or Svāyambhūnāth in Kathmandu Valley is a catalyst to a higher state of conscious-ness. My educated roommates Sonam and Ye Shes had a great feeling of compassion for these folk who would endure many hardships to reach Nepal—some of them would die on the way. Their own feelings toward pilgrimage was one of respect. They also realized its inherent educational value. They believed in the magical qualities of sacred substance and places, but despite their belief they found difficulty in expressing what seemed to be a superstitious notion. As I saw the pilgrims' attitudes as an-other reality that reflected my own quest, we developed a crosscultural dialogue that I hope was as edifying to them as it was to me. The enthusiasm the pilgrims had for the sacred was a support for my own quest for an understanding of The Great-Black-One's Tantra.

Connected with the guest house was a Tibetan restaurant managed by Kham-pas; that is, they were from the region of Kham in Eastern Tibet. They are well known for their directness, military prowess, and great spiritual fortitude. The restaurant was like a window into the not too distant future with my teachers and friends in Nepal, many of whom were of the same region. As all Tibetan restaurants, they specialized in Tibetan noodle soup called thup-pa, juicy meat dumplings shaped into small twisted-top-like change bags called mo-mo, and an especially potent hot sauce called ping. It was here where I drank my first cups of Tibetan tea and did my best to follow the stories of the energetic devoted veterans of the Asian war in Tibet. Many of the Tibetans who frequented the restaurant had narrowly escaped Tibet at the time of the Sino-Tibetan conflict. The hot sauce, tightly-packed buffalo meat dumplings and occasional bowl of barley beer (chang) went well with the lusty, humorous and sometimes scary stories that coagulated the atmosphere of this very unique tea shop. Only a few feet away was the monastery where mo-mo, ping or chang were not allowed. Lama Lobsang was very strict about this age-old Buddhist rule; that is, for monks not to take aphrodisiacal substances, which all of the above are considered. I found that the restaurant, with its fun-loving atmosphere, and it's hidden dimensions of secular and domestic intrigue a characteristic of all Tibetan restaurants throughout South Asia. If there was a Tibetan monastery in sight there would also be a restaurant.

It was one evening after tea, mo mos and a little chang that Sonam and I engaged in a conversation with some Kham-pa pilgrims on their way to Nepal. They had a wealth of stories about the war in Tibet and their escape to Nepal and India. What stimulated the conversation was the presence of an American, me, and my interest in Mahākāla—not the usual topic of conversation. They told of an airplane that bombed their village, of ambushing enemy patrols from high in the mountains, being caught on a small path thousands of feet above a gorge while receiving fire from automatic weapons; but most of all, they awed at the miraculous nature of their escape, which they attributed to the blessings of Mahākāla whom they referred to as protector (mgon-po) The Great-Black-One. In particular, they told how the bullets of the enemy would pass through the bodies of some without any wounds whatsoever. I was touched more by these stories than my Ladakhi friends. They had heard them many times before. In private they portrayed a certain amount of skepticism—after all, they were students at the university. Yet beneath their skeptical breath was great belief of the possibility of such miracles.

I guess I was somewhat of an enigma to my friends. The magical dimensions and popular beliefs captured my interest, and yet, the philosophical and linguistic were obviously important to me. The discussion in the restaurant stimulated my own memories of an Asian war. The image of Rudee came to mind. I remembered that some of my fellow soldiers carried Bibles with them—sometimes small ones with metal covers that they would place over their hearts. I think my mother gave me a little Bible when I went into the service. How she must have worried and suffered. Miracles do not surprise me. It is a miracle to survive a war of any magnitude. If you are on the front lines where the demons are erupting out of the ground from all sides, the odds are against you. I shared my experiences of the Asian wars with these co-survivors, and later on that night I looked at my Mahākāla-Tantra manuscript and reread the sections on mantras to utter for surviving a holocaust.

I felt that I had made a connection between the Tantra of The Great-Black-One and the living tradition. A year later in Nepal, I heard many similar stories. I would like to add at this point, that the truth of miracles caused by the repetition of mantras is not in the telling of the story, or even in the belief that the mantra works. Between the story and the reality is an in-between space and time, where the truth waits for disclosure, which is in the experience itself. The truth of the miracle is in the passing on of the experience of which the story may or may not be an intrinsic part. The story is always relative truth, but not the experiential results of mantra, wherein lies the ineffable. Who knows except the person or group having the experience. It was both emotionally disturbing and stimulating that the Asian wars came up so unexpectedly in connection with the mantras of Mahākāla. I had a brief period of unpleasantness when I thought about this war-god dimension. Because of its magical and destructive countenance, it must have scared the communist Chinese, I thought, but momentarily they were the stronger. Although, nowadays, the words, sounds and gestures that are coming from communist countries betray the impermanence of political systems.

Conflicts have a larger meaning. The victor may only be a pawn in the hands of another victor hidden away in some future event. There seems to be some cosmic-karmic force that is using the conflict as a means to an end. I thought deeply about the thoughts and behavior of my grandfather. I did not want to mix up the Indo-European spirits with the Asian wars, but here I was the receiver of some teachings about The Great-Black-One from the survivors of an Asian war.

It occurred to me that if I participated in activities centered around food, one might learn and adapt more quickly to another culture. In the East, food has a closer proximity to religious practice than in America. In the East, food is hardly ever just food. The food chain is a river that connects the person with the gods (the images)—both good and bad. Food binds and glues images. When you think about a particular food, cooked or raw, images of various types will come to mind. Food has a closeness to the invisible and is more conducive than nonfood to catching the power of the floating images—and Im.

As there is an intimate connection between food and divine beings, there is also a unity between gods and nature. Nature contains the food. Much of the lifestyle of South Asian people is a continual involvement with ritual; most ritual in one way or another involves food. By the time I left the East, it was hard for me to exchange food without some kind of presence to ritual. For me relationships are food-empowered—food is the stuff of ritual. Dining becomes a kind of pūjā.

At the Ladakhbudhvihāra I was introduced to the rituals of the community; that is, pūjā. Pūjā means respect within social and religious connotations. Pūjā is to show devotion and to make offerings—which practically always include food offerings. Pūjā can be a part of a very large, sometimes massive festival called in Sanskrit "yātrā," which can last for days on end, and is the object of pilgrimage. On the festival of Sivarātri (the night of Siva), pilgrims flock from all over India and the Himalayas to the temple of Pasupatināth in Nepal. This usually happens around the beginning of March (the lunar month called in Newari phalguna).

I was familiar with the various styles of Hindu dress, and could spot pilgrims from Gujarat, Mahārāstra, Punjab, Assam, Bengal, Himalpradesh and other states or regions in India. In the context of this or any other festival, the pilgrims make offerings. The most common offerings are flowers, incense, light (that is, pieces of cloth soaked in perfumed oil or little candle-like lamps), or make-up paste (gandha) for anointing the statue as well as worshipers' foreheads made from mercury sulfide (sindūra), and edible food (naivedya). Regardless of the offering it is considered food.

The first large pūjā I ever witnessed was the celebration of Tsong-kha-pa's birthday (December 26, 1967), the day I was informed that there was a place for me in the Ladakhbudhvihāra. When I came to the vihāra with my bag, about 7:30 in the evening, there were literally thousands of burning candles in every nook and corner and lined up on the railings of the vihāra. I walked into the courtyard of the guest house stunned by the myriad flickering lights and the murmuring of the famous man- tra *om mani padme hūm*. Except for the small children starting wax fires, the Indian caretaker chasing them away and extin- guishing the fires (the caretaker, incidentally, looked exactly like pictures of Gurdjieff), the atmosphere had the same dream-like quality as on my first night in India when I heard the music of Krishna. Beneath the stairs a whole family was camped. The mother got up to run after her children, and the father, sitting on a Tibetan rug, leaning against his supply pack, was reading a Tibetan devotional. I joined in a circumambulating procession around the main temple, where different intonations of the man- tra blended with the sound of flames flickering in the wind and the gentle lapping waves of the Yamini River against the cement stairs.

On New Year's Day 1968, I was invited to attend a Ladakhi grade school celebration in the village of Alipur where the older and younger generations, including the head lamas and visitors, sat in a large circle and paid honor to the Buddha, dharma and community of monks and lamas (sanga). This was an extraordinarily auspicious day because it was also a celebration of the opening of a new section of the school. Food was offered in many ways. Roasted barley was thrown into the air after the hoisting of protective prayer flags. Mounds of rice, pretzels and some blocks of butter were placed near the icons of the deities. The food to be eaten, in other words, was first offered to the Buddhas for the sake of all sentient beings. We took off our shoes and followed the lamas to a designated spot in the dining room. After the head lama arrived, the children recited a melodious and beautiful prayer, after which we began our feast of goat's meat, rice, potato and cauliflower curry, fruit and yogurt—a very filling and tasty meal. The next day the children performed Ladakhi, Himalchalpradesh and Punjabi dances.

In Asia, social occasions are more often than not based on the dynamics of pūjā. New events are empowered by the ritual: it is through the relationships in the ritual as perceived by the participants that enables the Im to empower the cultivated images; the substance, thought, being and the momentum of the process.

The monks and lamas at the vihāra would do pūjās almost every day. There was a continual murmuring of dharmic chants, smell of incense and butter lamps. My first contact with the actual practice of Mahākāla was on Tibetan New Year's. I had not been initiated into the practices, so I did not expect any intimate teachings or explanations. I learned that there would be a seven-day ceremony to invoke The Great-Black-One and his retinue.

The ritual would clear the atmosphere of malicious forces and bad feelings, create good karma for the remnant consciousness of the dead, help them to a better rebirth and prepare the way for an auspicious new year. My friends did not feel that there was much to learn, scholastically speaking, from the ceremony. Most of the pūjā was performed either by rote or chanting from the text accompanied by Tibetan musical instruments. Copious offerings were given in the ceremonial circle to The Great-Black-One.

The following year I was introduced to the ceremony. Mean-

while, in my spare time I would entertain small-sized observances that I gleaned from the sādhanās that I had translated in
New York. I imagined, not without some trepidation, through
my experiences with Rudee that permission to practice the teachings had somehow been granted—at least in some small way. I
recycled this thought, because it signified the dark force of the
unknown which was frightening. At the same time it provided
me with the confidence that I was about to ascend to a new
platform. To pursue on my own would bring me as close to the
darkness as possible. At some point, I would establish that link
my mind's eye needed to truly become one with Mahākāla.

It is easy to develop false confidence. Sometimes I imagined
being on the path to paradise, ready to disclose the pot of gold at
the end of the rainbow, and to attain that ineffable bliss that can
happen with the practice of Buddhist meditation and ritual.
Among beginning serious converts to the Eastern religions, especially of the tantric or taoist varieties a feeling of false confidence is common. I was brought up with the idea that with
God's help one can do anything—even become president of the
United States. I wonder how many men who have run for
president were empowered in that same way by their mothers.

During the time I was in India over the next two years, there
was a great deal of turmoil in Southeast Asia, especially the
Vietnam War. In Delhi I spent a fair portion of time reading and
writing in the coffee shop at the University of New Delhi. I was
approached by a variety of students who wanted to know why
America was getting involved in Southeast Asian affairs, especially in Vietnam. Many of the students who were politically left
wing were just plain belligerent. Because I was a Fulbright
fellow, the students assumed that my views on war and peace
coincided with Richard Nixon's or Lyndon Johnson's.

I came to South Asia to pursue a scholarly spiritual quest, to
develop a practice and philosophy that could produce peace of
mind and an approximation to enlightenment. I did not want to
get involved in political discussions. Sometimes, to use an image
of the novelist John Keeble in his book Yellow Fish, I felt like a
giant white beluga whale stranded, almost lost in a pitch-black-
ness of the current of ordinary time. But this feeling was a cue to
accept this dark power that has potential shape—a possible ally.

Actually, I was somewhat of an enigma to the Indian students: they thought my residence at a Buddhist hostel peculiar. After all, didn't my scholarship fund give me an allowance generous enough to live in a hotel or at least a middle-class neighborhood? For them it would have been quite natural for a hippie to stay in a hostel with Tibetan refugees, but not a scholar.

I was anxious to travel to Kathmandu where the traditions of tantric Buddhism in many ways were still an unbroken living tradition. I had heard many stories relating how difficult it would be to use the national archives in Nepal. There was one rumor the library would be closed for some time. Fortunately, this did not turn out to be the case. I needed to see the Mahākāla manuscripts in the national archives, for there was the possibility of finding not only a palm leaf manuscript, but many other versions as well: maybe, even the fifty chapter version. I had already bought a plane ticket to Kathmandu, which I cashed in after deciding to go by train and truck with my friend Yeshes. It was important to find out which day would be the most auspicious to leave. The astrological dimension is as important to most Tibetans as a DOS manual is to a computer user. I have seen pilgrims at the vihāra consult their rectangular astrology books with great seriousness before moving on to the next place of pilgrimage. And, now, as we prepared for the journey, the older lamas out of respect for Yeshes and myself, made sure we departed on an auspicious day. When I still had my plane ticket, I was told by one of the older lamas that the day the plane was scheduled to leave was not a good one. Then as fate might have it, I find out that the flight schedule was changed due to mechanical problems. Later I found out that we had left the day after a Great-Black-One ceremony, just after the new moon, in March 1968.

I remembered how my grandfather was aware of the moon and planetary cycles and how he related them to his activities. I had never taken his star-gazing activities very seriously, but now as a student living close to my own dreams I had touched an order of things connected with the planetary forces. The astrology had it's lasting influence. To this day, even in matters of business I have caught myself turning to the planetary forces. On several occasions, I have done business and profited partly from a decision based on the position of the moon. Yet, in my own family upbringing, astrology was not highly regarded.

At least 50 Ladakhis and Tibetans came to see us. We were sent off with a tremendous aura of good luck. We worked our way through the usual confusion at the Delhi train station and boarded the train around eight o'clock in the evening. We arrived in Lucknow about 12 hours later. Then we transferred to a mail train which was so overcrowded the conductor had to remove several people who had not paid for sleeping privileges in our compartment. The mail train took us to Muzaffapur, where we took another train to Singali, which ended up at the Nepalese-Indian border Raxaul.

We met a Sikh on the train, who was traveling to Kathmandu. He was about six feet tall and wore alligator shoes and a turban. He reminded me of the caretaker at the Ladakhbudhvihāra. He said with the aura of supernatural knowledge that we would see him again in Kathmandu, and we did.

Raxaul reminded me of a very small town in South Texas where the dust always blew and people reacted to the heat by just hanging out. At the station there was a group of seven Americans waiting for the customs official to return from breakfast. Yeshes who wore his Buddhist robes, was eyed with suspicion by the officer and with curiosity by the Americans. I was embarrassed and incensed when one of them asked loudly where my coolie came from.

Americans are remarkable in that they never feel like they are offending anyone as long as they are direct, forthright and honest. Everyone was apologetic over the fauxpas, but Yehes was not phased—at least on the outside.

The official sat down behind his desk, borrowed my ballpoint pen and complained about a bad cold. I gave him a codeine pill (available over the counter at any drug store), which he dropped into a jar of cluttered broken pens, pencils, aspirins and bidis (an inexpensive Indian cigarette). He suspiciously scanned Yeshes' passport. The official thought that he was a Tibetan refugee attempting to cross the border into Nepal, which was illegal. Ladakhis, who look like Tibetans with their monastic attire, but are Indian citizens always have trouble with border guards. The Americans were a missionary team that traveled all over Asia in a moving Christian library bus.

The truck ride from the border town Raxaul to Kathmandu had many daredevil curves over the mountains. Our Sikh driver boosted not only his abilities to race trucks, but to drink wine and carouse with women. His English was not so bad, so we received a detailed history of his exploits, especially with hippie girls—he tried to convince us that he had cracked the secret of how to seduce hippie girls all on his own.

In those days there were quite a stream of hippies and missionaries coming through the borders. The name of the truck, painted with gold, red and blue letters, Suvarnāvajra; that is, golden vajra. I thought I would get in a few words and began to discuss the name of his truck. I told him that vajra had a philosophical meaning among the Buddhists. He said, oh, sure, and pointed to his penis. Yeshes showed his annoyance and said it was a stupid gesture. My Sanskrit classes at Columbia University once translated the name of a bar on Broadway called the Golden Rail into it's literal Sanskrit equivalent Suvarnārambana. The students preferred the Sanskrit name. We had long discussions over the word "vajra" and its tantric-sexual connotations. Of course, vajra is a very important word—the way or vehicle of vajra (vajrāyanā) is the school of Buddhism, I was practicing and studying. Actually, our Sikh driver and his truck named golden-vajra scared the daylights out of us. He was quite a character.

The first day in a new place was always full of sensations and thoughts. Since we arrived in the morning the day was spent in settling ourselves, strolling about and locating the nearby tea shops and markets. Through a letter of introduction, we found a place to stay in a Sherpa's home in the very center of the commercial part of Kathmandu. Even though I had read a number of books about Kathmandu, I was still astonished to find myself in the middle of the city where large parts of buildings seemed to be carved with the images of gods and goddesses, stimulating memories of myths (I remembered grandfather's artwork and seeing the totem poles of the Northwest). The streets of Kathmandu were just large enough for the passage of wandering cows and bunched-up cyclists. There were icons and reliquaries on almost every corner that were crowded with devotees. The marketplaces were bustling with peoples in a variety of dress and who spoke an assortment of dialects.

The atmosphere was extraordinarily congenial and spiritual. Compared to the marketplaces of Seattle and New York, the people were relaxed, polite, friendly and smiling with sparkling eyes. As we turned one corner and the next, the smell of incense and the rhythmic sound of bells cascaded over us. I saw a chariot about 50 feet high that was slowly being pulled through the city. It was like the skeleton of a moving pyramid. Throughout the city and near the chariot were the local priests who performed the rainmaking ceremonies common at this time of the year. The generic name for those rituals is homapūjā, common to both Hindus and Buddhists with its origins in the early Vedas.

The air was rich with odors from a fire sacrifice that consumed large quantities of herbs and medicines. Each time the priest poured clarified butter or herbs into the fire, he recited a mantra.

My interest in manuscripts developed from my personal quest to find a palm leaf manuscript of the Mahākāla-Tantra. Whenever someone in the valley wanted to sell a manuscript, it was easy to locate the Fulbright scholar. All the messenger had to say was that it was a Buddhist dharma manuscript—it could be concerned with Mahākāla.

Our first day in Kathmandu was at the time of the Matsyendranāth festival, in honor of the deity who assissted The Great-Black-One in making the valley fertile. I knew that the contentment and wonder I felt veiled local anxieties over the imminent planting season that depended on the right amount of rain. Shortly after having watched the homapūjā, Yeshes and I wandered through a maze of small paths and circumambulated a Mahākāla statue (called Mahenkal in Nepalese). That evening we ate our dinner in the Globe restaurant. It was famous for its good Sino-Tibetan cuisine and friendly atmosphere.

Over the next few years a few manuscripts of the Mahākāla-Tantra passed through my hands. Most of them were not concerned with Mahākāla, nor were they ancient. Eventually I photographed a number of Buddhist Sanskrit manuscripts which are now loaned out to the Institute of World Religions in Stony Brook, New York: two years later the institute got wind that I had cultivated some important contacts and gave me a grant to do a report on Buddhist Sanskrit manuscripts in Nepal and India.

In my search for manuscripts I traveled to some very obscure parts of the valley; drank tea with mysterious persons who wanted to meet the scholar from America who was on a quest for the secrets of The Great-Black-One. One of these mysterious persons was an elderly Buddhist priest in Patan. I rode part of the way by taxi, and then walked for about a half a mile. This priest was said to have a palm leaf copy of the Mahākāla-Tantra. When I arrived, he had just finished his morning pūjā. As we walked into the courtyard and up the ancient wooden stairs, I smelled musk incense and heard the lingering and recurring echo of a Vajra-bell. I waited, seated on a dark blue Tibetan rug with a red dragon that had spindly feet and black-rimmed orange popped-out eyes. I accepted tea and flattened rice. The priest was over 85 years old, though he looked younger. He did not know English, but he was somewhat conversant in Tibetan. Like many Newars, he had spent a number of years in Tibet—at that time I did not know any Newari or Nepalese, so we had a very slow, but not tedious conversation about the Mahākāla Tantra and The Great-Black-One.

He told me that years ago during the Second World War a plane had crashed fairly near his home and that the two pilots had survived and stayed in Kathmandu. Well, I couldn't help but think of the movie Shangri-la. One of them died after a few years, and the other had settled in Bhaktapur and was still alive, he said. The old man thought that he was a practitioner of The Great-Black-One.

I only heard of three instances of Caucasians living as Nepalese and practicing a Newar version of Tantric Buddhism: the aforementioned pilot, an apostate Catholic priest who became a Vajrāyāna priest and married into a Nepalese family, and a now deceased friend of mine who had become a tantric yogi and married a Nepalese girl. The ex-Catholic priest was pointed out to me twice over a period of three years—both times I saw him doing a pūjā. In one case a fire sacrifice (homapūjā) near the Matsyendranāth temple, and in the other case, a hārītī pūjā to ward off disease—at the Hārītī shrine at Svāyambhūnāth. The third, a dear friend of many Americans, Tibetans and Nepalese;

was Keith Redmond, an independent scholar, accomplished sarodist and yogi. He died at a very young age. Besides myself he was one of the only Caucasian practitioners who was greatly influenced by the Newar tradition of Mahākāla.

The old priest mentioned guns: he had heard Americans were experts on firearms; that all Americans had guns, and that there must be something like Tantra in America in order for Americans to create the atomic bomb. He added that "it couldn't be just science". He knew the English word for science. I told him I had a friend named Bob who had thousands of dollars worth of guns, who wasn't interested in science—was, in fact, a poet—and had not the slightest idea about Tantra and probably would not hurt a flea, let alone drop an atomic bomb. The old priest seemed to understand. He got up and returned with an old photograph of Hitler. His children, he said, finally convinced him to take it off the wall near his alter. They convinced him that Hitler was not an incarnation to save the world, but more like the demon Ravana whose head is imagined to be split when a pumpkin is chopped during the planting festivals, and during the durgapūjā. After he sat quietly for a time in a meditative composure, he said he had a palm leaf manuscript of the Mahākāla Tantra, but he could not show it to me because he loaned it to some friends at the National Archives. The manuscript had been in his family for many generations and that only a few initiates were able to see it. No one except himself and one other person really understood the contents anyway, he said. He promised to at least show it to me at a later time. I probably would not be able to photograph the manuscript or have it copied. The meeting with the old priest not only made my day, but still lingers on in my thoughts and dreams. It is not only the dream of a palm leaf manuscript, it is the hidden dimension of the search for experiences of the riddles and paradoxes that present themselves in life. I still imagine the feel and image of an original palmleaf manuscript of The Great-Black-One.

When I finally received permission to use the National Archives, I naturally wondered who was reading the palm leaf manuscript of the Mahākāla Tantra. When I went to the National Archives I met Pandit Sukrarāja, who would hand-copy the manuscript. As I suspected, I would not be allowed to photograph the manuscripts. This was all right with me, for providing jobs to the scribes had a definite place in my sense of economic fair play. I had desperately hoped that the palm leaf Mahākāla Tantra would turn up at the National Archives. My heart raced when Pandit Sukrarāja brought out the manuscripts and laid them before me. He pointed out that he thought there was a palm leaf manuscript, but unfortunately he had been mistaken.

Part of me thought the palm leaf manuscript would never be found. The more optimistic side thought it could appear at any moment. I was impelled to keep searching. I never really gave up looking for the manuscript. It still might show up; especially one that has the first four chapters in the Ngor version.

Pandit Sukrarāja brought out two manuscripts written on Nepalese rice paper with a light coat of haritāla (arsenic) to protect the paper from paper-eating vermin. Many of the manuscripts I looked at in the marketplace and individual's homes that had not been prepared with haritāla were partially eaten away.

The two manuscripts had 29 chapters and no date. The language and style were similar to my other manuscripts—all copied in the Nineteenth Century; that is, 1803, 1805, 1830 and 1868. The other Sanskrit manuscripts, except for the Ngor version were not dated. Sukrarāja spent the next few months copying them for me in an elegant Sanskrit hand. His reverence of the written word enhanced my sense of the sacredness of the written and spoken word. He copied the manuscripts in the spirit of the gods themselves. It reminded me of the meaning of the most common name for the alphabet, devanāgari (the realm of the gods). The Buddhist and Hindu rituals in Nepal are conducted mainly in Sanskrit, Newari and Tibetan. Even the Tibetan rites have their most secret utterances (mantras) in Sanskrit sounds. Wherever there is Mahāyāna or VajrāyānaBuddhism, Sanskrit words are used in the form of sacred syllables. So, many of the Newari rites are a combination of Sanskrit and Newari—Mahāyāna Buddhist traditions the world over have been careful in retaining the mantric tradition. The Japanese form of Tantra is best known as Mantrāyāna (Japanese Shingon); that is, the way of mantra.

Grandfather used to say that if I learned a new language, I would absorb its spirit. He felt that his mother tongue, Bavarian German, was difficult to learn because only a few people understood its underlying spiritual connotations. I think he went a little far in the rating of the esoteric qualities of his own language, but so be it. Despite grandfather's eccentricities, I could feel the truth in his opinions when I worked with languages and cultures that had a historically continuous spiritual tradition and mystique.

Although many forms of Buddhism and Hinduism are practiced in a varied linquistic context, their classical roots are Sanskrit and Pāli. These languages have their very discernible origins in very early Sanskrit (Vedic), and what is sometimes referred to as Indo-European; going back several thousand years B.C. In Nepal I lived in a culture where the Sanskrit language was used on a daily basis by Hindus, Buddhists and a hybrid Hindu-Buddhist-Shamanistic population.

The art of the scribe is a kind of meditation. Copying the manuscript correctly and with care creates good karma—maybe fame and fortune as well. In copying the Tantras, a scribe has to be careful that the proper initiations have been undertaken, and that his motives are in accordance with the practice as it has been handed down. In order to know this, he needs to be in communication with the teachers who understand the configurations of the rite and philosophy therein. For the teacher, the yogi or the priest, in the last analysis, it is the feeling that one receives in meditation or the vision which carries the final weight. The scribe accumulates good karma with every focused stroke.

The language of liturgy with its accompanying gestures, sounds, images and overtones fill and satisfy the empty spaces within: The images and sounds are fed back to the participants in an aesthetic and transpersonal manner. An example is a common gesture that became automatic for me after a few weeks in Kathmandu Valley: When you pick up a manuscript it is raised to the forehead. In and around the holy spots the priests sit cross-legged and read out loud from their holy books. A passer-by may stop and take blessings from the priests; that is, he will lift the book or a leaf to his or her forehead—sometimes the priests will present the book in such a way.

Each syllable of the Sanskrit alphabet is considered sacred; that is, the alphabet is transpersonal. I am cautious of the term "magical," but after all, transpersonal could be a sophisticated translation of magical. Personally, despite literary or academic caution, the term magical for the way I felt along my own path comes close to reality. But I want to distinguish pulling bunnies out of hats from that deep feeling of contentment and satisfaction that one derives from a sudden discovery, saying mantras, meditation, falling in love or beholding a giant redwood.

My grandfather believed in sacred syllables; that is, runes. He said that the use of sacred syllables were one of the cultural secrets of the hidden tradition in Bavaria. He hardly ever talked directly about mystical subjects. In those days in my parents' circles even the word mystical was translated as just plain horse feathers. I know that grandfather whispered mantras (runes) because he told me so in defense from another member of the family who accused him of talking to himself—a sign of senility to some people. This was an odd behavior for a predominantly protestant environment. It was a common occurrence to catch grandfather with his lips moving and no sound.

After overhearing grandmother criticize him for talking to himself, he took me aside and explained that he was not really talking to himself, but to the nature spirits.

He had already convinced me that indeed there were nature spirits. He had mentioned the word "rune" before. He couldn't explain to me in detail, he said, but eventually I would learn about communicating with spirits. He pointed out that it was the kind of language that would not be in the dictionary. At that time, I had not even heard of the syllable "om."

At the Ladakhbudhvihāra all the monks, lamas and pilgrims constantly uttered mantras, both quietly and audibly. Most of the time they fingered the beads of Buddhist malas (rosaries) in their left hand; repeating the mantra for each bead. I remembered grandfather using his Catholic rosary on Sundays. Somehow he felt an obligation to do the stations of the cross and Hail Marys. Yet, he would precede and end his prayers with his runic syllables. I still am not sure what they were. He told me that these ancient Bavarian sounds purified the distortions of the Roman Catholic traditions. He did not mean this in a pejorative sense. They brought out the truly compassionate and spiritual nature of Jesus and the saints.

When I was studying Sanskrit at the university, it never occurred to me to make the connection between my grandfather's runic utterances and the mantras in the Buddhist tradition, Yet, the syllables of the alphabet are used quite commonly throughout Asia as empowered syllables. The syllables of the Sanskrit alphabet can be written on rice paper mandālas, folded into amulets that are sewn into little cloth bags, drawn in books, put on the wall or used in numerous protective rites—both Hindu and Buddhist.

Among Tibetan-speaking people the Sanskrit syllables are transliterated into Tibetan script: actually, the Tibetan alphabet was derived from the Sanskrit alphabet in the seventh century A.D. The Sanskrit alphabet was accommodated to Tibetan phonetics. The alphabet is used as a ritual or meditative device, not only in protective amulets, but in many other ways. One of the more interesting ways it is used is in the ritual-meditation called ātmayoga, or self yoga. "Self" in this case means the image of The Great-Black-One. In this phase I imagine the rising image of Mahākāla's form uniting with my body. During the process, each Sanskrit syllable of the alphabet is related to a corresponding iconographical part of the image of Mahākāla. If I emit the sounds in just the right circumstances and mental attitude, I can become The Great-Black-One.

It is a spiritual song of syllables that calls forth Great-Time, which releases practitioners from being attached to the outward structures of existence. Great-Time arises as an extraordinary state of being. Ātmayoga can be practiced by itself or in the context of larger rituals, such as the one performed every Tibetan New Year. In other words, the atmosphere that one breathes through the medium of mantra is empowered with the sacred word. The act of copying and reading manuscripts, uttering prayers and mantras, circumambulating holy objects and uttering even the most public mantra om mani padme hūm has an ecstatic effect on both long-time and new devotees.

During the time the two manuscripts were being copied by sukrarājavajrācārya, I moved into a house with a beautiful view that lies in between the City of Kathmandu and Svāyambhūnāth (the Monkey Temple). The owner Ratnabirsingh was a Tibetan-speaking Newar who lived as a merchant in Lhasa for seven years. He took a humorous but sincere interest in my pursuit of knowledge about The Great-Black-One. He had an uncle who was a well-known Buddhist priest, Jogmunivajrācārya. Jogmunivajrācārya lived with his wife at the vihāra at the very foot of Svāyambhūnāth. His wife had a reputation for having been a yoginī who made friends with man-eating tigers that not so long ago lived on the outskirts of the valley. The first time I went to see him was with Ratna during the summer monsoon season festival of Gunla. Sometimes this observance is called Nityapūjā; that is, "Always-pūjā", because it goes on continuously for 30 days. It is also the name of pūjās that is performed every day. During this time the Newar Buddhists visit and pay respects to as many temples and holy places as possible. Traditionally 108 places are visited. There are 18 locations that are considered particularly sacred, and visited on a daily pilgrimage. The first day is called "decorating the temple day" (Newar bahiboye). The religious centers are not only decorated with cloth and paintings, but display their sacred images to the public. At six o'clock in the morning the streets are already crowded with pilgrims making their offerings and taking blessings at each shrine. Jogmunivajrācārya was too busy celebrating Gunla for a lengthy interview, but he was especially interested in seeing the photocopies of my manuscripts.

Ratna's uncle mentioned that he heard of one palm leaf manuscript of the Mahākāla-Tantra, but doubted that the old priest really possessed a copy. Meanwhile, manuscripts of various texts kept coming my way. I was often approached in a very circuitous manner, usually through a friend of a friend of a friend, who assured me that the manuscript I was about to inspect was very rare, with secretive material, and if I didn't purchase it right away, I might never see it again. Business is the same all over the world—even when dealing with religious folk.

During this month of Gunla I found myself drawn into the vortex of the daily pilgrimages and ceremonial atmosphere. I woke up, sometimes as early as three o'clock in the morning, to the music and singing of the worshipers making the rounds of the vihāras. One year later, I stayed at the Svāyambhūnāth temple during this festival, and heard the singing and instruments drift their way to Svāyambhūnāth in the early morning. When I encircled the temple complex at Svāyambhūnāth during Gunla, I often imagined being in the paradise of celestial musicians as artistically depicted by the carvings around the Hārīū shrine. Music, dancing, imbibing and an atmosphere of aesthetic eroticism are very important dimensions of tantric Buddhism, but not in a socially offensive or personally indulgent sense. The aesthetics of the Gunla Festival illuminated the Tantric or Vajrāyāna sensibility.

Life in protestant America was so devoid of an outward devotional aesthetic, that Asian religious observances catapulted me into an entirely different universe. For some, the observances of various offerings seemed odd or superstitious. Because of my experience with grandfather's nature worship and Catholicism, I found myself on familiar ground. I imagined grandfather's community in the Bavarian Alps as they brought flowers and incense to icons of forest deities placed throughout the village and countryside, uttered runic syllables and performed complex ritual-meditations in remote areas. I have met several Bavarians and am only vaguely familiar with the history of that region. I realize that Kathmandu cannot really fit into the Bavarian Alps—or could it? I am sure that grandfather would have felt at home with the myriad icons and the pleasant manner in which the people practice their spirituality in Kathmandu.

The imagery was not totally unfamiliar. At first, I entertained the possibility of having a similar experience in a past life, but as I sipped memories of my life with grandfather, my past life approached very close to this life.

These imagery of Tantric Buddhism can be compressed into a space the size of a dot—like the compressed knowledge in a compter chip. Such a compression of images and ideas is represented by the center of a mandāla which is realized within the invisibility of oneself. The images of the deities and their multidimensional spaces (mandāla) have an almost infinite number of "other realities" and corresponding informational systems. The culture itself is one of these realities. An initiation into The Great-Black-One's universe, like gaining access to the files of a computer, gives the initiate access to the rest of the information.

Every cultural event in Nepal and India contains the code to the whole spiritual system—like one cell in the häman body contains the chromosomal code for the whole person. For example, one of the most common rituals is Nityapūjā; that is, the "Always practice." It is not just the name for the above-mentioned thirty-day Gunla festival, but for the everyday practice. It is one of the most discernible ritual acts in Nepal. During the early morning the woman of the house carries a pūjā tray (Newari pūjābā) with five offerings for all the icons in her locality. This particular scenario is sometimes referred to as mapūjā. The offerings are flowers (pushpa), scented paste (gandha); that is, a kind of make-up or ointment that is rubbed on the icon; and incense (dhūpa), which is sometimes made special for particular deities, but usually whatever incense is on hand is okay for the mā or nityapūjā. There are also small burning wicks (dīpa) offered as light and edibles (naivedya). When Buddhists make offerings to The Great-Black-One, they will not sacrifice an animal, but offer duck eggs instead. The ritual of mapūjā is like a computer chip, it has the information of the more elaborate ceremonies and ultimately the whole culture, and indeed, information about oneself.

The most common offerings are called in Sanskrit the five-fold ordinary oblation pūjā (pañcopahārapūjā, sometimes pañcopacārapūjā). As I strolled the streets and pathways during Gunla, I experienced the rising of an image on a collective and cultural level. It seemed like the words of Grandfather were beginning to make sense, at least in an intuitive sense. I began to make some connections between the offerings being made to icons—an activity based on superstition according to the protestant way of thinking—and a larger cosmic exchange system. I sensed the connection between offering to an image and letting go of attachments. Maybe this type of offering is the link between devotional intention and nature's system of transformation: the sun lets go of its heat to the plants (photosynthesis) and humans (vitamin D, which is necessary for human life); and then, the plants let go to the earth and the animals.

Here is a manner of thinking where memory, experience and a little abstraction come together. I am not sure where one begins and the other ends. My own rising image was involved in the exchange system itself. That is, what I offered determined what I would receive. The process of the offering contained the code and was part of the meditation which generated the chemistry to create the image and the underlying Im. The crucible for generating image, at least at some point in life, is not only in oneself, but within the exchange with persons, thoughts, substances and being. The past, or karma, is at work in the process. It is for the most part a hidden spectrum of life.

The Gunla festival is a model for offering observances for the outward image. Every day during the festival there was both rain and sunshine. There were rainbows that hovered and shimmered above the pagodas and rice paddies. The streets were muddy—I saw muddier in the Asian wars—but if I carried an umbrella and wore zoris (plastic sandals easy to take off and wash), I could survive the daily pilgrimage quite well in this subtropical monsoon. When I first came to the Mahākāla shrine, I passed by, thinking that I should come later with an introduction from one of my Nepalese friends. Who would believe I was a true practitioner of The Great-Black-One—a sincere scholar looking for truth.

To most Nepalis I was just another big white foreigner who had some strange need to pry into others' secrets. The place where Mahākāla landed from a flight from Tibet was a sacred spot. I finally received an introduction to meet and take blessings from the officiating priest. The insides of shrines and temples were always very mysterious and very dark with vast numbers of candles burning. Because of my own quest and karmic preconceptions, the Mahākāla temple was a mystery of mysteries, and on some level created in my own mind an unattainable symbol. I flashed back to my dream about Theos Bernard and pulling the palm leaf manuscript from the tummy of Mahākāla.

The shrine itself was relatively small; only a few worshipers could be inside at the same time. When I entered with my friends, Ratnabirsingh and Yeshes, it was like stepping into another time and space caked with ointment offerings and laden with the perfume vapors of incense made from musk. The priest read from a Sanskrit book—most certainly the Mahākāla-Tantra.

During the next few weeks I wondered about the text the priest was reading. When I finally met the keeper of the book, he told me that there was no palm leaf manuscript left. However the one that belonged to the temple was probably the oldest Mahākāla-Tantra in the valley. He could not actually show me the book, because another priest, as usual, was reading it at the temple.

Actually, the manuscript was an ordinary nineteenth century copy. When a young man brought me the same supposed manuscript, telling me that he snuck it out of the temple for me to see, and said it was an ancient one, it was somewhat perplexing. Nevertheless, one can never be sure of the contents untill it is studied. I offered to pay him to keep it long enough to photocopy. He said he would try and arrange it, and quickly with an ambience of quilt slithered away. I never heard from him again. Maybe it was the temple manuscript.

Shortly after the Gunla Festival, I became a student of Jogmunivajrācārya. He made it quite clear that there were many aspects of the manuscript itself that were not clear to him, but that he definitely could guide me in matters of ritual and meditation. It was also clear that if I were willing to suspend my academic attitude, I could gain empowerment. What I learned was how to sense my own limitations and how I might expand them.

CHAPTER IV

Jogmuni's Images
And Initiation

It was early morning, around three o clock—a few hours before the complete descent of the moon: it was an appropriate time for the ritual of The Great-Black-One.

Ratna and I wound our way along the upraised paths of the rice paddies to his uncle's vihāra at the foot of the Monkey Temple complex. This would be my first formal Buddhist initiation. On that night of the no-moon I imagined the events that could take place in my initiation. I had already been assured that I would not have to drink blood, eat human flesh or have intercourse with the local witches. In a way I was disappointed, but at the same time relieved.

Many of the Buddhist rituals are mechanically complex, but every ritual recycles the basic Buddhist principles. Some of these concepts, such as the four noble truths, the doctrine of nonself, impermanence, and the cycle of dependant origination were in some way already a part of my everyday mentality. My expectations were to experience the ritual-meditation dimension of Mahākāla and receive a mantra from the vajrācārya.

When we were invited into the room where the vajrācārya Jogmuni was sitting crossleged, flanked on each side by the various ritual implements—his head and eyes motioned us to seat ourselves. As we sat cross-legged, Jogmuni seemed to be in a state of altered consciousness. His altered state imparted a psychic force to the ceremonial circle and all those within its

78

boundaries. The setting was prepared for the raising of the Im. Jogmuni would become transfigured into Mahākāla. Not that he looked like the pictures of Mahākāla that we see in the plates in this book, but he had a feeling and charisma that I associated with the image of The Great-Black-One as I imagined and felt at the time.

The altered state is called samādhi. Those who practice Japanese forms of meditation are familiar with the Japanese translation of samādhi—satori. The expression in Tibetan is ting-nge-hdzin. I like the Tibetan rendering because of its poetic sense and the logical connection with mantra: it translates "seizing the sound." I take seizing the sound to mean a swelling, bursting and breaking through to the Im within oneself—the Im of The Great-Black-One. If the experience is authentic, it allows one to empower the ceremonial circle. Authentic empowerment offers one the power to expand one's ceremonial circle, to extend it into the world. There are many different kinds of samādhi and a variety of explanations on how samādhi is supposed to work.

My initiation into the Newari ritual complex and meditation provided me a reference from which I feel I can describe a part of the process. I want to emphasize that the events of both the ritual and the meditation flow together like the structure of a piece of music and its instrumentation. When one experiences samādhi without any support whatsoever it is called the "samādhi without support". This latter can be thought of as the initial insight and state of being which allows the creative impulse to flow, like the presence of the composer at the moment the creative impulse is generated.

Jogmuni was in a state of samādhi. In front of him was the ceremonial circle which consisted of a clay dish full of curd (dadhipatra), a small brass saucepan turned upside down (used for making special offerings to one's teacher and deity) called a gurumandālapatra. There was another clay dish with a fivefold mixture of substances from the cow (pañcagavyapatra): they are milk, sour milk, butter, urine and feces; the latter two were substituted by honey and sugar. There was a burning wick and some rice and flower offerings that would be for the world protectors (lokapālabali) and an offering cake of Tibetan origin called a tor-ma (spelled gtor-ma), meant to be a temporary dwelling place for the deity while enjoying the offerings of rice and flowers. In the center there was a human skull on a tripod. In the pot was placed an offering of cooked rice, an herb called karavīra, garlic and different kinds of meat and beans. Because the ritual was designed to allure The Great-Black-One, the beans were black. Miniature blue and red flags hovered over the vessels, the tripod and double triangle. The blue flags represented the dimension of wind called the vāyumandāla, and red ones represented the fire mandāla (agnimandāla). At a certain point we were instructed to contemplate the fire and wind combining to cook the above offerings. Off to one side is a circle with a red svastika, on top of which was placed the dish of curd.

By the way, in the Buddhist context the svastika has nothing to do with fascism. In fact it means quite the opposite: literally, it means "well-being" stemming from the prefix `su' meaning well or good and `asti' which is the verb to be. The suffix `ka' is placed on the end to make the word a noun or adjective. The reason for `sva' instead of `su' is that the `u' changes to a `v' when it comes before a vowel. In its vocative form, svasti, it is used in the sense of a "peace be with you greeting". The four arms of the Svastika in Vajrāyāna Buddhism have the meaning of the four Brahmavihāras (compassion, friendliness, joy and equanimity). There was another clay pot on which a serpent (Nāga) was painted, who is called Vāsuki, the protector of Kathmandu Valley.

Vāsuki is one of the serpents that drapes The Great-Black-One's body. The curd is symbolical of that ineffable quality of enlightenment-called bodhicitta (enlightened mind). Bodhicitta represents the utmost purest thing within the body, and is associated with spermatozoa, but that energy beneath the visible substance and attributes—the Im of the image of sperm.

The ceremony lasted for several hours in a very relaxed manner. When I seemed perplexed he would add an explanation to the process. On the other hand, when I insisted on an explanation, he would simply continue with the ceremony. There were some phases of the ritual that he wanted to explain. He provided explanations, gestures, and tossed out a number of surprises. I felt like I was being rewired to the cosmos and that life would never be quite the same again.

He had never initiated a foreigner before. As a foreigner I couldn't expect to be an initiate in exactly the same way as the Vajrācārya or other Newaris. Jogmuni said: "since your head has not blown up I will take it as a sign that you can continue your sādhanā and move on to the next step". That is, he would take me over the threshold into The Great-Black-One's practice.

Every action in a pūjā is a variation on a theme. The theme is a set of very broad and fluid conceptions and assumptions about life: these ideas and working principles are genetically bound by the material culture reflected by language. Incense, edibles, images of deities, expressions of the people, the social relationships in the ritual, philosophical interpretations are all filtered through the sounds and shape of language sound and breath.

Buddhist ritual harmonizes the participants and the surrounding culture. The music, the song, or more precisely the chant is one of the most important dimensions. The personal mantra is like a personal song; one does not sing it in just one way: the mantra can be sung in any key and take on a number of variations. The subtleties within the variations stimulate the spirit. The ritual is also like a recurring dream, or in a larger sense like the recurrence of life cycles themselves. They stimulate memories and at the same time drain them away. That is, there are the daily evening rites of satisfaction and fulfillment that last for an hour and then the monthly one that is performed for a whole day. And, then, there is the same rite performed in an expanded version of seven days at the end of the year. The rite ends with the burning of the former year's karma—the burning of the image of The Great-Black-One. There are the in-between rites and contemplations that build dreams and take them away on a daily and momentary basis.

In Asia, ritual and music are not separate, at least in the classical religious context. I was pleasantly surprised when the Vajrācārya broke out in song. The song was called "Madhyameru" which refers to the symbolic center of the universe which we were ritualistically building with our little mounds of rice and flowers. It was the gurumandāla or teacher's mandala we were constructing. It was a transubstantiation that brought together the substance of rice, flowers and water with one's geographical and spiritual center.

Descriptive Analysis of Nepalese Buddhist Pūjā

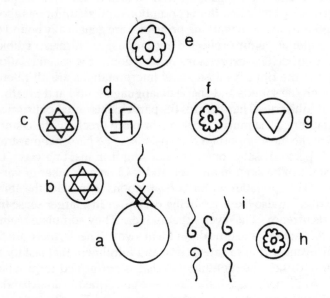

a. *Gurumandala* [of Guru Vajrasattva]
b. *Samādhibalimandala* [of food offerings for the divinities to produce the curing ambrosia]
c. *Krodhagaṇabalimandala* [of food offerings for the group of wrathful divinities]
d. *Dadhipatramandala* [of the pot filled with curd]
e. *Kalaśamandala* [of the main divinity's flask]
f. *Nāgabandhamandala* [of the divine serpent's flask]
g. *Dīpamandala* [of the light]
h. *Pañcagavya* [the five substances of cow]
i. *Dikpālabali* [food offerings for the protectors in space]

In America and the West, outside of Catholic liturgy, opera seems to come the closest to being a remnant of ritualistic proceedings that incorporate music. As ritualistic ways fade into history, art becomes more isolated. Ideas and conceptions also become fragmented from the world around us. For me the experience of the rite was a breakthrough in the sense that conceptions and ideas took on a meaning in the action of bringing together substance, being and thought.

In the ritual all the senses and the intellect are brought into an interactive play and game of balance. Outside of ritual; or, in some specialized therapies there are conditions where a spontaneous spiritual combustion will evolve or erupt into altered states of consciousness—occasionally it will take place in one's everyday routine. The rite is a way in which a universal symbol, an archetype or transpersonal idea, can be translated into experience. If the Vajrācārya wants to share an experience (not just show or teach its structure), he needs to either have an already-made ritual or create a structure that might involve other spirits of nature or so-called supernatural beings (that is, images).

Jogmuni explained that it was a waste of time to do rituals or meditate unless there was a strong intention of purity. If I did not have that clear and pure intention, the ritual can be detrimental. It could harm my karmic process in a significant way. Our initial act of purification was to sprinkle ourselves with water and chant an accompanying mantra.

The water for the sprinkling came from a nearby sacred well. There are supposed to be 8,000 wells in Nepal. In each well dwells a naga, a divine-like serpent. Use of tap water in a sacred rite is taboo. Water from the rivers is especially sacred. I sprinkled the sacred water and chanted mantra which purified the body (Kāyaparisodhana). Then I reiterated my intention to be initiated into the cycle of Mahākāla and to dedicate myself to the vows of one practicing the sādhanā of The Great-Black-One. At this point Jogmuni talked to us about some of the basic Buddhist precepts. Every Buddhist ceremony, he said, includes the dedication of one's skills and positive characteristics for the sake of all sentient beings: a purpose implied by the vow to become a bodhisattva (whose being is enlightened).

The few points that Jogmuni mentioned to me at the beginning of the ceremony were very important. He did not ask me if I understood. He would just stop and watch me absorb what he was teaching. Either I understood or I did not. He allowed me to ask a few questions, because he knew that I would not ask unless the questions were important to me.

I had learned that the meditation and ritual were for the sake of everyone—even though, it seemed that I· was not actually doing anything altruistic. Yet whenever I practiced the rites and meditation, I was helping others-indeed, the whole world. This was an encouraging thought: to be of benefit, all I had to do, was to meditate—or was it?

I used to meditate in a Zen temple in New York. The priest of that temple used to say: "when you are enlightened the whole world is enlightened". I thought that Jogmuni's answer was very clever and probably true. He said, "That is why you are here, William. Due to the meditation of others you are now part of the process. Even though you are not a Newar, you are in the family of those who have taken the Bodhisattva vow. Furthermore, you are in the family of Mahākāla, whose father is the deity Akshobhya (the unshakable one)." He used the Sanskrit word gotra for family, which like the words Brahmin and Ārya were redefined by the early Buddhists: The Brahmanic meaning of gotra is a person descended from a male line whose original ancestor was a recognized holy person traceable to vedic times. But, the early Buddhists saw their ancestor, indeed, their spiritual progenitor, as sākyamuni Buddha. His other name, Gautama, could be traced to a vedic seer with that same name. I enjoy the feeling that I can belong to a universal brotherhood that indeed has its origin in the Vedas; this was a notion of grandfather's which always intrigued me.

The beginning of every ritual is not only concerned with purification, but also with the reiteration of vows. It was important to Jogmuni that he take out the time to teach me more about the Bodhisattva vows. The Bodhisattva vows are ritualized into a structure of agreements with the self and one's teachers: they are then extended to the world and even the universe. That is, a commitment is made with the latent underlying image (the Im) . The vows are supported by symbolic ritual actions. The ritual complex itself becomes the image, i.e. the utensils, substances, pictures of deities, and the assumptions behind the rite and the participants forms a vortex of channels leading to the possibility of the ineffable.

We recited a mantra to the deity Vajrasattva (whose being is vajra). Jogmuni then gave a short talk on how Vajrasattva could be thought of as a single deity; or, as any of the other Tantric deities, including Mahākāla. From this point in the ritual Mahākāla was thought of as The Great-Black-One whose being is Vajra that is, Vajrasattvamahākāla. Actually, in the purification process, Vajrasattvamahākāla is visualized as white. Jogmuni repeated several times that the complete world is in the nature of Vajra: the goal of the practitioner is to realize the Vajra nature through the means of sādhanā. The phenomena of the universe in its external essence is composed of the five elements: air, water, earth, fire and the space (or subtle energy between the elements called ākāsa). Sometimes a sixth element is added to include the psychic processes. The ritual instrument vajra designates the empowerment and flow of these six elements.

The word for element in Sanskrit is "dhātu". The phrase earth-element then, is translated into Sanskrit prithivi-dhātu. However, in the ritual-meditation of Tantra, earth-element becomes earth-vajra; that is, prithivi-dhātu becomes prithivi-vajra, and wind-element, vāyudhātu, changes to wind-vajra,i.e. vāyu-vajra, and so on. In fact, in the ceremonial circle everything that is elemental, i.e. dhātu melts into the nature of vajra—everything.

The priest chuckled and smiled his way through a great deal of information about Vajra. He would discuss it tongue and cheek. He said that I could wander around, study and teach my way through existence, but that I would never realize the true nature of Vajra until I married someone suitable to a practitioner's nature. We laughed. I thought, Oh! a hidden dimension embodied in the mystery of courtship and procreation. ·

We then read a passage about revealing our misfortunes and errors before the gods. This part of the ceremony, called pāpadesanā, is sometimes translated confession of sins. Jogmuni was aware of the power that this phrase has in Christianity, and mentioned that I would have to be very careful with this part of the practice.

The confessional is not as much the relationship between the confessor and priest, as it is between the confessor and the order of things represented by and in the ceremonial circle. The distortions in my life were laid open and made bare, and it was as if the ceremonial circle was an oversized third eye scrutinizing the self-conscious karma of my existence. Before my own eyes there came an array of past events and people that were filling up space in the recesses of my mind, which reminded me a little of the old fashion garbage dumps that were always burning and casting off the odors of rot and waste. The images were vivid and I could smell the dump of my own creation. But these set of images and odors were part of my karma and like the garbage heap served as a place of transformation. It was clear that my past had lacked serenity, sobriety and compassion for all sentient beings. Yet, now, that it could be seen not only by myself, but by the invisible images brought alive by the ceremony, the dump could be offered and purified. The waste could be cultivated into the image of The Great-Black-One.

The ceremonial circle contracts and expands. It can be a larger ceremony, festival; or, ideally it spills into the self so that we can practice within.

Jogmuni gave the bodhisattva vow a bit of a psychological twist. He said in some ways it would be difficult for me to do bad things; after all, I would take on the image of Mahākāla. Yet, bad actions could result from my good intentions. Even the effort to help another person can result it their suffering: the intention must be very clear. I had heard this before from grandfather, who was always complaining about the "do-gooders who usually create a thicker pile of garbage". For me it was a full circle. I wanted to escape from the do-gooder's karma. I received the same message in a different way from my future Tibetan teacher, Petsan. Jogmuni said the best thing I could do after I finished my sādhanā would be to relax and enjoy life in a casual and ordinary way.

We read a prayer paying homage to the five Buddhas. Since the five Buddhas represent the five elements (incorporated in the symbol of the vajra) in the natural universe, the prayer is a recognition of the raw structure of the universe. Furthermore,

Mahākāla himself is composed of the five Buddhas. We then requested Buddha for the proper teachings in order to become a Bodhisattva. When a Bodhisattva's time has come to reach Nirvāna, he or she refuses it's isolation and bliss in order to stay in the world and work for the sake of people and other creatures.

The bodhisattva maintains his presence in the world for the sake of helping others. Jogmuni reiterated-a boddhisattva story: Once when his wife was young and when Kathmandu was surrounded by forest she was confronted by a tiger while meditating in a pine grove. She thought: "this is the end of my life and I will finally be able to attain complete nirvāna". So she offered herself to the tiger as food. The tiger, who was actually Mahākāla in disguise communicated to her that her vows were intact, but that she was needed more in the world than in a state of complete nirvāna. She could, however, have her choice. The tiger, like in many of the Jātaka tales, was really a disguised image—an image that blended into the environment. The question she and the tiger discussed was this: would she be food for the tiger or stay in the suffering world for the sake of other beings. She was developed enough in her meditation so that food for the tiger would have meant the happiness and bliss of total extinction (parinirvāna). Jogmuni's wife chose the latter, and here she was to confirm it as she helped to arrange the ritual offerings and occasionally serve us tea. Tigers had not been seen in the Kathmandu area for ten years. On the other hand, I had experienced a bit of anxiety as to what my choices might be the rest of the night. The importance of the Bodhisattva to Jogmuni was that one's merit (punya) could be channeled to others through the power of the ritual-meditation. Even if the ritual is done without great concentration of mind, merit by virtue of the charisma of the ritual would be routed to the world. He said that the practice of ritual is like that of a painter who does a big painting. The painter reproduces the image in his mind's eye for himself and the rest of world. He not only has a picture, but the Im or inspiration behind the picture. Like the construction of a painting a ritual expands the original thought; that is, the thought of being able to reach enlightenment, and then to expand that thought to the very limit of the ceremonial circle which can be reproduced in other places in a variety of ways. "The ritual is necessary", he said, "because it is the only means we have to pass on true knowledge from one generation to the next". When I replied that higher education also passes on knowledge, he retorted it to be only mechanical knowledge, which has not done the world much good. At any rate, I had an edifying feeling being the recipient of the type of experiential knowledge that is passed on from generation to generation and from culture to culture. I had never thought of a ritual as a means of passing on knowledge except in a mnemonic way. But grandfather too admitted the passing on of knowledge in ritual not just as a way to help remember paradigms, but as an aid to healing and mystical experience-indeed, as a way to the attainment of extraordinary powers (siddhi).

In Kathmandu pūjās continue throughout the day. There are thousands of ceremonial circles radiating merit—all at the same time. If the teacher was right, and I think he was, there was a constant flow of merit moving throughout the atmosphere.

Jogmuni then showed us how to do karanyāsa (touch ritual), which establishes the body as being in the nature of Vajra. We touched various parts of our body, uttering the appropriate mantras for various deities. Each part of the body touched activates the elements in their transformative and sacred dimension. This was in preparation for the teacher's mandāla pūjā (gurumandāla), which is done in every ceremony.

The gurumandāla (circle of offerings for the guru) is a replica of the perfect world offered to the guru. Essentially, the guru is Vajrasattva (whose being is Vajra), and is hence referred to as the AdiBuddha (the first or primordial Buddha). He is also called Vajradhāra, the Vajrabearer. Both Vajrasattva and Vajradhāra are depicted in the Iconography as holding a vajra and bell. At the same time he is Vajrasattvamahākāla (Mahākāla whose being is Vajra), as well as the officiating priest, Vajrācārya, and all the teachers from the past who were initiated into Vajrāyāna. The guru can be any one of these or all of them. He showed me the passage to be uttered in praise of Vajrasattva, which we then read. He did the five ordinary oblations pūjā on top of a conch shell filled with water, rice and flowers. Each offering gesture is made with the appropriate mantras. For example, when the incense is offered the mantra *om Vajradhūpa āh hām svāhā* is uttered, and so on. The conch shell and its contents are then in the nature of Vajra, and hence empowered for the ritual process. In fact, all of the ritual items at some point must be empowered by the fivefold oblation pūjā. Another way of putting it is that the ritual objects must possess the life of the five Buddhas. This transfer of raw energy does not happen just through the saying of the above mantra. That would be too easy: the transfer is made by means of the Vajrācārya offering his own Vajra-body. Every pūjā represents a cycle of offering initiated by the ritual specialist whether he be a priest, yogi or married practitioner who has received initiation. There are many sub-events of rite and language that were lost to me that early morning. I had already made up my mind not to take notes or photographs. I did ask questions at the beginning, because that seemed to be part of the process.

The five ordinary oblations are done at the beginning and end of every major part of the ritual. I did not know this at the time and marveled at the repetition of offerings. In the beginning of the gurumandāla I was asked to join in the fivefold offering. The cycle goes on. The priest takes the conch shell, sprinkles some water and flower petals on his head, and sips the sacrament.

In Nepalese ritual, flowers represent purity; even the deities themselves. The reason for this is not only their abundance and natural beauty, but their internal biology having evolved into a unity. The flower with its two central extensions inside the bloom (stamen and pistil) contain both its male and female parts. It is a perfect and aesthetic symbol of the reconciliation of opposites, i.e. the union of insight (prajñā) and means (upāya)— indeed the union of the practitioner with the deity.

Because the flower is androgynous, it depicts the male and female within each other. Males have female characteristics and vice versa. When the Vajrācārya takes a consecrated flower from the conch shell and contemplates the sound *om* and then puts the flower on the head, the action symbolizes the purification of the psycho-biological self (kāya). Kāya is usually translated "body," but kāya is not just flesh, but the internal energy and invisible structure of the flesh. Another flower is tossed to the right as the mouth chants *ah* designating speech (vac). Everything pure and sacred has the power of speech (vac) that is, rocks, water, wind, lightening, the planets all possess speech. After that, another flower is tossed to the right, which stands for the nature of subtle thought and feeling (citta). The Chinese translated citta "heart," and this is much more accurate than mind. It is heart in the sense of the total feeling that one emanates or experiences. The phrase "he has a big heart" approaches the general feeling of the word citta. The Tibetan translation "sems" is also closer to the idea of the Sanskrit. Sems is not only a technical word, but is very common in colloquial speech: a person who is well liked will be said to have a good sems (sems-yag-po). Occasionally a mean or dishonest person will be said to have a black sems (sems-nag-po). The above mini flower pūjā is called the purification of body speech and mind (kāyavāccittaparisodhana). This short and quaint little ritual activates the purification of these three primal energies. Hence, every religious painting that is conse-crated has on its back side the syllables *om ah* and *hūm*.

Newari rituals use a small double-cupped vase (tikabandhu) with red powder in one cup and yellow powder in the other cup. These powders are rubbed on all the statues in Kathmandu and are used in every ritual. Mixed with a bit of the holy water they become pastelike. Jogmuni pinched the yellow ointment in the right hand with his ring and index finger and pressed it into the gurumandāla in front of him. He then dabbed a bit on his forehead. He repeated the same with the red sulfide ointment in the left cup. He let me repeat the action and explained that we should realize ourselves, now, as both male and female. He emphasized the "now" to understand the importance of the event. That is, the red stood for the strength of the female, and the yellow meant the strength of the male. I have written in my diary that for strength he used the word for spiritual power—that is, the Sanskrit word "siddhi." He saw that I was surprised and explained that male and female strength (bala, the usual word for strength) was in everything of nature, which is the Vajra of a thing (of all phenomena). When the male and female strengths are in union they have the potential not only for bal-ance, but for spiritual power. He used the metaphor of a medici-nal weight measure where just the right amounts of medicines are balanced out to make a prescription. One type of medicine, like the haritāla, the yellow powder (arsenic), is too powerful to take by itself. Another ingredient must be added to neutralize the potential harmful effects of the first medicine; or, to help the first medicine be more localized. This makes the compound work and emits a balanced power. The yellow stands for upāya, usually translated "means" or "skill-in-means"; and the red stands for prajñā, usually translated "wisdom" or "insight": they represent male and female energy respectively—the delicate bond of relationships and the ensuing procreation of image.

In Tantric ritual and meditation each phase implicitly represents this interplay and potential union of the two energies that generate the image—that helps to raise the underlying Im. Without this intermingling there would be no extraordinary power (siddhi); no heterosexual image.

The procreative metaphor in a ritual meditative context is a key for conveying the idea that spiritual practice can transform a person into an aware individual on the path to wholeness, salvation or enlightenment. There is a not-so-hidden feeling that sexual energies can be redirected into a higher level transformer than the gonads: some people have interpreted Eastern eroticism and Tantra into a permissive semantics and behavior; others have used this relatively new cross-cultural influence to go to the opposite extreme and entertain varieties of celibacy.

Individuals who are fragmented from their roots and who are looking for a new way of relating to the opposite sex and society will take what they think they understand at the moment and adapt it to their own existing circumstances. In my counseling practice many people experienced themselves as being dilettantes and had a dark miasmic feeling of guilt about their lack of seriousness. In actuality their feelings of insincerity and dilettantism were simply a cover for an underlying and more important feeling to get it together. They felt a desperation to change and a concomitant frustration in finding an excuse or a way to initiate the change. Many times a foreign or exotic spirituality legitimizes an action as a catalyst to attempt a personality change. The dilettante and cynic part of ourselves has been a major obstacle to spiritual sincerity. On the positive side there is usually a glimmer of hope that these deep and dark emotions and energy that surround the procreative can really be worked with in a beneficial way. The obstacle is the structure of conditioned thoughts, feelings and mental pictures about the role of sexuality and relationships.

The idea that Tantra may support a more permissive attitude about sexuality comes from the desire to be more permissive; not from the teaching. Awkward and distorted parental and marriage relationships are rooted in the culture from which they evolve. We sometimes look to other cultures for a cure, but before the healing process can truly begin, the medicines must be accumulated, mixed, balanced and empowered. If there is an overabundance of disharmony and strife, then how can the rituals of life, be conducted in a beneficial manner for oneself and others? If our life and social environment are confusing and fragmented with equally confusing corresponding pictures and thoughts that relay double messages and unworkable directives, we need to go through a debriefing phase—an emptying process that allows one to suspend their own pictures and thought sets— be they parental, religious or political. Also, assumptions, dreams and values about male-female relationships need to be suspended. The rites and meditations of The Great-Black-One allows one to do just this.

The practice pulls us away from stereotyped structures. The yellow and red blend denotes a kind of raw structure symbolizing semen and blood. Thoughts and pictures arise from such a depth that the image erupts as an archetype.

At this point in the morning ritual the priest did not really convey much verbally. He merely pointed out that the Gurumandāla had to be a pure spot before we could begin to make the offerings; that is, to build the mandāla into a perfect universe as an offering to Vajrasattvamahākāla.

As mentioned before, many Buddhist values are implied in the ritual. For example, when we purified the ritual spot, we called to mind the six perfections. For this reason the purification of the place ceremony is sometimes called the six perfections pūjā (sadpāramitapūjā). Here is the way this pūjā was done. The first perfection was called the perfection of charity (dānapāramitā). We dropped a steady stream of flowers and waters on the mandāla, and thought that the mandāla was washed free from impurities. We thought also that the ceremonial space was being purified with cow dung (there was no actual cow dung): It was not uncommon to actually use cow dung. Yet, the Nepalese Buddhists did not place the same emphasis on the purity of the cow as the Hindus did. When the first stream of water and petals was finished, we picked up more petals with a little water and sprinkled the mandāla, with the thought that the mandāla was now clean. This was the perfection of morality (silapāramitā). The third perfection was the perfection of peace (ksāntipāramitā). Here, while we sprinkled the rain of holy water and flower petals, we contemplated that all the insects were gently being removed from the mandāla. We actually brushed aside any burrowing or wandering bugs. The fourth is the perfection of effort (vīryaparāmitā), which means that now the pūjā materials were arranged properly—the flowers and water fell continuously. Again we picked up the flowers and water, contemplating with one pointedness of mind on the relative and empty (sūnyatā) nature of the universe. This was called the perfection of meditation (dhyānapāramitā). The sixth perfection was the perfection of insight (prajñāpāramitā). While the rain of flowers were dropping, we thought that this is the wisdom behind a blooming flower.

We often replace an activity or behavior with a symbolic action or thought, or to mentally act out an event in the hope that the event will manifest itself in another space and time. Much of courtship is daydreaming the images of desire and love. The Army plays war games in order to reappear victorious at a future time. Goal setting involves the mind in the projection of images that will stimulate the person to follow a certain course of action that will lead to success. Without images and symbolic activity we would not be aware of other realities. The Christian eucharist points to an experience beyond ordinary space and time. What seems to be important for humans is expression, i.e. the creation of images and then the acting out of the fantasies with which they are connected. Not so many years ago the rocket ship was just a fantasy.

I contemplate the ceremonial circle is purified and that it extends to the world. But here I am conditioned by the material world to the extent that at times I place more of a value on the material than on my own expression that gives the material a transpersonal meaning. It is clear that in order to exercise patience, peace and compassion, the surrounding emotional quagmire can only begin to be transformed with the symbolism and values of transformation.   To some extent worldly action is replaced with a symbolic or ritual action; yet, the purpose is not to replace but to enhance and alter one's attitude to the point of generating an enlightened mind.

For example, instead of doing the dirty dishes, with the help of any number of symbolic actions, I could ritualize doing the dirty dishes with the thought of increasing one's perfections (the above patience and so on). The dirty dishes might not ever reach their state of cleanliness. Maybe this would improve my discipline to do unsavory chores; or, maybe I would never do my chores, thinking that I am increasing the quality of my perfections, which would mean becoming ritually pure. Ritual purity would be unacceptable in a community where the dishes were just laying around dirty for days on end. It would be acceptable in a group where designated individuals either by custom or agreement were assigned to the task. Since the work is getting done, everyone is free to pursue ritual purity. Someone will do the dirty work anyway.

Religious rites are transpersonal. A ritual substitute for cleaning the dishes might, indeed, not remove the effluvia from the kitchen or clean the dishes. On the other hand, a ritual substitute could very well create a more balanced and harmonious atmosphere—an atmosphere that may or may not be conducive to cleaning the kitchen, but could open other possibilities in relationship to the household and oneself. What if this reasoning is extended to a love affair? Maybe a ritual substitute could contribute to the serenity of a relationship? And, then, what if one had a ritual and meditation as a substitute for actually murdering someone? The ritual could avert a hideous crime. Substituting one act for another one is not such a bad idea—especially, if the substitute is motivated by friendliness, compassion, joy and equanimity. If it is not motivated by these Four Keys of Balance and Harmony or similar values the shadow side of the ritual could predominate, i.e. become ritual abuse. It could work either way. But then South and East Asians have been playing with these arguments and polarities for thousands of years. Their rites and meditations have not been destroyed and polluted as in the case of the European prechristian traditions. As an outgrowth of Catholic doctrine and ritual, we have the black mass and the fear of inquisition. Hitler was obsessed with ceremonies and esoteric rites— examples of massive ritual-abuse that were often alcohol and drug supported.

Constructing a ceremonial circle and performing rites and meditations is tantamount to the generation of an atmosphere. Atmosphere is the partial goal. Of course, atmospheres just seem to happen. They are usually realized after the fact. In the case of our Tantric rites and meditation, the atmosphere is consciously created and yes, the process is formalized but not strangulated—not every Vajrācārya, for example, would purify the mandāla in exactly the same way. Jogmuni wanted to emphasize the perfections. The gurumandāla is supposed to be a perfect universe. He said that no matter what kind of pūjā was enacted, the six perfections were of the utmost importance to always keep in mind. Actually, there are ten perfections he pointed out, but that the other four, skill in means (upāyakausalya), resolution (pranidhāna), strength (bala) and experiential knowledge of the underlying Im (jñāna), were implied in the previous discussion of the transfer of merit. Atmospheres constitute not only qualities of temperature, light, landscape and local customs, but also behavior and feelings that arise from affirmations of values and all those gestures, sounds, playacting and mental creations. The image or dominant spirit that dwells in a particular atmosphere will have many faces to reflect the various dimensions of a particular place and time.

We try to recover what we feel has been lost in our history and to mend what is perceived as fractured through the means of creating specific shapes and masks. The ritual specialists (Shamans and some educators), artists, children and psychotics consciously create new forms. The rest is unconscious and evolutionary.

My own initiation into a Buddhist practice was also part of developing a craft that makes atmosphere and image: a craft that preserves tradition and at the same time initiates change. I discussed this many times with my teachers, and although for the most part they chose to emphasize a more traditional approach, they encouraged me to pursue The Great-Black-One and to share it with others in an innovative manner. Jogmuni had a religious painting of Mahākāla hanging on a nearby northern wall. It is thought that Mahākāla dwells in the northeast. There was a vase with a picture of Mahākāla and we constructed a gurumandāla. Each ritual event was a new whiff of atmosphere.

"Your hands will be instruments for the sake of others", he said. When the priest asked me to think of the right hand as an embodiment of the sun, the male principle and symbolical of skill and means (upāyakaudlya) I flashed back to grandfather. "Think of the left hand as the moon and as insight, the female principle (prajñā)", Jogmuni said. Grandfather had a similar idea, the right hand is the moon and the left is the sun according to him. The sun was female and the moon was male. But both the sun and moon could represent either male or female energy; depending on the astrological circumstances, in grandfather's mind. This reverse symbolism is sometimes true in Tantric Buddhism. I held back my desire to ask a question.

It seemed like we looked at our hands for a very long time. I was urged to see the dark forces in my hands. I saw them. I don't know why, but tears came to my eyes. I saw a collage of what I call the dark phases of my life. There were shapes and happenings that took me back to my childhood, teen years and the Asian war. I saw clouds of activities that produced deep and hidden sensations—even smells, that went beneath the incense and flower-laden mandāla. Maybe these were structures and configurations of past lives. It seemed to happen for a very long time. I think somehow I moved into Great-Time, but in clock time it could not have happened over a span of more than a few minutes. I felt a strong feeling coming into my arms and hands. I knew the feeling. I had experienced it many times doing tai chi, only now it was stronger with a very warm temperature. My right arm was warm and my left arm was slightly cool, and from my hands there emitted commingling auras. I touched a flower. My hands were now as pure as the sun and moon (candrārkavimāla). We put a flower on the spot where the gurumandāla was to be constructed (mandālapushpanyāsa) and dropped some water and flowers on the food offerings—a ritual action called the removing of obstacles (vighnacchedana). The actual construction of the gurumandāla is simply to drop little flower petals or rice in each of the directions and the center to make up the perfect universe. Each action is accompanied by a mantra.

The process can be done mentally. The gurumandāla is within each practitioner. Many of the vihāras have a built-in metal disk in the courtyard where the gurumandāla pūjā is performed. Most practitioners have little copper plates, which they use for their private worship.

Jogmuni drew a circle with white chalk for himself, Ratna and myself. We followed his instructions and constructed the mandāla.

First of all, as we let the petals fall from our fingers, we each contemplated that it was our own body that was being offered. It was almost as if we were reaching inside our own body pulling out the same body, and then, decorating it with flowers. We were actually going to offer the perfect universe within us for the sake of all sentient beings. We put together ideas, substances and beings to generate the most impeccable universe. The first few petals dropped in the mental image of a circle of colored jewels (ratnacakra) that make up the very center of the universe in the form of a mountain called the "Great Middle Meru" (mahāmadhyameru). This central mountain emerging from the center of our own being stood for the Buddha Vairocana. Next to this central mountain we projected a mountain of turquoise called the "Middle Meru" (madhyameru), which symbolized the Buddha Amoghasiddhi. We then offered a mountain of rubies for another mountain called the "Small Meru" (sūkshameru), which designated the Buddha Amitābha. Above these consecrated mountains of jewels we projected a blue and red aura. The blue stood for wind and the red for fire. We projected that the wind was fanning the fire into a yellow mountain called Sumeru, which designated Vajrasattva.

My thoughts turned to the sun and wind and their effect on the earth. I wondered how I could symbolize ozone and what kind of ritual might save our environment.

We then created the continents. First of all, we projected the Eastern continent, called the Videha, to be in the shape of an arrow. Next, we created the Southern continent, Jambūdvīpa, as a triangle; and then the Western one, Aparagodavari, in a round shape. Finally we projected the Northern continent, Uttarakuru, as a square. In the subdirections, i.e.northeast, southeast, northwest and southwest the subcontinents were then created as an offering. We did not mention any particular names of countries for these, but rather we simply projected seed syllables. For example, in the Southeast we thought *yam*; the Southwest, *ram*; the Northwest, *lam*; and the Northeast, *vam*. We then created the traditional eight jewels of regality: in the East, the elephant jewel (gajaratna); in the West, the stallion jewel (asvaratna); then in the southwest, the man jewel (purusharatna); in the North, the woman jewel (strīratna); in the Southeast, the sword jewel (khadgaratna); the Northwest, the Dharma wheel jewel (cakraratna); and in the Northeast, the cause of all things jewel (sarvanidāna), also referred to as the flask jewel. To complete the process we then mentally offered the celestial regions, primarily the sun and moon on the outside of the mandāda.

Jogmuni sang. I found out later the tune was titled "Middle Meru" (Madhyameru). Newari singing is extremely energetic and full of the same kind of feeling that I heard when I was young during the caroling season at Christmas time. I have not heard caroling with that same spirit for a long time. The teacher finished his song with a smile and gave me a brief lesson on how to sing and say mantras and related that everything sacred can be sung or chanted into existence. It was a very useful teaching that initiated me on an in-tune path to uttering mantras. The gurumandāla was then further consecrated by the fivefold ordinary oblations and offered to all sentient beings. The offering of the gurumandāla was an outward expression of the vow to do my work for the sake of all beings. The universe I ritually created was an ideal of the perfect world.

To the right of the gurumandāla was a balipot (balibandha) filled with cooked rice. Below was a tor-ma (gtor-ma) on which was placed some of the rice: it was mentally projected to attract the protectors of the world (lokapāla). Another offering of curd was placed on the tor-ma for the world protectors (lokapāla). At this point Jogmuni asked us to think of the world protectors as spirits from the past now coming to aid us because of our vows and sacrifice. I thought this was quaint: I cajole our ancestral god through my ritual-meditation, and then throw him a party with the idea that he will, like us, work for the sake of all beings. Grandfather would have appreciated this little drama. His ancestral gods, teutonic nature spirits, and personifications of life cycles were maintained and cultivated in his consciousness. "Without their presence," he said, "the Judaic-Christian illusion and its parallel materialism would destroy nature and humanity." This concept might be a little harsh, but is the reality of today's world. He believed that the five elements were spirits or gods. Grandfather had a sacred well with strange runic markings and ritualistic paintings. He said the waters protected him from the bad spirits of mechanized civilization.

He had a curious idea that the old Germanic gods were a purifying force for Christianity. He used to mention the thunder and lightening god Donar, known better as Thor, and of course Wotan—so celebrated in the Wagnerian epic The Ring. He used to tell grandmother she was like Frau Holda, which would have been a compliment if grandmother was not so passionately against paganism of any kind. Frau Holda, who represented the sky, haunted my grandfather's natural spring, moved about in unison with snow flurries, and like the Chinese Kuan-yin, is a compassionate goddess. Grandfather perceived Frau Holda's spirit as a nature spirit and a divinity that gently moved us from one life phase to another.

I'm not really sure how much grandfather ritualized this remnant of Teutonic tradition, but it seems similar to the conception of the protectors of the world (lokapāla). The protectors of the world are the old guards. They are Vedic deities that throughout time found themselves very active in the Buddhist fold as protectors of the inner circle. The inner circle in the case of the gurumandāla designated the Mt. Meru complex at the center of the universe; that is, one's own center of the universe.

There were ten world protectors. Almost all of them have a role in Vedic myth and rite. Six of them a have a place in the Rig Veda. The most dominant of them are Indra (war god), Agni (fire), Yama (death), Vāruna (the waters, and possibly has etymological connections with the planet Uranus), Vāyu (wind), and Prithivi (earth). The remaining four, though Vedic in origin, are extremely popular in later Hinduism. Kubera is depicted as the god of abundance, and some of his earliest references have him as a somewhat questionable deity who presides over robbers. He is termed a rāksha. The rākshas are beings who tend to move against the Vedic order of things and spread disharmony and sometimes disease. Of the remaining three, Nirriti is the most important, because she is the personification of disease—the forerunner of Hariti. The remaining two, Brahma and Īsāna are also Hindu deities.

Attracted by the cooked rice, the ten protectors descended into the ceremonial circle and took up their positions in a circular fashion. Following Jogmuni's example, I put ten flowers in the mandāla concentrically near the center of the mandāla, which represented the atmosphere of the ten protectors. Jogmuni explained that my meditation had to be very powerful to channel the ten forces into my consciousness. Sometimes it took an extra effort to generate the feeling that I had cajoled the ten protectors into my sacred rite. He performed four hand gestures along with the uttering of four seed syllables, *jāh, hūm, bām, hoh*. Jogmuni said that we should perform the hand gestures and utter the mantras slowly. The ten deities were old warriors not easily allured into one's universe. He said he would take responsibility for insuring their working presence. But I would not be capable of doing it until I received my mantra. He taught me the hand gestures and gave some further instructions on meditation. These old Vedic gods are always reticent.

The protectors of the world were traditional culture archetypes that evolved their significance in the process of historical change: Indra and Agni in the old Vedic milieu, protected and generated fear in the hearts of the everyday Āryan, now were called from the chthonic depths to be soldiers in the Buddhist pantheon. But the soldiers need to be supervised by the Buddhist deities themselves; they would only be given limited controlling power. Jogmuni explained that we were installing ten more Buddhist deities around the innermost perimeter; and were called the ten angry ones (dasakrodha). They were considered to be Buddhist deities and the first guardians of the perimeter. As the protectors of the world reluctantly take their stations, these ten angry ones nudged them into a sentinel position. Since these Vedic warriors were reluctant, they were sometimes said to be nailed in their place: But, Jogmuni explained that the protectors

and the ten wrathful deities did not have an adversarious relationship—just a family one. He said it was like a family squabble
where one party needed to be restrained to maintain the order of
things, the dharma. This part of the rite is sometimes called
kilanābhāvanā, which means cultivating the nailing. It was a
case where traditional forces can be thought of as both obstacles
and assets at the same time. The Vedic deities were pervasive in
Buddhist rites, and like the Sanskrit language itself, preserve a
sacred dimension—even when they are called obstacles.

After arranging the world protectors and the ten wrathful
deities in our consciousness, we performed the five ordinary
oblations pūjā for them, hence establishing them in the nature of
the five Buddhas. Then there came an offering in the form of a
celebration. The sixteen musical goddesses, pleased with our
performance, were then thought to descend into the mandāla
playing their orchestra. To show this, Jogmuni did sixteen hand
gestures which stands for sixteen goddesses and their musical
instruments. The priest then rung the bell. He offered the bell
which revealed the nature of insight, after which he chanted a
praise (stuti) to the world protectors and the ten angry deities.

After he was satisfied that the Vedic warriors had come into
the ceremonial circle and joined forces with the ten angry deities,
he offered them holy water. He dipped his ring and index finger
in the holy water and snapped the water into the air. This is
called tarpanā, which literally means satisfaction. This offering
was a signal for the world protectors to enjoy the fruits of the
ceremonial circle. As we called them aloud to take the edibles,
they were imagined to begin their feast. After this, all the gods
were offered the five ordinary oblations, the 16 musical instruments, the bell (as insight), praise, stuti and holy water until
there was mutual satisfaction between men and divine beings;
there was a compatible feeling with the arising images.

The remainder of the evening was centered around the skull
bowl on top of the flask that was placed on the tripod. I would
sit in a similar ritual four years later without the skull where the
flask portrayed a painting of The Great-Black-One. This latter
event was my marriage ceremony. In the present ritual there
was just the religious painting on the north wall. It was understood that the spirit of The Great-Black-One would be coming

into the flask—an outward connection with the center of gravity of our being. I would cultivate The Great-Black-One in the pot of my own self. In yogic terms the flask indicates the center of gravity of one's own body which is part of the meaning of meditating on the area of the navel—actually just below the navel.

The flask and the skull bowl were loaded symbols. They carried the associations of emptiness, and at the same time form, completeness and abundance. The flask and skull bowl symbolized procreation, and of course the skull generates the feeling of death in some way. The pot, or flask, was said to be the cause of all things (sarvanidāna). It is the eighth jewel, a good luck symbol, also outlined on a silver flag in the ceremonial circle. The common water jug, shaped like our clay flask, was a commonly seen article—usually carried to and from wells and rivers by the women. The water jug, or flask, had the ambience of a mother goddess. A Nepalese bride who has not conceived after about a year may call the Vajrācārya to perform a flask pūjā (kalasapūjā). In Mahākāla ceremonies the skull can be employed.

Since this was essentially a Mahākālapūjā, the skull was appropriate. The priest took liberties in the ritual process. I received an initiation, in the community of followers of The Great-Black-One, and the Buddhist Tantric order of things and its dharma. However, in Kathmandu Valley the other Newar Buddhist priests would not take my initiation very seriously, Jogmuni explained, for I would not be able to participate in social functions where caste rules concerning sharing of food applied. The Newars, at least at that time, did not have a community of devotees which was separated from marriage and family. This was one reason why occasionally a Newar would become a Theravādin Buddhist or join the Tibetan monastery. There was no other way of becoming a member of the Buddhist community that was detached from the concerns of ordinary domestic life. I naturally gravitated to the Tibetan community whose social structures allowed for a more diverse Buddhist practice and fluidity of thought and movement. But it was my Newar instructions that allowed me to receive a sense of how the worldly and sacred can commingle.

When we had reached the moment in the rite where the usual practice would be to share meat offerings from the same skull bowl, we had instead our individual bowls. Then we had a rest period. Jogmuni's wife poured something that smelled like alcohol, and began to serve the food. I was startled by hearing my name called several times. Apparently I was in a kind of trance and maybe just becoming sleepy in the lull period. I moved closer to the priest so that he could whisper the secret mantra into my ear. He did.

The already familiar mantra was quite short. And had now come to me in an unexpected, surprising and dramatic manner. Although I had expectations to receive a mantra I was never quite sure about the next step. The rite focused the energy around these thoughts. When I received the mantra, I was catapulted from a slightly awkward and sleepy frame of mind into an energized state. The fact that I knew the mantra from my personal study did not detract in altering my consciousness. I was slightly surprised at finding the secret mantra as one that I already knew. The timing was just right. Jogmuni read from the Mahākāla-Tantra, conversed with his wife, who was still preparing some food and drink, and for a while we just sat. My thoughts were cleared and the mantra seemed to automatically turn through my mind's eye. At the same time my eyes remembered a former instruction about the circular movement of the ritual action: the flow, from the gurumandāla to the protectors of the world offerings, the five substances of cow, tor-ma, the flask with the skull bowl over the six-pointed star, the curd offering, flask for tutelary deity, flask for divine serpent, and finally light for clarity. Near the flask were the eight symbols of good luck and abundance.

My mental process seemed to be taking care of itself. Then the nature of the rite changed. There were smells of spicy meats and liquors. Small clay dishes and cups of delicacies appeared in the ceremonial circle. The priest began to utter mantras and bits of meat and tasty solutions found their way into the skull bowl. The smell and sight of the food and drink excited my senses. Then, instead of partaking of the delicacies, the Vajrācārya explained that there was really no difference between Vajramāhakāla and Cakrasamvara, the Grandfather Tantric de-

ity of the Vajrācāryas, and that Cakrasamvara would appear in
the form of the Buddha Akshobhya with his consort Māmakī to
enjoy the offerings in the skull bowl. Akshobhya was one of the
five Buddhas and the father of Mahākāla. Mahākāla was often
depicted growing out of his Akshobhya's head. Each of the five
Buddhas represented the transformation of a strong human emotion. Akshobhya stood for transformation of anger or hatred
(dvesa). Hence, he was looked on as the chief of the class of
deities called anger (Krodha). These were of course, the protectors. Every rite in some way was a ritual-meditation on the
redirection, transformation and relationship to one of these five
dominant emotions: anger (dvesa), lust (rāga), jealousy (irsya),
confusion (moha), and envy.

I wasn't comfortable listening to the priest at the same time
that these tasty morsels were being offered in the ceremonial
circle. My mouth watered, but just because there is food on the
table did not mean that we should immediately devour it. The
negative emotions though universal, are responded to in a
variety of ways according to how the senses are trained, and
underlying values. On one hand, this is a matter of upbringing
and culture, and on the other, the willingness to have new experiences, be self-reflective and open to change.

The five meats and drinks represented the five Buddhas, the
five elements and the five directions (four plus the center) i.e. the
fivefold nature of the universe. The essence of the whole world
was being empowered by the already empowered ceremonial
circle, and shared in its transubstantiated form by the participants. We started out with Cakrasamvara and his consort
Vajravarāhi (the sow goddess) whose images or essences were
projected in the center skull bowl. Jogmuni read from one of his
ritual texts called Pañcasālipūjā; he stopped occasionally and
explained. The food was spread corresponding to the directions.
In a larger ceremony there would be a different kind of bowl in
each direction: oyster shell in the East, in the South coconut, in
the West a tortoise shell, and in the North a brass bowl. In the
center is a human skull bowl. Each bowl respectively (placed on
a pot with a tripod) was empowered with the goddesses Rūpinī,
Lāmā, Khandarohā, Rāmadevī and in the center Cakresvarī.

This phase of the ritual was a recycling of what we had

already completed in the gurumandāla and the samādhipūjā. We had opened the back door of the senses. We smelled, tasted, listened, saw and caressed our way into a door of perception. Now, the continents of the gurumandāla were offered: the five traditional breaths of Ayurveda were offered which are breath (prāna), lower body breath (apāna), upper body breath (udāna), life breath of the fetus (samāna), and the breath of the total body (vyāma). The offering of the gurumandāla set the stage for offering the five-fold universe: The five elements, the five castes, five different kinds of knowledge, the five senses; and I added some of my own, which included grandfather's Bavarian forest, my father's library, Columbia University, and five parts of America. There was more to offer—both in the text and in my mind.

As a part of the offering preparations the priest put a little curd, salt, oil and sour into the skull bowl and on the food. The curd represented the essence of the sperm, the male principle, called bodhicitta. The sour substance represented the female principle which is red in color and called rakta (blood). The salt and oil were meant to designate the creation of beings. The mental exercise of synthesizing these substances, thoughts and beings into a cultural and psychological stew was a process that could be called psychic cooking: here was an extension of the beginning goal of the rite; to activate the thought of enlightenment (bodhicitta) in its unifying form.

I couldn't help but wonder if the food was getting cold or not. I think this is an American hang-up. My family relations, except for grandfather, always preferred to have hot food. It was just one of the odd crosscultural thoughts that drifted across my mental screen.

The process of the ritual was the flow of a rising image. The rising of the bodhicitta was the rising of The Great-Black-One. I am not sure exactly what happened, but as soon as the offering of projected beings and substances was completed, my perception changed. One traditional way of expressing the goal of the ritual was the attainment of the experience of equanimity of taste (samarasa). Yet, at this point, I was not thinking what was supposed to happen or when I should attain such and such a state. I can only say that it was exciting, pleasant and unusual.

Maybe it was just being overwhelmed, but I don't think so, because there was no confusion or anxiety and there was a definite phase where nothing really seemed to be all that different—despite the variety. All the thoughts, substances, beings and processes blended into each other. Then it came time to share in the feast.

But first there was another surprise. I was instructed to project a copulating Akshobhya and Māmakī within the skull bowl. I think the priest felt a little self-conscious about initiating me into this phase of the rite. This is near the culmination of the rite. Māmakī is the consort of Akshobhya. She represents Prajñā (insight), and Akshobhya is the embodiment of hatred. When embraced by the personification of insight, hatred is transformed into skill in means. But not until the practitioner projects that he is killing Akshobhya, i.e. killing hatred and then joining with Mamaki himself. I was now one with The Great-Black-One; I had the permission to kill my father; Aksobhya and unite with Prajña (insight). The erotic and violent metaphor takes into account the worst of human nature. Yet, the transformation of hatred into the skill in means to generate the healing ambrosia and image assumes the best in human nature: it is the near magical ability to tap the raw energy of our emotions, regardless of how negative, and rechannel it for our own and others benefit. This spiritual intercourse between oneself as The Great-Black-One and Māmakī transforms the offerings into an abundance of bodhicitta that would flood and transform the offerings into a healing ambrosia. This part of the ritual was a reenactment of a primitive urge to become one with the female at all costs, indeed to attain wisdom by neutralizing the hatred within ourselves.

The episode, ironically, made me feel that I had not loved my own father, for a moment I felt sad. I thought of the <u>Tibetan Book of the Dead</u> where it states that the new consciousness about to be reborn will hate the parent of the same sex. It will see its future copulating parents, then, feeling jealousy and hatred (if to be reborn a male) towards the father. If reborn a female there will be hatred toward the mother and lust for the father. So, here I was, practicing the art of neutralizing hatred through the medium of images and rites. It was working through the darkness and creating healing energy at the same time. The drama served as a model for using my raw negative emotions as a means to neutralize and transform the negative part of ourselves. It showed me in a subtle manner how I can utilize and transubstantiate these dark phases of my life.

When it finally came time to share in a sacrament, a feast of healing ambrosia, Jogmuni smiled and said we were going to eat the five different kinds of meat. He pointed out that the meat was called go, ku, da, ha, and na which stood for the meat of cow, dog, horse, elephant and man. I had a brief regression. I thought of the time I ate red dog meat during the Asian wars. I imagined what it would be like to cannibalize—I had never done that. I remembered the tear-ladened eyes of a dying elephant shot by a great white hunter in a Clark Gable movie and had a brief flash of self-consciousness for having been a beef-eating Westerner. I looked up and across the atmospheric bed of offerings, projected deities and ritual paraphernalia into the smiling faces of Jogmuni and his wife. Ratna seemed to be elated and also surprised. He was also initiated. The feast was intoxicating. I was ready to continue my sādhanā.

CHAPTER V

Sādhanā: Recycling The Suffering

The sunrise scattered streaks and droplets of pure light through the shutters and across the ceremonial circle, creating a flow of natural energy that intermingled with our aura of gifts. The sun made me aware that I was chilled. We sat there in pleasure massaged by the limbs of the sun's rays. My state of mind was broken by Jogmuni's wife shouting, *"phat, phut, phat."*

When one performs ceremonies (pūjā) in the Svāyambhūnāth area, the monkeys and stray dogs are sure to get wind of it. Jogmuni's vihära was at the foot of Svāyambhūnāth. A half dozen or so monkeys were conniving their best to sneak through the shutters and doors...phat, phat, and the game continued. As in all pūjās, the deities were discharged. Some of the remains would be burned and carried away to be put in the river. We finished our chai and left. Ratna and I circumambulated Svāyambhūnāth. We uttered Mahākāla mantras and chatted. I thought of the Vedic hymn to Sūrya (the sun): "Sūrya rises from the bosom of the dawn. Shining, he is honored with joy by the singers". That is what we and the other worshipers were doing.

Around 5:30 in the morning the atmosphere of the pūjā still lingered in the air and the sounds of Newari singers drifted in the atmosphere. When we walked through the village of Kimtole, a small procession formed along the path. The devotees passed us or fell behind: the dialect of the murmuring had changed. The sounds were now Tibetan. According to the Newari way of thinking Svāyambhūnāth is the ideal center of the universe. Lhasa is also the center of the universe, it is said by many Tibetans; and Hindus sometimes purport that Mount Kailāsa, northeast of where we were about 500 miles, is the center of their universe. Mecca, Rome, Babylon, Jerusalem, and even New York City have become the centers of the universe. I felt that Svāyambhūnāth was Sumeru, the center of the gurumandāla, and that the great caitya on its top was its essence, with its two eyes surveying and piercing the mist in the valley. I always thought of those two eyes as the sun and moon, appropriated as the all-seeing wisdom of Avalokitesvara: From this sacred place I could hear every day the Tibetan horns and Nepalese drums that drifted over the valley. The markings between the two eyes is very similar to the marking used by the Newars for their offerings when they design their ceremonies: the offerings are gifts that are exchanged between men and the beings of the hidden dimensions—the deities who constitute the totality of one's personal universe. These offerings and the blessings received are considered to be unlimited. The sacrifices are extensive and the profits are boundless.

Here we were, the initiation pūjā completed, but I was still in the process of making offerings. The circumambulation (pradakshana) was a form of offering. Svāyambhūnāth itself was the offering. What Ratna and I were feeling was our inner center. We floated into the warming subtropical morning.

The Svāyambhūnāth area, which includes the village of Kimtole, was pervasive with the sacred. At the top was the Karmamahārājavihāra the most visible temple in Nepal. It's golden spire peaked like an iceberg in a sea of humanity. Surrounding it was a small complex of temples with an active community. The large caitya gazed over the valley. Just a few feet away was the temple of Hārītī, the goddess of smallpox. Behind Hārītı was the sacred entrance to the underground tunnels where Vāsuki, the nāga serpent, was believed to guard over the valley with her coils stretching throughout the area. There was also a space set aside for the Newar musicians who came there every morning around dawn to play their sacred songs as an act of worship and fellowship. The musicians, in the same sacred place on the top of Svāyambhūnāth where the kam-tsang monks would bring in the new year with their long horns (dung-chen), pole drums (lag-rnga) and large cymbals (rol-mo). We caught the sounds of their music as we continued our circumambulation.

I used to follow after grandfather in his Bavarian forest while he inspected and talked with his bushes and trees. He seemed to always move clockwise as we were doing. Sometimes he would move counterclockwise but not very often. He had a penchant for doing things backwards. It seems to me that whenever he was troubled by the events of the time he would walk around his well counterclockwise, and of course he would be mumbling some ancient syllable. I learned later in my studies and life that counterclockwise was a necessary movement for achieving goals and helping others, but, often it was inappropriate and harmful—as I found out sometimes the hard way. The sun goes clockwise, but sometimes human conventions are out of order and some opposite motion is needed to balance out the relationships between man and nature, a strong consideration in Buddhist Tantra.

I had recently moved to the smallest of the three hills of the Svāyambhūnāth complex. In accordance with the local population of Kimdol, I perceived the hill where I was living as the little Meru (Sūkshmameru). Then, there was the second hill compared to middle Meru where there was another Tibetan monastery, and slightly above it to the west there was another monastery. The son of the priest of that temple now lives in Seattle and is the author of a very funny and ribaldish book called Uncle Tompa.

Both Ratna and I were quite tired in that special out-of-this-world sort of way. We finished one round and walked up the stairs, known as the thousand and one steps, to the top of Svāyambhūnāth. As we arrived at the top, the Newari musicians played their final melodies for the day. We walked around the main caitya and decided to enter the Tibetan temple where the monks and lamas greeted the new day with a pūjā of Tārā.

The insides of most Tibetan temples are constructed so that one can circumambulate the ceremonial circle and take blessings from the monks and lamas.

We slowly and respectfully entered the temple where an older monk motioned us to come forward and continue our circumambulation. We respectively walked towards the incarnated Lama sitting in an elevated chair. When Ratna realized that we did not have a white scarf (kha-btags) offering, the traditional manner in respectively approaching an incarnated lama, we quickly returned to the old man who supplied us with two scarves. As we approached the incarnated lama on the raised wooden chair covered with carvings of lotuses and the five colors that represent the five sacred knowledges, we bowed and presented our scarves. The lama who would soon become my sponsor into the future teachings of The Great-Black-One, took my scarf and then gave it back, briefly placing his head against mine. I don't want to seem overreactive and romantic, but I will just say that I felt a warm wave of energy going through my body. At that point, I knew that I was going to be spending a great deal of time in this temple.

Both Ratna and I had more than enough spiritual ecstasy for one night and morning so we politely refused tea from the old monk and went on our way. The joy I felt that morning had an underlying darkness. There was an atmosphere of illness that seemed to pervade the Tibetan temple. I mentioned this uneasy feeling to Ratna before we went to our own dwellings. He pointed out that many of the monks were sick from tuberculosis. He said there were many diseases in the valley and told me his own story about how his family, during a smallpox epidemic, gave him up for dead when he was just a baby. He pointed at the pox marks on his face and smiled. Ratna had plenty to smile about—he survived the smallpox epidemic and became healthy, wealthy and wise. The death rate from smallpox in the valley was 80 percent until vaccination was introduced. But many people still did not take the vaccination for fear of spiritual pollution.

One of the busiest shrines in Kathmandu is the Hārītī temple at Svāyambhūnāth. Hārītī as we mentioned before, is the goddess of smallpox. It is the belief of many that only her blessings can ward off the disease. Of course, I was filled with the usual inoculations. I was also filled with contentment and sure of my quest with a one-pointed mind. Yet, at the moment, I was somewhat sidetracked with my feeling that here was an environment that could not only lead me to the continuation of my understanding of the Mahākāla-Tantra, but one which was not without its challenges in terms of old-age, sickness, disease and death. This dark trinity manifested itself differently than in America where old age, sickness and death are kept undercover. It is also different than in a life and death crisis, like soldiers in combat, where one can expect physical trauma at almost any moment. But here was a lingering suffering that was endured year after year—it was in the open and accepted as a part of one's karma. I was discovering a new dimension of darkness: a way of relating to old-age, sickness and death. Although it is the same the world over, its treatment, relationship and appearance is different.

I was being reminded by The Great-Black-One of The Four Noble Truths: One, the world is in a state of suffering regardless of the apparant situation, and two, despite any momentary sense of happiness one might feel, there will arise, at some point in one's life, a sense of suffering. The third truth has to do with coping and transforming the attitude and feeling of suffering that will inevitably arise: The third truth simply states that there is a way of coping and transforming both physical and mental suffering which is indicated by the Sanskrit word Nirodha which literally has the meanings of "to stop", "to hold back" or "to confine". The basic idea here is not to repress or even suppress, but "to stop" and pay attention to what is going on with one's inner emotions and thoughts. It is through this stopping and attention that can eventually lead to an enactment of The Fourth Noble Truth which is the eight-fold method of coping with suffering: The eight ways of coping and transforming are: viewing the life around one in a balanced and harmonious manner, having good intentions, speaking in a clear and nonagressive manner, conducting oneself with poise and good will toward others, engaging in a livelihood that relates to positive thinking and the welfare of other sentient beings, to exert and extend oneself in a healthy and solid manner, to contemplate in a way that is conducive to mindfulness and to practice the kind of meditation that allows for the growth of others as well as oneself. The Eight-fold path is often explained by the adjective "right". Petsan used to tell me that if there was any problem in deciding what is right or what the Eight-fold path means to convey, just apply the four keys of balance and harmony to each of the eight, but even more important I should practice stopping and transforming the arising of thoughts and images. Then, there would come new thoughts and images that could be more easily transformed into peace of mind, and a further knowledge of oneself and the human condition, that is, acceptance and realization.

The Tantric tradition interprets the neutralizing or stopping the cause of suffering through the affirmation and embracing of those very causes in a skillful and often aesthetic manner. At any rate, I decided to employ a simple skill in means and a few days later I took a dying monk to a tuberculosis hospital. Eventually, after establishing a cross-cultural clinic in the monastery itself, the tuberculosis was neutralized.

According to the life history of the historical Buddha, Gautama Buddha, he formulated The Four Noble Truths after discovering that the world was full of old age, sickness and death. His discovery was quite typical. His father tried to shelter him in his princely palace from all forms of suffering. Hence, after running away from home, he discovered that life outside the palace was full of unpleasant surprises of horror and suffering. His father, the king, had the means to keep the world of impermanence and pain from his son's consciousness. Because of his isolation in his fathers palace, endowed with all the comforts that one could possibly imagine, the darkness of the world came as a culture shock to Gautama. Gautama Buddha might serve as a model for some of the runaway teenagers who run away from home to discover the streets to be shockingly bleak. His surrealistic perception of this other reality led him to a lifelong quest for an antidote to the suffering that he perceived and experienced. Gautama found new kinds of relationships to have with the confronting world. Because everyone recycles the experience of confrontation with suffering, Gautama's adventure and the spiritual quest is archetypal. And like Gautama, almost everyone seeks a way to overcome the suffering that they often unwittingly create themselves or discover. Gautama's initial question was heuristically put in a simple manner: What is the cause and remedy of old age, sickness and death?

When Gautama decided that the practice of yoga would not answer his question as to how to neutralize the cause of suffering, he decided to meditate on his own, i.e. improvise. After a long and arduous contemplative practice, he had a vision that allowed him to conceptualize his own new way of relating to suffering: a translation of the system of yoga—a variation of the contemplative experience.

As Gautama practiced under the bodhi tree on the night of his enlightenment, his primary realization was liberation from the feelings of absolute existence (bhava), lust (kāma) and ignorance (avidyā). Some versions of the enlightenment expand these three into the twelve worldly connections, which is both popular and instructive. His meditation on the twelve-fold circular chain was both clockwise and counterclockwise; that is, with the hairs (Anuloma), and against the hairs (Pratiloma). He asked the question, how could anyone live in spiritual bliss without working on the suffering of the world? I was recycling this archetypal experience that morning when I sensed the dark side of Svāyambhūnāth's spiritual atmosphere.

The sun came out, I had chai at my favorite local tea shop which was located at the bottom edge of Svāyambhūnāth near where I lived on the hill called Vulture's Peak. As it grew warm I was naturally beginning to unwind and tire, and I remembered that the priest still had the Calcutta edition of my Sanskrit manuscript. Then I circumambulated Svāyambhūnāth once more by myself. Ratna had walked home on the east side of the Bagmati River.

Every Newar and Tibetan Buddhist has the idea that he or she has a spiritual practice. Even though there is great variation and freedom to add and subtract from one's practice, most Buddhists of the Himalayan regions will practice mantra, circumambulation, offering to the deity or priest (pūjā), and in connection with those three, some dimension of deep contemplation. Categorically speaking there are four general kinds of meditation: calming the mind (samatha), insight (vipāyana), mindfulness (smriti) and through image cultivating the Im (bhāvanā). The first three are conventionally practiced before contemplative concern and cultivation of an actual image and the arising of the underlying Im (bhāvāna). The process of cultivating an image (bhāvanā) is more than a technique; it is an attitude.

Ever since that morning, when I slid through an atmosphere of an awareness of suffering and at the same time maintained that feeling of joy, I have had the thought that Buddhist practice, regardless of its method or sect, has the goal to recycle Gotama's awareness of suffering and the noble truths. How should we practice to gain the knowledge of the cause of suffering as well as its neutralization, and maintain happiness in that same life?

That evening as I read through the Sixteen-Handed Mahākāla Sādhanā it took on an unusually alive character. The history and sense of each word seemed to carry a multitude of living spirits that had their origins in a remote past. That same evening, the images and words of grandfather seeped between the words of the Sādhanā. I soaked in the contemplative energy until it became almost oppressive. I read the last few words of the Sādhanā and fell asleep with the following sentence on my mind: "This is the offering mantra of the Sixteen-Handed Mahākāla equal to all the Buddhas." That night I dreamt profusely. According to Jogmuni, I was supposed to dream the night before my initiation, but did not. But this particular night I dreamt of a deer that had been shot in grandfather's Bavarian forest by two pesky teenagers in a pickup truck. The deer was bleeding to death in one of grandfather's favorite creeks. The creek turned blood red and began to flood the property until it seeped into my room where I was sleeping. Grandfather appeared as a dark shadow who went to his well. Next to it was a statue of Frederick the Great (there actually was a statue on the property). Grandfather turned the well on its side so that the river of blood was running into the well. By that time, I was almost drowning in the red waters. Grandfather or his shadow, began to murmur some teutonic runes and the well then sucked up the blood. About that same time the boys who killed the deer had become spirits in the sky. I did not see them in my dream; I just had the feeling that they were there. Just before I woke up the deer had turned into a killer whale and was escaping into Puget Sound (not far from where we were geographically). I found myself looking for a magic wand that grandfather had given me (he had given me a Bavarian hiking stick when I was very young). When I found it behind a heap of Mahākāla manuscripts, I reached for it and woke up.

Someone was knocking at the door. It was Sotup, one of the monks from the monastery. He was knocking on the wrong door, so I got up, walked onto the little balcony overlooking the house owner's courtyard and golden shrine. I directed Sotup to come upstairs. I felt a little embarrassed for having slept so late, and was pleasantly surprised that a monk from the temple came to see me. Sotup noticed my sleepy eyes. He asked me if I was okay—literally—is your body good? His dialect was the same as that of the owners and frequent patrons of the Ladakhi restaurant in Old Deli. I was not really set up yet for offering morning tea and Chinese biscuits—the usual civilized morning snack in that part of the world. Sotup noticed my Sixteen-Handed Mahākāla Sādhanā. It was lying on a low Chinese table next to where he was sitting. It was in Sanskrit, so he could not read it, but we used it as a device to discuss dharma and The Great-Black-One.

He mentioned that his teacher, the head teacher of the temple, was the best person with whom to study The Great-Black-One— exactly the information I was seeking. Petsan's fame, I came to find out, was far and wide among the scholastically-inclined monks and lamas. Due to the difficulty of the subject matter, Sotup was not sure I would be able to study Tantra with Petsan. Sotup said that Petsan knew Sanskrit and that I should meet with Sa-bcu-rin-po-che and let him know what I wanted to study. He thanked me for taking his friend to the hospital. Sotup and many of the other monks in the temple had lived most of their lives in Nang-chen in the high mountains of Eastern Tibet. As refugees from the Chinese-Tibetan conflict, they escaped across the Chinese-Nepalese border and finally found a home in Kathmandu Valley. The temple had a long history of associations·with the karmapa lineage and was a natural holy spot for the settlers.

Mahākāla is very important to all Tibetan Buddhists, but for these survivors their very life as a monastic group had depended on their practice of The Great-Black-One. After Sotup left, I decided to write down my dream, and thought about the cultural and psychological impact of Mahākāla and the other fierce tantric deities. The fierce deities were there to support us in the translation of our base emotions into a more neutral and finer emotional complex for helping oneself and others. It was also very clear to me that the potential to turn the dark forces against another person was inherent in the practice. This is almost never discussed in this manner of potential ritual-abuse. There is a history of ritual abuse in every religion. Rather, the ceremonial circle, whether it be in the form of an outward rite or an empowered protective amulet worn on one's body, was considered more as a meditative and preventative measure than a weapon. Yet, in South Asia, the layman, indeed, has healthy respect for any priest, yogi or sādhu who might have a knowledge of Tantra.

Grandfather used to say that because of his own pagan tradition of rites and meditation, he could never confront the Catholic priests with the same awe and indeed fear as many other lay Catholics seem to do. I do not mean to say that Catholic priests are tantric, but all spirituality has this hidden dimension of power that can easily be misused on an unsuspecting or naive victim. Traditionally speaking, Tantra is reserved for the initiate, and it is still not surprising to note that there is even today very little written material in Western languages on the subject. I know too, that my own fears of losing my head were justified. Also, there are among both Tibetans and Newars, as in any culture, a minority of individuals who make their living in sorcery. Sorcery, or magic on the dark side, is quite common in Tibetan and South Asian Buddhist literature. Most of the same literature either frowns upon the activity of sorcery or has its methods placed in a context where it is used against the negative emotions in oneself. We have had an example of this in the Māmakīpūjā; that is, the killing of Akshobhya (i.e., the killing of hatred) and the joining in union with Māmakī (uniting with the wisdom within oneself) and the generation of Ambrosia (the healing and creative fluids).

Grandfather also said that the destructive forces in the universe were really agents of transformation and not killers. According to him, snowstorms, floods, hurricanes, forest fires and earthquakes are our teachers. Living only a few miles from the San Andreas fault which recently gave us a few lessons in earthquake survival, I often think of grandfather's neo-taoist and Tantric wisdom. They also give us clues as to how to utilize energy. Isn't this what the physical sciences are all about? It is not in the order of things to wish harm to another person. It was even unnatural, grandfather would say, because our wish to do harm is not a function of the elements, but of self-centeredness.

The negative outflows (āsravas) within us are like the natural forces except that hatred, lust and jealously, as we are normally aware of them, are to a great extent conditioned emotions. For the most part we do not know their unconditioned natures—their primordial states or raw structures. The anger we feel when someone steals from us is not quite the same as when monkeys and dogs take food from each other. And, then, compassion, love and altruism are complex, for example when we are giving something away.

When it comes to sorcery or any other practice that seeks to tap into the hidden dimensions in order to reach out to control, predict or change forces in society and nature, the practice of Tantra crosses from the spiritual and psychological over to the social—to the domain of relationships. The path of Tantra is the path of the aspiring Boddhisattva—it is working in the world, even in the state of deep meditation. Yet, if the practitioner performs his practice (sādhana) purely from the motivation of compassion, friendliness, joy and equanimity, the whole environment will benefit. When one attempts harm to another, it is pure and simple—bad karma. The goal of Tantric practice is to be able to utilize human energy for the sake of others regardless of how it is categorized. The tradition recognizes that one's health can be a factor in one's ability to help others, and that the etiology of suffering is beyond any specific symptoms. The concept of healing and gaining extraordinary powers is based on such an assumption. This is expressed by the emphasis on translating and transforming our dark sides by means of our understanding and skill in order to gain the success needed to produce a healing energy.

Several weeks after my initiation ceremony with Jogmuni, I was asked to visit the head lama. When I am asked to describe Sa-bcu-rin-po-che, in all respect, I always say that he looked like the fantasy figure E.T. What I mean by this is that his image definitely has the ambiance of a compassionate space creature. There is some resemblance in looks as well, but my perception in this case is very much formed by my subjective feelings. Steven

Speilberg probably did not have this in mind, but E.T. could very easily have been an incarnated lama or accomplished yogi—he had that ambience.

That morning was another watershed. Karma, one of the monks, led me to Sa-bcu-rin-po-che's room. It is the same room and setting as described in Chapter One. It was always the same. The space became a positive state dependence—it was part of the rising image. The Rim-po-che sat on his pile of carpets accompanied by three senior monks on the floor, my future guide and teacher Petsan. Also in attendance was O-sa, the brother of the Rim-po-che and a hero chieftain of the Nang-chen group. With his black red-on-the-inside silk chu-pa, cowboy hat and sporting a dagger, he was a symbol of the secular authority. We were served sweet tea and Chinese cookies and went through the communication ritual of finding out what kind of questions and answers we were going to trade. The initial stages of a first meeting are much the same throughout the world: feeling each other's vibes, having something to offer, wanting something, and always a potential hidden agenda.

A person's authentic teachers reflect their own image. One's teachers do not always fall into conventional relationships. They can even be adversaries, and forces of nature, or a combination of these. We can only realize who and what our teachers were after some years have gone by and we are able to reflect on the significance of past events.

I remarked during our meeting that indeed Petsan looked like my grandfather. They all thought that was both funny and quite possible. Enjoying the humorous side and at the same time understanding the serious aspect of events is a usual characteristic of Tibetan-speaking people and Newars. I described my grandfather to them, using Petsan as a visual model. They were both short sometimes with thin mustaches, black hair, sort of bluish-brown eyes and soft thin bodies with an uncanny ability to adjust and mimic their environment. But a more important comparison was an underlying nondiscursive feeling. If I had to pick a dominant trait that indicated the similarity, it would be the chameleon character of both grandfather and Petsan. It was almost as if they had multipersonalities. Good teachers are often good actors. They can take advantage of their moods to make a point or get a job done. My father also had this quality, but he confined his personality to a strict set of boundaries that he never crossed. I responded well to Petsan. He was full of surprises and always striving to do his best to pass on the knowledge of The Great-Black-One.

We talked for over an hour. They asked me many questions. Sa-bcu-rin-po-che asked me what I really wanted to achieve? I related my aspiration to learn about the practice of The Great-Black-One. I specifically mentioned that I was learning about Tantra, not only from a scholarly point of view, but as a way to reconnect with my own spirituality. I pointed out that there was a tradition in the West that attempted to recover one's history from classical texts; hence, I gave him an oversimplified yet correct definition of humanism. I am not sure I explained this clearly, but Petsan, especially, seemed to understand. He commented that there is an original Buddha nature in all of us, but that it is covered with a miasma created by rtog.pa which translates "mental fabrication". I asked him if that meant interpretations, descriptions and scientific enquiry? Petsan pointed out that even the Tibetan religious texts are rtog-pa if not read and practiced from the basis of The Four Keys of Balance and Harmony, openness to one's shortcomings and the realization that "We are of the nature of Vajra which originates from the experiential knowledge of sūnyatā."

I explained that I was making a critical edition of the Sanskrit text and did not feel that the edition could properly be done without a thorough reading of the Tibetan version, as well as doing the practice. I wanted to read the Tibetan text over and over again until I felt comfortable not just with the grammatical apparatus, but with the subject matter and practice as well. Sa-bcu-rin-po-che replied that my desire to study The Great-Black-One was probably the most difficult task that I could embark upon, yet it was the most important process in life. He then pointed his finger at Petsan, and explained, "Petsan will be your teacher."

It was not long after the above meeting that I began the new routine of going to the temple every morning to study and meditate with Petsan and Sa-bcu-rin-po-che. Sometimes we would read from the Tibetan version of the <u>Mahākāla-Tantra</u>.

Occasionally we would talk with Sa-bcu-rin-po-che about a particularly esoteric aspect of our study; and on those days of important rituals I would join him in the preparation, which included the making of offering cakes, thread crosses and place-
ment of ritual objects. Once in a while Petsan would give a class
concerning a particular topic which I would attend. Sometimes
we would read commentaries. For the first six months or so he
liked to see me sit with the monks and read the text aloud in the
cyclical ceremonies of The Great-Black-One. Quite often we
would just-sit—in the Za-Zen manner. I never knew when we
would do this. It would usually happen in the context of reading
a text or giving an explanation. All of a sudden I would find
myself just sitting and not thinking about anything in particular.
This was Petsan's method of introducing to me meditation that
has no support and the Zen aspect of what the Tibetans call
completion-yoga (rdzogs-rim).

The work with Petsan was exciting and gave me the confidence that here was a Buddhist family of teachers that had all the
knowledge and channels available for my quest and study. I also
knew that study and practice was basically my own work. I was
accumulating a basket of jewels, and at the right side of some
highly esteemed teachers. I realized later that the responsibility
to live up to these opportunities could be quite difficult indeed.
Everything that I was learning and practicing would be capsulized
in a single breath of sādhanā.

If for some reason all the Tantras were destroyed or lost, but
individual practitioners either had in their possession or remembered some sādhanās, the essence of the Tantras could be rees-
tablished. The sādhanā can be a single breath or a very long
recitation and practice. Implied in the Sādhanā are the four
stages of meditation: calming, insight, mindfulness·and the
cultivation of oneself as the image of the deity, i.e. Buddhahood
(the Im).

My own practice included various sādhanās. At first the two-
handed Mahākāla sādhanā, and later on the sādhanās of the
other Great-Black-Ones. The following is a translation of the
Sixteen-Handed-Mahākāla composed by virupaksa from the
Sādhanāmālā Number 312. At the beginning of every Sādhanā
there is a phrase that indicates the respect and worship of the

deity to be invoked, in this case Mahākāla. What and exactly who the devotee is invoking will depend on the image system of the devotee. It also depends on the Im. The first expression "Om Praise to Mahākāla" (Om Namah srīmahākālaya) opens the door to the complete process of sādhanā as one understands it. The word Namah implies a humility to one's higher power and the invisible.

To begin, one should experience friendliness, compassion, joy and equanimity (The Four Keys of Balance and Harmony). Immediately after realizing emptiness, when the sun arises from the flickering murmur of ri-ri-ri, one should cultivate the sixteen-handed lord Mahākāla as oneself arising from the syllable *hūm*. He has eight faces, twentyfour eyes, four feet and 16 arms. The right arms hold a chopper, vajra, buckler of elephant hide, mallet, three-prong spear, sword and the staff of the vedic god of death. The left arms hold a human skull filled with blood, elephant hide buckler, bell, elephant goad, white fly swatter, drum and a severed human head. With the remaining two hands, Wisdom (a female) is embraced. He appears as a blue-black dwarf who shouts *ha ha, ha ha, he he, ho ho*. Mahākāla is The Great Howler (Mahāraudra). He wears a crown of the five Buddhas and is characterized by the three dimensions of Buddhahood. To the world this is a dreadful image.

To the East, sitting on a lion with her left foot forward and right foot drawn back (like an archer or a marshal artist) is the great goddess—The Great Sorceress. She has four hands. In her first left hand is a human skull bowl. The other left hand plays a drum. In her first right hand she holds a chopper, and in the second a mallet. She has three eyes, disheveled hair and monstrous fangs. Her color is blue.

To the South, sitting in the same way on the powerful god of death is The Naked Female Messenger Of Yama. She has four arms. The right hands hold a lotus staff and chopper. The left hands carry a human skull bowl filled with blood and a flyswatter. Her color is blue and her hair is disheveled.

To the West, again positioned in the same manner mounted on a horse is The Female Messenger Of Time. Her left hands hold a human skull bowl and cow's head; the right hands a mallet and three-pointed spear. She has three eyes and disheveled hair. Her color is red. All of these divinities are adorned with garlands of snakes and have monstrous fangs.

In the Southeastern corner positioned in the same manner mounted on a corpse is Kālikā. She has two arms holding a human skull bowl and chopper. She is blue-black.

In the Southwestern corner is Carcikā. The description is the same as the former except that her color is red.

The same goes for Candesvarī in the northwest corner. Her color is yellow and she carries a wild beast.

In the Northeast corner is Kulikesvarī. She holds a staff and vajra. She is white. Again, her stance is the same. All of these divinities have three eyes, monstrous fangs, disheveled hair and are naked.

After conceiving oneself as the lord, surrounded by eight yoginis, with his left foot forward, right foot back, existing in a trance of emptiness with a fine vajra, trampling the corpse (vajrabhairava) in joy he should utter a mantra. Here is the mantra: *Om for the 16 armed one hūm, hūm, kīḥ, kīḥ. For the sake of the gigantic formidable one whose, fangs are frightful, and violent. For him who gives all powers, kīḥ, kīḥ, kīḥ, kīḥ, he svāhā.* Indeed, one should utter this mantra.

If this victorious of mantras is constantly uttered, it will give enlightenment in one's lifetime and innumerable past lives are remembered. With the above mantra, the eight great powers (siddhi) are realized.

If an offering needs to be given, one should project the lord Mahākāla with his retinue. Then, one should give eight offerings while uttering the offering mantra:

Om praise to Mahākāla, to the gigantic terrible one with great fangs, to the lord of the great angry ones, to he whose erected hair is flaming yellow, who has 16 arms and who has 24 eyes. Om please be quick, please be quick. Kha, kha. Please devour, please devour. Please seize, please seize this offering. Hā, hā, he, he, hu, hu, hehai, hohau, hamhāh to the Great Vajra Buddha. In the body, please bless me. Please bless! Tata, tata, mata, mata, kata, kata, please do the work. Please do the work. Please roar, please roar. For the ferocious one, master of the great angry ones, please destroy all the enemies. Oh, you who tames the wicked beings, please protect, please protect me. Please give, please give, please destroy all of them. Hūm, hai, kīḥ, kīḥ, bhah, hūm, hūm.

(All the genies, ghouls, demons and manbeasts. Please make all of them peaceful. Ham, hah.) Please destroy, please destroy. For Mahākāla whose form is black; who is the great frightful one. Please tame, please tame the feared one. Please cause them to be destroyed, please cause them to be destroyed—destroying. Oh, destroyer of all wicked beings, please rescue, please rescue, for the master of the snakes. Please destroy, please destroy, please rescue, please rescue. Hah, hah, katah, katah, khatah, khatah, phatah, phatah: please cut, please cut. Please kill, please kill. Please burn, please burn. Please cook, please cook. Please agitate, please agitate. Please destroy, please destroy. Please strive, please strive. Please flow, please flow. Trām. The angry one. Svāhā.

Now here is an important point: each day, during the night, while uttering this mantra, one should respectfully fold one's hands into the shape of a small bowl and make offerings. Also one should offer generous portions of meat and wine into a clay dish filled with water. This will nullify all the malicious forces that are one's impediments. Because of the offering, those beings who are enemies and flesh-eaters are neutralized and dissolved.

Now, immediately after the offering whatever that one desired, not yet attained, will come to be realized. Certainly it will be possible to attain the eight powers (siddhi).

If (there should remain) all the flesheaters, nature demons, disease carriers, deities, underworld creatures, humans and all the rest, they will be put to flight. Then each one's head will burst and they will disappear into the atmosphere.

Mahākāla, for sure, predicts what is auspicious and inauspicious in one's dreams. He knows the past, present and future, and can be channeled from anyplace.

With this offering, even the Buddha is not able to count the accumulation of merit of this victorious mantra of all the Buddhas. In its continuous flow day and night even the gods cannot count its merit. This is the river of the 84,000 dimensions of phenomena.

If there is no success because of a distortion (or mistake in one's sādhanā) in the flow, one should make an alcoholic beverage (mead), and using the beverage as ink write the spell with a bone pen. Now, that hand will hold, touch, grasp and nullify the difficulties in one's breathing that are afflicted by disease, starvation and enervation.

Why is it said that the body becomes healthy for a thousand years like Mahākāla's? It is because this is the victorious offering mantra. When drinking water is blessed 100 times with this wisdom-mantra, it protects the pregnant woman, and she will easily give birth. Certainly for a thousand lifetimes it destroys sundry torments and fears—just from reciting the mantra they are destroyed. While reading the mantra, if one anoints the two eyes with the sacred substance, men, tigers, horses, elephants, buffalos, serpents, dogs, insects, lions and the rest will go away. Yet, they will certainly return after having realized one's goals.

This is the offering mantra of the sixteen armed one who constitutes all the Buddhas. One should recite the 100 syllables and make an offering of forgiveness-discharging the spirits. This completes the sādhanā of the 16-handed Mahākāla.

The reader may begin to feel some similarities between the activities of grandfather, my own process as it evolved into a Tantric path and the written word as expressed in the Buddhist scripture (the above sādhanā). The words we write and expound can be intermeshed with our experiences and life. They can also be disconnected and abstract. Buddhism, despite its voluminous canons and commentaries has never been without a strong oral and experiential tradition. Our teachers and ancestors have passed on to us images of enlightenment, and despite their own shortcomings the clear, ecstatic, and authentic has been made available for us to cultivate and pass on to others. I feel fortunate that my scholarship and practices were able to accommodate the images of grandfather's spiritual lifestyle into the Buddhist path. I have come into contact with many people whose family memories and ancestors are forgotten, almost to the point of obliteration. One of the reasons that Buddhism was able to grow in Asia was the affluent and copious suitcase of Hindu, Confucian and Shamanistic images that the Buddhist teachers and yogis had at their disposal—a wardrobe accumulated over centuries. If we imagine how Tantric Buddhism at the time of our Mahākāla-Tantra in fifty chapters (12th century) might have developed in Europe before influenced by the Bible, we might have had a cultural and religious development similar to the growth of Buddhism in Nepal and other regions of the Himalayas. It is also conceivable that if Buddhism had signifi-

cantly influenced the Gnostic and Jewish parts of the population
from about the 1st to the 5th centuries in the Roman empire,
without the development of Christian dogma and imagery, Buddhism would have evolved on European soil with a different set
of images. When the indigenous traditions of one's ancestors
has been forgotten or repressed new ideas and practices are
welcome and exciting, but until the deeper images in one's
chthonic well are confronted and translated it will be difficult to
achieve harmony and balance. In my own search for a lost
manuscript and image, my own depths that contained
grandfather's imagery and Im were touched. Like the images of
the Indian Buddhists were cultivated from vedic lore my own
arising image has some seeds within that illusive and miraculous Bavarian forest.

If one asked grandfather about metaphysical matters, at some
point, in the conversation he would reply, tongue in cheek, that
he was just an ordinary Catholic who had a special appreciation
for nature. His penchant for nature, however, was linked with
some arcane ritualistic behavior. To those who were closest to
him, he always seemed a little out of the ordinary. Grandfather's
lifestyle demonstrated a hidden spirituality—not secret in the
conspiratorial sense, just a very personal way of life, based on
some very old traditions that he was willing to discuss to a
receptive audience. I realize now that I developed a similar
attitude.

Grandfather's behavior was conditioned by his Bavarian childhood. Even to this day in certain parts of Bavaria, his style might
not be considered so idiosyncratic. In South Asia similar idio-
syncrasies would have gone unnoticed.

Grandfather did not have a written text that one could call a
sādhanā-no personal prayer book. Likewise many of the practitioners of sādhanā who still wander the Himalayan regions, do
not use written texts. On the other hand, there are yogis who
carry written sādhanās with them, sometimes tied into their rolls
of hair; but others refuse to write the sādhanās down, considering them too sacred. I have often wondered what images and
meanings grandfather's practices would have generated in the
written word. He did not write or keep any kind of diary. His
ideas, rituals and runic uttering evoked a pure oral tradition. If I

had not traveled to Nepal I might have never realized the scope of grandfather's wisdom. If his wisdom had been put to the pen the authentic experiences may have been lost. Sometimes the written word unwittingly serves as an obstacle to the true experience. In hindsight, I can only say that grandfather's spirituality approximated my own reoccurring experiences concerning the idea and practice of sādhanā.

Words like "mysterious", "arcane" and "esoteric" are loaded and sometimes confusing. I like the word hidden because it accurately contains all three meanings—like an ancient Roman well which is arcane and mysterious with esoteric implications. There is a well in the former sādhanā—in every sādhanā.

The images that bind the sādhanā to our normal perceptions are the bricks of which it is built. The text is esoteric, but the implied practice lets one see; even immerse oneself in the well—the practitioner becomes one with the hidden.

Grandfather's well was an example of the hidden because like most wells, I couldn't see very far into the depths. The sometimes gurgling sounds would bubble up in the darkness and burst forth with a plethora of images that would both haunt and excite my imagination. In general, the hidden has the propensity to stimulate superstition, but in every superstition is a realty. The imagination soars in the sky and is treasured in the earth. The healing waters of the earth evolve from the dark energies of our own creation. But, now that a parking lot has taken the place of grandfather's well and forest, I wonder how long it will take for the healing energy of the earth to restore the magic that directed me to the Land of Pagodas. The well is not forever sealed in darkness; it is not irrevocably covered by cement.

CHAPTER VI

White Rice

The sādhanā is similar to the well which seems to have no bottom. The abyss of terror and darkness, the bottomless pit of angst is occasionally felt by everyone. The possibility of the dread and terror lies beneath the outward trappings of daily life. The Buddhist Four Aryan Truths stating that the whole world is suffering and suffering always arises is not as pessimistic as it sounds; but does point to the underlying dark space that contains the panic within everyone's possibilities. Dread and apprehension also arise amidst the subtleties of relationships and communication, through gestures, sounds and letters, through food, shelter, clothing and all the stuff of intimacy. Material existence can take on a gruesome ambience.

Petsan once assured me that even the tiniest emotional bits of hatred, jealousy, fear, lust and selfishness were miniature time bombs. He liked to use the image of the atomic bomb; he often pointed to a photo I gave him of an atomic explosion as an example of what could happen to an inner emotion. For Pechan (and for me), the bomb is a good illustration of how knowledge could be used in the wrong way, how a demonical force can be unwittingly unleashed over time. For Pechan, the bomb was just a gigantic megabullet, and the explosion was an extension of some irregular karma which originated in the emotions and ego.

The person engaged in the practice of sādhanā confronts the conditioned self with all the possible distortions, uncontrollable emotions and addictions. He or she knows that these thoughts will not disappear, nor can they be denied. They will continue to play an active role in one's life and environment. The sādhana becomes a function of one's higher power and can create a new kind of relationship with the dark forces—a transforming and positive one. The practitioner understands that becoming one with the Great-Black-One is to realize the dark side of consciousness, and a confrontation with the darkness can be an antidote to disease and suffering. Then one will be able to transfer the healing energy to others.

In my counseling practice I sometimes ask my clients to list the negative aspects in his or her life. Although these can be listed on a piece of paper, most people do not have the perspective that enables them to communicate how these distorted impressions actually work in their lives. Organizing the negatives is to get to know them, and understand that they have a partial life of their own. Hatred, for example, can arise unexpectedly, It can produce a frown, tighten the connective tissues between the ears and head, narrow the eyes, constrict the cheek muscles, tighten the lips or even bare the teeth—"whose fangs are dreadful". Hatred may stimulate threats, weapon wielding, curse shouting, and may generate images of inner and outer conflict and violence.

Hatred is usually repressed, yet the energy behind hatred needs to be expressed. On a profane level, hatred constantly threatens to produce a violent and antisocial manifestation, which can often be channeled through political and institutional means into accepted ways of warfare and brutality. Hatred, by definition, is pathological and not indefinitely tolerated by society. Even so, hatred is learned through cultural upbringing, in much the same way as one learns mathematics or history. Hatred is learned through curses and gestures—"whose fangs are dreadful". Is there a raw structure of emotion, which is beyond cultural conditioning? Can hatred, like hunger be related to an almost irreversible need? But, then, unsatisfied hunger creates anger. Anger becomes hatred when catalyzed by prejudice and intimidation. Do the bared fangs of the tiger express the same feeling as the bared teeth of a human shouting curses at a potential competitor or attacker? The possibility of converting the reservoir of energy that lies behind hatred and the other emotions into a new kind of feeling and constructive way of being is a large part of Buddhist practice and sādhanā—in all schools of Buddhism. In Tibetan Buddhism, it is common to believe that after death the soul wanders in the atmosphere: It is a space between death and rebirth (called in Tibetan Bar-do). A part of this soul is looking for a rebirth in the earth's copulating couples on whom it is gazing full of emotions. Another part is attempting to detach itself from the images of lust and enjoyment in order to continue its journey to a possible state where there will be no rebirth. When the wanderer finds him or herself looking down at an embracing couple it has the desire to enter the womb which of course will entail another rebirth. The soul, if female, becomes jealous of the woman being embraced and feels lust toward the male. If, male, it will have jealousy for the male and lust for the female. Such an emotion for the wandering "desire body" is an opportunity to consciously move away from the object of desire to a clear mind—a clear light as contrasted with the dull lights that produce terror and confusion as the soul is tempted to dive into the sensual energy that the couple is exchanging. The clear light is a distant, but everpresent image showing the way to a state of being that indeed has no rebirth—a condition of Im.

Ordinary rebirth is fraught with the extension of this original desire, hatred and jealousy. The sensual images of the copulating couple, and the matrix of the emerging life overpowers the concentration of most wandering souls, as well as those of us on this earth. If these wandering souls are unable to work their way into the clear light, freeing themselves from attractive images; flowing continuously through ordinary time and rebirth, they will fall back to earthly rebirth. They will become dependent on one image after another—a Buddhist description of a deterministic life. It is a description of archetypal co-dependency. In the world between life and death, we have an archetypal imagery. In order to be reborn as a bodhisattva, the attraction to clear light must be very conscious and empowered with The Four Keys of Harmony and balance: compassion, friendliness, joy and equanimity. Yet, to be reborn a human being, instead of a plant, insect, animal or a spirit is an auspicious opportunity, since only

a human has the ability to truly help other creatures to enlightenment. Only a human being (or potential) can bring others to a
condition where the primordial emotions of hatred, lust and
jealousy can be experienced as antidote to pathological behavior.
Hatred and lust are clusters of energy that can be tapped for
medicinal, spiritual and communal goals.

The invisible conduits that are formed between the five senses,
the thought process and other beings, substances and ideas are
pipelines for the healing energy generated by the sādhanā practice. This healing energy is called in Sanskrit "amrita". It makes
sense that a word which is often translated "immortality" would
be applied to various forms of healing energy. Invisible realms
of medicinal power are activated by mediums as touch, sound,
symbol, ritual, and by forces within the raw structure of nature.
It evolves as psychic energy. I like the Tibetan word "byin-rlab"
which denotes, on one level of meaning, an invisible movement
from one thing to another, i.e., "splendorous ripples". The phrase
"splendorous ripples" is an appropriate image that conjures in
the mind's eye a rippling pond, heat waves in a desert, or a rising
shimmering sun—"immediately after realizing emptiness when
the sun arises from the flickering murmur of Ri Ri."

One of the antidotal images that symbolizes the neutralizing
aspect of hatred (its cure) is represented by the figure Akshobhya,
the spiritual father of The-Great- Black-One. To show this relationship, some of the images in Nepal display a sculptured
image of Akshobhya on top of Mahākāla's head, sometimes
drawn between the eyes. Kinship terms such as father, mother
and the other usual familial terms are used to portray relations
between humans and other beings. More than once, I have
heard my grandfather call the animals that roamed his Bavarian
forest his brothers and sisters. My father did the same with the
rattlesnakes of the Arizona desert as well as the eagles of the
Pacific Northwest. These kinship expressions are powerful images in the sense that they help our proximity to the transpersonal,
i.e., the Im itself.

There are five transpersonal families that correspond to the
elements; each one has a father who is an antidote to one of the
toxic emotions: For example, the image Vairocana is the antidote
of confusion, Amoghasiddhi the antidote of envy, Amitābha of

lust and Ratnasambhava of jealousy. The Great-Black-One (Mahākāla) is an Akshobhya family member, the antidote of hatred. An image of one, however, implies the character of all five—"he (Mahākāla) wears a crown of five Buddhas."

The visible and symbolic natures are always empowered by hidden streams of energy. The sādhanā also has a hidden flow which clears the psychological miasmas and transfers the power— "in its flow day and night even the gods cannot count the merit. This is the river of the 84,0000 dimensions of phenomena."

Since the empowered substance will be communally shared, the empowering of the visible (or the conceivable) is initiated with great care. Each person, though maybe not as inspired as the actual practitioner who empowers the substance, will never-theless benefit in their own way. Initially an empowered object has the specific goal of being shared with a designated person or group. The purpose of the ritual-meditation is clear—it may benefit a specific donor or group; or it can ameliorate a particular disease or harmful condition. Yet, in Buddhism this type of ritual always has the more universal purpose of being for the sake of all sentient creatures. But unless the empowerment is enacted in just the appropriate manner, an unpredictable and distorted situation could arise.

My friend Ratna told me many times to be very careful on my walks around Kathmandu, "Don't accidentally walk into or put your hands on leftover ritual items!" Pieces of feathers, cloth, leftover incense, charred paper, and bits of string were often left along the road. These seemingly harmless objects could contain a terrible spirit or curse, and consequently might harm anyone who touched them. On the other hand, Petsan often said that demons harm people who are attached to their negative emo-tions. For example, a person who goes through each day holding a grudge, hating another person or blaming others for their mistakes will use anything that happenchance comes their way to legitimize their negative emotions. Eventually they will be-come ill. Actually in every day life we encounter situations where a person does great injustice to self, body and others because of their own attitude. We strew the path with images of greed, hatred, jealousy lust and bitterness for the world. What we bring to the world will add to the world. It will be not only own future but everyone else's as well.

Petsan insisted that the images and thoughts concerning the Great-Black-One are misinterpreted by the majority of people outside the fold of Tantra. Even practitioners themselves can misread the signs within the texture of the visible and conceivable, wherein may lie a powerful medicine. We learn to read words and images literally and visibly (at face value). Some people are surprised at the monster-like countenance of the wrathful deities, and never stop to think of the terrible possibilities within themselves. Many in the West think of evil as a force that is sent from an outside place of evil. Therefore, sometimes when one perceives something unusual or just plain different, the sense of the exotic can be imagined to be terrible, and may even have the ambiance of a plague or destroyer, an omen to the end of the world—"To the world this is a dreadful image."

It is important to clean any invisible colonies of spirits in one's chosen place of ritual—if someone crosses that path and misreads the signs, they may end up in a state of dread, the victim of psychic cannibals. One must clear the space and time of any substance, thought or being that could give an impression which might be translated by other sentient creatures in a malicious context.

My grandfather realized his drawings and pictures were considered weird by most of the people who visited him. Many of his pictures portrayed dwarves; they were all different and had various functions. Like Snow White's seven dwarves, they played musical instruments and carried tools to show their avocations, e.g. a shoemaker, logcutter, fisherman. Most of grandfather's dwarves had a spiritual or occult significance, and were identified with the forces of nature. He used to point up to the rafters, to his mural of a dwarfish stout figure with oddly shaped ears and a Frenchman's goatee. The dwarf was featured lying on his back grasping his legs looking at the sky; the eyes appeared to be stretched out from his head by a very thin cord and seemed to be searching for something in the heavens. "He's looking for rain," grandfather said.

The dwarves were pictured in all sorts of awkward stances, each holding natural objects from nature such as a twig, rock, crystal or a planet. Some carried rainbows, clouds, or raindrops and wore halos in the manner of Christian saints. Grandfather shunned the serious side of Christianity; his paintings and explanations made visitors uneasy. Despite the humor associated with many of the pictures, most who saw them felt an aura of the macabre. Although, for anyone familiar with Hieronymus Bosch, the medieval German painter, grandfather's folk art would not have seemed quite so strange. Like the Tibetan imagery of the protector deities, the dwarves were meant to be benevolent protectors of the Bavarian forest—"The Great-Black-One commonly appears as a dwarf; he appears as a blue-black dwarf who shouts Hā Hā He He Hā Hā Ho Ho."

The family and visitors alike were disgusted with grandfather's images of dwarves having sexual intercourse with other dwarves. These images were hidden under the rafters and between the railings of the house. I also found them painted on rocks in dark places in the forest and behind his liquor cabinet.

Concerning the images of procreation and sexual union, Tantric Buddhism communicates a transpersonal, dimension. As one cultivates the meditative process, the erotic is understood in a new way. That is, the image of Mahākāla portrays the experience of Great-Time and Space which in turn can produce an oceanic feeling of oneness; it is where the conjunction of opposites takes place—the transpersonal marriage, so to say, demands an expression of poetry, words and phrases that denotes the inexpressible. There are many such terms in Sanskrit and Tibetan; one of them is Mahamudrā, Great-mudrā (the sense of mudrā comes close to the meaning of "sign" or "seal"). The image of the copulating gods in tantric Buddhism is a sign that denotes a transpersonal bond in the minds eye which may softly explode into an extraordinary sensation of bliss (of various degrees)—"with the remaining two hands wisdom is embraced."

In the ordinary or exoteric sense, the copulating gods can remind us of the effluvia of disease that can arise from our ordinary sexual proclivities—AIDS, venereal diseases or genetic deformations that a wandering consciousness may encounter when forced by karmic desire to enter a diseased womb. The word venereal is related to the Greek goddess Venus. It reminds me of the sometime consort of The Great-Black-One, Srīdevī, who carries a bag of diseases. We are constantly reminded of the possible bliss that comes with the embrace as well as the risks that come with the territory of common sexuality.

In the middle of this century American readers of Oriental philosophy were zapped by the starkness of Asian sexual imagery and the underlying mysteries of tantric and taoist lovemaking. I say zapped, because the images of the gods in conjugal embrace reflected the wish fulfillments of young people of the late 1960's. The truth of this image called in Tibetan the yab-yum image is experienced through practicing sādhanā. The concepts of yab and yum (these are honorific terms for father and mother) do not stand for any of our common notions of sexuality and permissive behavior. Yet in a cross-cultural sense the images denote an awareness of a new though misunderstood way of relating to sexuality that further ruptured the bedrock of puritan repression.

The image of the Great Black One is organized through the deeper energies of our primordial consciousness—an ineffable state. Yet the very process of writing about it gives the appearance of an image which we think we can understand in the usual discursive manner. Like the image, the writing is an indication of a process and a hint as how to practice—or, how not to practice. This complex of images and signs are a map that could lead one to the circle of the Great Black One—the mandāla within. But the practitioner is always confronted and tricked by appearances. The appearances of more images and books make the map more complicated and confusing. If we could do an internal photographic study of the Great-Black-One, a kind of cat-scan, a process that looks at the body in slices, we might find a multitude of configurations that reflect the human condition and the cosmos. We might see a flash of a historical process, maybe a cross-section of the future, a picture of how hatred and the other emotions will be embedded in future evolution—how they will come out of hiding and make their secret transformations.

The image is conceived to work antidotally and religiously (transpersonally) at the same time. Imagine going to your doctor and having a religious experience. Imagine getting a physical or indeed a surgical operation, and at the same time receiving a dose of spiritual enlightenment. On one hand it initiates a healing process, and on the other is conducive to spiritual enjoyment. Its aftermath, so to say, is the kind of reflection that could be called philosophical and aesthetic, and has an ethical nuance as well. It is the results of sādhanā that the practitioner brings to the world. Therefore, regardless of the level of the practitioner, the sādhanā in Tantric Buddhism is emphasized—in the same way that prayer has a focus in the Judaic-Christian religions.

Explicit or implicit in every sādhanā is the context for relationships. I prefer the word relationships rather than ethics, which I hesitate to use since it is loaded with conflicting meanings passed down to us over the centuries. The original meaning of ethics or ethos in Greek is "cow pen." Cows relating to each other within boundaries: This reminds me of the Chinese character for family which illustrates pigs under a roof. The raw structure in these images is one of relationship, i.e. the dynamics of interrelating sentient beings. It is within this context of relationships that every sadhānā explicitly states "The Four Keys of Balance and Harmony" which is the glue of positive and peaceful relationships. In the Buddhist practice, these Four Keys are the precursor for the rising of image—"to begin with (at the beginning of every ritual or action), one should experience friendliness, compassion, joy and equanimity".

The image, though still an imagined or created form of this world, has an Im beyond appearance. Image acts as its own antagonist. The Im has released itself from the image, and generates the healing energy. Since the practitioner cannot completely control his thoughts and feelings, let alone the mechanical functions of his automatic nervous system, the Great Black One in this neutral form goes to work on these uncontrollables. In the Tantric way the practitioner focuses through the female side of image: It can be the earth, the five elements, the Image of the goddess, the bell, a female sound (like the seed syllable Bhyo), or a dedicated spouse. However, embracing wisdom is not so easy, nor is it automatic.

It is a process of meditation, which cannot take place, at least in the Buddhist sense, without the generation of compassion, friendliness, joy and equanimity. If the substance or flesh is embraced without these four qualities embedded in one's consciousness one may be pathologically attached and dependant, i.e. co-dependent. As one cultivates The Four Keys of Balance and Harmony the negative emotions or the demons, move from a position of absolute power to a phenomena that is possible to change. This is expressed in the representations by The Great-Black-One trampling on the demons.

Every sādhanā has the means to generate as well as to reduce image. Reduction in the ideal sense is to develop a closer proximity to the underlying peace and power of healing. Precisely the manner in which this is done depends on the guide, the proclivities of the student and the environment. The generation of the image means to realize in a visual and conceptual manner the totality of the deity. For example, one can visualize a salad, simply by remembering a salad that a waiter carried to the table. It is not difficult to develop the ability to remember images as you see them. But if you did not taste the salad you might not realize that it was mixed with the finest of ingredients. There are many ways of describing the process of creativity. Reduction of the image, the salad being our example, does not mean its demise. Long after the salad is eaten it will still be there in the mind and experience of both the eaters and the salad-maker. Regardless of how beautiful the appearance of the salad, the salad-maker knows that the salad is going to disappear into the invisibility of the stomach. The salad-maker accepts the process with equanimity and joy; he offers the creation in a friendly and compassionate manner. The thought that others will enjoy and benefit from his work adds to the dimension of his own perception of his created image. He has come close to realizing the creation as ephemeral beauty.

The image of the salad is basically impermanent, yet is empowered with the qualities that will make other people happy. Through compassion, friendliness, joy, and equanimity, the salad or any created image is drained of the negative energy, and becomes a receptacle for healing and happiness. The image is reduced, not only to ephemeral beauty, but through the cultivation of the compassion, friendliness, joy, and equanimity the negative emotions are emptied and transformed. For the cook who makes the salad the salad could be said to be empty.

Petsan once handed me a single grain of cooked rice, then ordered me to cut it in half. I cut the grain in half with a chinese pocket knife that was lying on a little shelf behind his slightly elevated cot. He said, "cut it again and again". When he saw that I was struggling to divide the grain into smaller pieces, he searched through a little Bhutanese bag and produced a razor. After I had made quite a mess, Petsan laughed and with his hand swept away all the morsels except one barely visible piece. "Keep cutting!" he told me. "I can't" I said. When I stopped, Petsan again urged me to keep cutting, halving each piece. I told him that if I were to maintain the exercise I would need an electron microscope.

Petsan had never seen a microscope let alone an electronic one. He knew they were used in hospitals and thought he had once seen one in a Chinese magazine. He asked me to describe the most powerful microscope in the world. "Like cars and cannons," I said, " microscopes have a history of invention." It was always a challenge to try to answer such questions in Tibetan. Since I did not know the details of the history of microscopes, I could not elaborate, but had heard about microscopic dissectors that could magnify aspects of the essence of life inside a living cell—even to the extent of dividing sperm into minute sections of the living organism. I mentioned telescopes which could magnify large areas of outer space and locate other worlds millions of miles away. Petsan asked me several times where microscopes originated? Despite my fumbling about for the right expression, Petsan perfectly understood. To make a point, he handed me a small tea bowl lined with silver and told me to put the leftover piece of rice in the bowl. I lifted the morsel with my ball point pen when, for a second, I lost it. Petsan was grinning from ear to ear. I remember thinking how both grandfather and my father had big ears. I tore off a piece of paper from my Nepalese notebook, fashioned a kind of wick and picked up the morsel which I carefully dropped into the silver bowl. He told me to keep dividing the morsel. Then he told me to reinvent the electron microscope and walked out of the room.

This new task seemed as easy as trying to thread a camel through the eye of a needle. In a meditative sense though, I took the task seriously.

I carried my silver bowl with me at all times, usually disguised under an American newspaper that had a picture of

Kissinger. After a few days I replaced the newspaper with a sheet of Nepalese rice paper. The rice grain cutting was a kind of sādhanā—definitely a supportive exercise. I didn't know how long I would be carrying my grain of rice around with me. In a way, I did reinvent the electron microscope.

Naturally the rice morsel had already been divided as many times as possible. But the exercise became the kind of meditation that exhausted all logical and imaginative conceptions. There was a moment soon after the first exercise of dividing the rice grain where a part of my conscious mind became totally inactive. Once I had accepted the task, the effort came from a deeper place, where I could divide and redivide the grain. The morsel by this time had become fairly disintegrated and unrecognizable. Since the bowl was always covered except when on the altar, I knew this small offering was still significant. And besides, by now it had assumed psychic and almost hallucinogenic proportions. A part of my thought process, acting independently and differently from my normal way of thinking emerged. I began to have a profuse dreamlife for the first time in many years, and I became obsessed with my work of dividing the rice grain. Like most of my major projects, I could stop and begin at will. What was different than the other projects in my life was the effort required to let go of all my mental constructs and be attentive to focusing on the morsel in the silver bowl.

It is curious how a person can graft new life onto an independent consciousness.

When the grain of rice began to divide into various geometrical shapes—at times like snowflakes, or crystals but always maintaining the texture of rice, I understood I was in a different time and space. Like some dream images, with no obvious logical connections, the snowflake-like motion swirled by in a surrealistic fashion. The silver lining melted and the wooden part of the bowl became black. Sometimes it was difficult to stop the motion of thoughts to return to a previous image. During my evening meditation, when I attempted to return to the memory of the original piece of rice, it quickly transformed into a life structure all of it's own.

The exercise possessed me for about three weeks. Was it possible to terminate the exercise with the feeling of accomplishment; or, would it continue indefinitely. Petsan did not seem much help. I would meet with him every day and he never gave me any indication that I should stop the practice, even though it no longer seemed unique or pleasurable. The rice cutting chore was a constantly incomplete project. Then on one no-moon day, the abbot invited me to dinner. Petsan and some other monks and lamas would also be there. Naturally, I arrived with my silver lined bowl, which I was not ready to use for dining. I was about to explain that I needed another bowl for eating, when Petsan insisted I use my meditation bowl. Suddenly the bowl was filled with white rice and an assortment of strongly curried Nepalese vegetables. The Tibetans have the custom of licking their bowls clean—they rarely use forks or spoons to eat. Occasionally in the company of Tibetans, I too, like a cat would stick my tongue out and turning the bowl obliquely, lap the silver lining as clean as a whistle. This aftermeal cleaning ritual was a daily purification.

After I licked the bowl clean, Petsan asked,"Okay?" as if to suggest that I did not have to lick my bowl if I did not want to. I answered by licking my bowl again to confirm that I was content.

Grandfather would have appreciated this Tibetan version of cleaning up food scraps. He was a stickler for cleaning up every last bit of food. Much to his irritation, few members of the family cleaned their plates to his satisfaction. Briefly I forgot about the divided rice morsel that had undergone a rather complicated process of transformation. Suddenly, I was animated and totally clear at the same time. Petsan, got wind of my momentary emancipated feeling. Petsan was always making faces. He looked at me, rolled his eyes, nodded in an approving manner and gave me a smile. For a brief moment, I forgot about those millions of grains of rice that had snowflaked their way across my consciousness.

Petsan said,"Look inside the bowl...What's there?" I told him there was nothing in the bowl—just the bowl. Then one of the monks poured some Chinese clear tea in the bowl. I mentioned to Petsan that now there was clear tea in the bowl. "What do hosts usually pour for guests in America?" he asked. "Tea, coffee or alcohol," I replied.

Petsan pointed at his stomach. Also, the rimpoche pointed at his stomach. Everyone laughed. A mantra that Petsan gave me spun through my mind. I drank my tea and felt very good— "Immediately after realizing emptiness when the sun arises from the flickering murmur of Ri Ri Ri, one should cultivate the sixteen handed lord Mahākāla as oneself arising from the syllable Hūm".

Petsan gave me the silver lined tea bowl, a reminder of my lesson in emptiness, creativity, and giving. An old Hindu theme about food came to mind: he who practices a form of meditation called heat (Tapas) will realize the creative principle of the universe (Brahma) as food. Literally, Tapas refers to the heat generated through concentrative meditation and the utterance of sacred syllables. The third chapter of the Taittirīya Upanishad says, "Having performed austerity (Tapas), he (the student) understood that Brahma is food".

I felt like I was seeing the world of being, substance, and thought in Great Space and Great Time. I experienced something of the inconceivable. In describing the phenomena of the Great-Black-One the adjective inconceivable is often used. Offerings to the Great-Black-One must be empowered with the inconceivable. The endless series of shapes, thoughts and beings that issued from my grain of rice were in their purest form inconceivable. Any thoughts or ideas imparted to the process were eaten up by the process itself. Through an ineffable offering, I had connected with a bit of the invisible. I had also been able to reach back into the Bavarian forest, and briefly taste again a little of the substance of that dark and light place and joyful childhood. The Image had merged across time and culture.

At one New Year's ritual, gigantic mounds of cooked rice were artistically shaped into a pyramid next to the Mahākāla altar, behind which was a golden icon of Sakyamuni Buddha. There were scores of burning candles which cast reflections of a million lights. Behind the altar, was the brilliant five colored thread-cross mansion of Mahākāla, which cast a lattice-like texture of red, blue, yellow, green and white light across the protector's black face; light flickered on his ivory white fangs. The effect was magical—a universe of imagery that lost shape within the total hologram. I perceived the rice as I did when that first morsel suddenly turned into a kaleidoscope and plethora of sacred form and content—"one should respectively fold one's hands into the shape of a small bowl and make offerings."

CHAPTER VII

Sacrificing The Image

In Himalayan monasteries there are rituals and events almost every day dedicated to The Great-Black-One and similar deities. I had the freedom to recycle these more communal ritual-meditations into the private domain of my own contemplations. It is Ideal when a person can move from community to personal space and back again with the ease I was able to do so in Nepal. There were and still are unlimited possibilities through the medium of the ritual-meditations of The Great-Black-One.

The Tantric ritual-meditations have spiritual and sometimes avowed material rewards. During the monthly ritual for the Great-Black-One which takes place on the day of the waxing moon, curiously, I felt an element of danger. The night of no-moon is considered a night when the ghosts and demons search for psychic food. It is a night when many folk feel uneasy. Even though the sense of danger is still there, the laity can, sometimes not so vicariously, participate in the drama of neutralizing the demons. For many it is an escape from the mundane and the conceivable.

The ritual specialists constantly deal with the inconceivable. They are empowered to pass on the experience of the Great-Black-One and his retinue. Their work is to arrange the world as an offering. The Lama or the Vajrācārya are embodiments of the god (the image\Im), but at the same time become themselves offerings. The ritual specialist cannot offer the world around

143

him as an offering, until he himself becomes an offering, which
in turn protects the ceremonial circle—"if one needs to give an
offering one should project the Lord Mahākāla with his retinue
(as oneself)".

For a long time, Petsan left me with the quandary that the
projection of the Great-Black-One was a kind of offering. How
could the deity be an offering to itself? Or, how could one make
an offering of an image to an image? I had to reexamine my
preconception of the nature of subject and object as well as the
nature of food. In other words, we are conditioned to think of
food as a primary offering, a main dish. It was somewhat of a
quantum leap to think of almost any substance, being or thought
as food. Petsan's rice project had assisted me in making that
leap.

The image of Mahākāla is a little bit like the grain of rice. At
various points in my meditations the image vanished into the
real but invisible Im. But if those were authentic experiences,
and I believe they were, those peak moments had great possibilities—as great as anyone could ever ask for. They were without
attachment, empowered to fabricate almost anything, or, empowered to generate absolute stillness. Yet, at the time, the total
magnitude of the experiences eluded me.

The Great-Black-One is created from emptiness, and then,
through internal heat (Tapas) reaches a melting point and merges
with the flesh of the participant; the image becomes the Im.
Sometimes the commentaries say that the ego of the practitioner
becomes one with Mahākāla, but ego here is not to be understood in the Freudian sense. There is a danger: It is not from the
dreadful fangs of the Great-Black-One, but rather from the full
blown negative power of one's own emotions unleashed against
the world. Those who go mad are indeed possessed by destructive dark forces i.e., demons, addictions or disturbed genetic
tendencies. Blending with the image and not the Im can unleash
these forces. The word used in Tibetan for this phenomena is
nga-rgyal which literally means "I the victor". In the context of
sādhanā it designates the victory over emotional and mental
obscurations and the emptiness of all projections and imagina-
tions, including the image itself. The closest I can come to
describing the process as a phenomena is to point out the ines-

capable polarity. Yes, I can become one with the extraordinary being so that at a specific moment in the sādhanā I can say: "I am Mahākāla". At the same time, there is total emptiness—"Arising from the syllable *Hūm*."

I often participated in the larger monastic rituals such as the weekly or monthly ceremonies called "Satisfaction And Fulfillment." At this time, the words and seed syllables would be uttered in complex and somewhat strange ways. I used to spend my evenings attempting to duplicate the sounds I heard. I mimicked those sounds uttered by the master singer who is called the Om-mdzad (literally he who makes *Om*). Very few could utter the syllables like him. I could never even come close. But with the help of Petsan and the master singer, and much to their amusement, I was able to reach a compromise. In practicing sādhanā, a primary importance is on proper meditation.

When the sound emerges from a state of emptiness (sūnyatā), it will not be an ordinary sound, for it is coming from an altered state of mind. Sometimes I felt like a small child experimenting with the universe. I would emit very strange patterns of notes. After some time, I was able to generate certain sound-vibrations from various parts of the body. I can do this with or without uttering the actual sound. A typical practice session for me would be to keep my mouth closed while focusing on a sound of a seed syllable. If you try to do this, you will find that breath, thought and other kinds of energy including heat (Tapas) will automatically begin to manifest in a new way. The appropriate sound is very close to the image. Emptiness is close to the Im. The combination of emptiness and sound are not accessible to logical thought. True emptiness is the rawest of structures. Sound is cast into the interface between emptiness and the senses from which the image is formed. The power of the sound directs and shapes the image which has an organic connection with the world and with emptiness. The sound is like a seed planted in the muck to grow into a living thing—into an image.

How does the image manifest itself as one is learning how to practice? In the passing on of spiritual knowledge, the image may be held back from the student in order to let the Im itself make an impression. Sometimes an image or idea is presented only because it serves as a bridge to another image or idea more suitable for the development of the practitioner. The true image or Im then, will always lie ahead. In my own experience with Petsan, there was always the element of surprise. In Buddhism this is an aspect of upāyakausalya, which is usually translated "skill in means". The world, indeed, The Great-Black-One becomes a tool for enlightenment. Mahākāla is not what I think, nor what I see. What I see is a vehicle for the actual realization of the next stage of invisibility.

For example, consider the faces on the images of Mahākāla. Petsan once asked me what it was that I saw in those faces? What I saw on the surface was anger, lust, greed and jealousy. I thought it a little odd that a deity in conjugal bliss should have those expressions. In my view the gods were not having that much fun. I felt that I was definitely missing something. I mentioned to him that I expected a more erotic countenance in the context of conjugal union. He asked me to show him what I thought an erotic countenance looked like. He wanted me to demonstrate the difference between an erotic look and an angry one. I was embarrassed when I could not do it. Petsan insisted that I try. When he saw that I really could not; that I was perplexed at his request, he told me to come back the next morning and try again. Actually, I did not return for several days. When I finally did return, about a minute after I arrived, one of the monks who was standing around asked me if my studies were coming along okay. Petsan seized the opportunity to engage him in a conversation and asked him the same question that he posed me a few days before. What is the expression of erotic loveplay? The monk looked absolutely dumbfounded. Petsan showed him a painting of Mahākāla in union with his consort. The monk said that was different, but did not explain exactly how. Petsan jokingly insisted that the monk demonstrate an erotic look. It was all in good fun, but the monk was embarrassed and stymied. Petsan pointed out that the monk, at least, had a valid excuse for not having learned such a expression. Maybe that was his way of pointing out that even his long time students could not carry out some of the same requests he was giving me; or, that some of the seemingly more apparent aspects of life were not so simple.

About a week later, I returned. Again, he asked me to mimic

the expressions. During that week I had explored a variety of expressions related to the ecstacy of lovemaking, but that particular morning I was still at a loss. I mentioned to Petsan that I had read some books on the erotic temples of India which had photos of erotic-spirituality. I pointed out that the temple images had a very peaceful and contemplative atmosphere about them. · The faces of those icons were contemplative in their loveplay.

Petsan's reply was that there was always the possibility of achieving complete serenity. He reminded me that there were also many Buddhist images in conjugal union that were the essence of serenity. It is the level of mind that reflects a deep and complex desire that accommodates the magnetism of sexuality. Again, in the right meditation, we can employ such a desire to realize the Im of peace and bliss to which the serene image is pointing. The Great-Black-One and his consort, however, show the dark and terrible side. Pechan then surprised me again by offering his own version of the expressions of emotion including the state of erotic pleasure. He changed his face with fluidity and accuracy.

During his performance Petsan must have shown me at least thirty different expressions. I had not been aware of it before, but through Petsan's gestures and fabricated appearances, I was able to see an interface between the bliss of serenity and the terror of lust and anger. Somehow I could feel the hunger of the one who can only survive on flesh and blood. The image of Rudee came back, and I began to have a new kind of relationship with the carnivorous side of the human personality.

After Petsan's performance was over he asked me the differences between the expressions of erotic bliss, anger, and lust. I thought of the famous American movie "King Kong". The monster at times had a look of serenity and compassion, but at other times, when he thought he would lose his beloved, he became enormously outraged and ferocious. The movie was a reflection of man's inability to cope with being separated from the persons to whom he is attached—especially in matters of courtship. Indeed King Kong, to his best ability was courting his lady love. The fact that the courtship could not have been biologically consummated added not only to the kinky side of our imagination, but also to the psychological reality that people tend not to achieve that perfect state of happiness they are seeking for in a mate, and at times, go through a period of frustration and often rage in coping with this feeling. The newspapers are filled with stories of individuals who go berserk when their would-be lovers abandon them for another person. Then there are sociopaths who, for reasons they themselves do not know or cannot control, are denied the normal biological manner of consummating a relationship with the opposite sex. King Kong could not have had normal sexual relations with this lady. I told Petsan this story. He said it sounded like a foible of the human condition and asked: "When does lust become anger?" "When is there complete satisfaction?" Petsan asked these questions rhetorically.

There were several sessions over the years when Petsan's skill at mime helped my ability to overcome my own self-consciousness. Following Petsan's lead I began a reflective study of how one's facial expressions and postures in general can stimulate images and feelings in the subconscious. I realized that I was going through a process of breaking down inhibitions and tapping into the hidden dimensions. The problem with breaking down one's inhibitions in a permissive culture is that one needs to be sure that one's fundamentals, intentions and vows are intact. The sādhana practice, on one hand, creates an attitude of freedom, because it provides a new latitude of action and thought amongst the jungle of dark forces, but on the other hand, for every step of new freedom there comes a new responsibility-a responsibility for others and nature.

Rudee kept appearing in my mind. I remembered my own lust and anger; and thought of an eccentric friend whom I knew a number of years before who would wave his hands in front of me and shout "where do your hands leave off and mine begin". The face of the Great-Black-One is my own face. It is my teacher's face—the face of Dharma.

Feeling is very much a part of the process of sādhanā. The words, images and one's presence come together in a variety of psychic and feeling dimensions. When the text states that Mahākāla's flaming hair designates victory over the demons of the three worlds: the world of desires, the world of shapes and the world of no form, the real purpose of the sādhanā could be forgotton in the process of speculation. This particular symbology was presented to me in an interesting way. I was asked to focus on everything I desired on the face of this earth that came within my vision as I was sitting crosslegged on the top of the monastery overlooking the valley of Kathmandu. It was two days before the Tibetan New Year. Some of the monks were weaving with red, blue, green, yellow and white threads the Great-Black-One's five colored mansion a few feet from where I was sitting. I could see in the corner of my eye the golden tiered spire of the great chaitya reflecting a bright and hot stream across the back of my neck. The wall of the monastery, dropping about five hundred feet below reminded me of the desert canyons of the southwestern United States.

Spread before me was the valley of Kathmandu. Petsan suggested that the valley I viewed below was really the whole world, an image within an image. My thoughts took over and the valley became a receptacle for my imagination. I played out the exercise and travelled through the mental processes of my ambitions and desires. Petsan left me there for at least an hour. The monks went to lunch. He finally returned to the roof top. He confirmed that the weather had turned very hot and invited me to his room where we discussed the meaning of the flaming hairs of Mahākāla: that is, the world of phenomena and its impermanence. It was all before me. There were the shapes of the valley, i.e. the images which seemed to absorb and transform my own thoughts and feelings into more images, which in turn did the same ad infinitem. The golden temples, rice fields, distant buffalo, maze of pathways, dung plastered huts and the Bagmati River fed back to me the whole array of seen and unseen desires. The shapes of the world are transmitters of both light and darkness. They not only manifest one's thoughts and feelings, but seem to suck up energy from hidden places beneath the earth. For example, one day, I was staring at an ancient Newari well, and all of a sudden water spouted from the sculptured mouth of a the mythical serpent called Makara. Everyone said it was a miracle. Water had not dripped from that well in a thousand years.

Petsan asked me if I knew how to build a fire. He asked me to describe the firebuilding process, and listened patiently as I explained and digressed with memories of Jack London's short story, How To Build a Fire. The main character in the story attempts to build a fire in one-hunderd degree below zero weather at a remote spot in the Yukon. He succeeds in building the fire, but he builds it under a fir tree which after some time shed it's bough laden snow, hence putting out the fire. The man's dog curiously looks on and watches the man go through the process of freezing to death. Petsan said that the man needed the powers of gtum-mo meditation which generates heat. There are many stories of Tibetan yogis who have this power to the extent their bodies can dry out wet blankets in subzero weather. It is normal to feel the uprising of heat in meditation, but the gtum-mo style generates heat in a more concentrated manner. Like any power the heat generation technique can be misused or simply not enacted in the proper manner. Petsan thought that the story was about man in samsara (the world). "The cold represents all the obstacles that keep man from enlightenment and the dog is a being of raw nature," said Petsan. The man (in the story he is called the man) knows how to build a fire but builds it in the wrong place so his efforts backfire and destroy him. Petsan liked the story and said that the practice of The Great-Black-One was like knowing not only how to build a fire but the time and place as well. As Petsan was talking, I recalled the cremation I had seen the day before at the side of the river.

The earth is a repository of decaying substance, but also a place of new life. In science, the exchange cycle that goes on deep within the earth is referred to as the carbon cycle. Grandfather used to say that the earth was one big cemetery or cremation ground. No wonder death is such a sacred concept, it is the transition to other forms invisible within the earth. But humans are fearful of death. Sometimes we are not afraid to die, but rather to live, which means to come closer and closer to death. It is, at least momentarily, easier to deny death, and live as if one were immortal. The Great-Black-One moves in the heavens, but concentrates his energy on the earth. When he embraces his goddess he is embracing the earth. In the mythology of Tantric Buddhism there are eight great cremation grounds. It is here that death is celebrated as new life; where the earth is charred and the cycle of life begins again. It is the most effective place to do the sādhanā of the Great-Black-One. One who meditates in the cremation ground will embrace the feminine counterpart of Great-Black-One, and begin a transpersonal procreative process.

In Kathmandu there are eight famous cremation sites. They are actual places where one can go and practice sādhanā. Our potential corpse is a hidden dimension: It is the accumulation of forces that transform the youthful shape into withering flesh, clogged arteries and collapsed brain channels-like an onion that spoils from the inside. The alcoholic-addict syndrome provides us with a bird's eye view of the process. Beneath this shape lie the malicious forces which trick our conscious minds into believing whatever we desire is okay, and that the world which we fabricate is real and eternally blissful. The burning ghat, a cemetery, the place where the body is placed in the ground or vaporized to the atmosphere; or, the bodies that are placed on mountain tops to be food for the birds (as they did in Tibet) symbolizes the immediacy of nature's way of purification and an aspect of the transpersonal. Also, the cremation place with its charred bodies, ashes, lingering smoke and place of many mantras become a place of the imagination—a receptacle of carnivorous spirits.

Invisible predatory beings seep into other invisible channels that flow beneath the earth, indeed, that flow deep within the food chain, and find their way becoming satisfied as they enter the female womb to start the cycle over again. Petsan always said that the real problems in life are deeply felt, but not very visible. One can use the visible only temporarily for overcoming and transforming the hidden demons. Killing one's apparent enemies, for example, may get rid of the bodies that are causing harm, but the killing is hardly an antidote to hatred or the potpourri of lingering spirits that may shadow one the rest of one's life. Practicing the sādhanā of the Great-Black-One will generate the Im or the spirit of transformation within the raw structure of hatred. The Great-Black-One becomes a positive spiritual and psychological force-indeed, a teacher of life.

I once heard a story of a young monk who hated a relative. He lost his mind and almost attacked the relative with a sword. He caught himself just in time, and short-circuited the action by reciting some Mahākāla mantras he learned while participating in ceremonies. After a few days, he again grew very angry and began to say his mantras, but this time he took a framed picture of his relative and smashed it against the side of his altar. He then proceeded to stomp on the already ripped photograph, and as a final gesture of madness grabbed a ceremonial dagger (phurbu) from the altar and began to stab the picture over and over again. Shortly after this psychic rampage, he overheard a conversation in a nearby tea shop. The relative had fallen off a precipice and died.

The story was told to me as an example of the thin line between the healing and destructive possibilities of the Great-Black-One's energy. In both instances the Great-Black-One's energy was not called upon in the context of sādhanā, but rather in the throes of emotion. In the first case, the monk was saved from committing a crime, but in the second, his anger had the effect of negative sorcery. I like to think it was purely coincidental, however the monk subsequently went into retreat and was never heard from again.

The person who told me the story explained that the crucial error in the monk's actions was not that he became angry, but that he did not know how to make the appropriate offerings. An offering that does not calm the mind, and generate detached compassion is food for the demons. It is not necessary for the offering to be edible. Almost anything will do as long as the offering is an extension of oneself, and dedicated for the benefit of others. That is, before identifying with Mahākāla, the devotee becomes food for the world. He becomes a corpse for the earth. So, in the meditative process, as the corpse is burned in cremation, the senses and emotions are burned. The transformation cycle (the burning) begins with the kindling of the ordinary ego and false personality and culminates with a phoenix-like experience, having the sense that one becomes one with the Im. There are then truly two beings: One with the appearance of an ordinary mortal, and another one who is able to relate to the invisible and to the extraordinary. Ultimately, the practitioner can act as the deity. The feeling is so powerful that the practitioner must be careful not to reidentify with his or her ordinary ego—a major problem for meditators. For example, if one has the urge to fly

into space without a hanglider or airplane, it behooves the practitioner to give it a second thought. It is the desire of one's
ordinary ego, and would prove rather disastrous to oneself, and
maybe to others.

In Nepal there are practitioners of the angry deities who are
not just yogis striving for enlightenment, but sorcerers who
make a business out of black magic. They also need to become
one with the deity, reborn from the ashes. They believe they
have special license from the gods to direct the rites of sorcery
against others. They have the power to harm and even kill. But
on the other hand, so do the producers and advertisers of Western material goods, despite the fact, that the psychological and
motivational process is quite different. Actually, the sorcerer is
more aware; he knows what he is doing and that his actions are
nefarious and dangerous. He knows that his work is going to
cause harm to an individual, yet he will have a logical and even
compassionate explanation. The food producer who uses chemicals and other artificial substances will argue, indeed, in a court
of law that his product is harmless. His contribution to society
becomes a guise for greed, and a channel for truly malignant
forces. He legitimizes his actions with legal and sometimes
religious paradigms. He or she is in toxic denial.The practice of
sādhanā is the combination of meditation technique, insight and
the four keys of balance and harmony. The goal is to attain
Siddhi which is usually translated "power". Petsan always said
that practicing a sādhanā would allow one to taste the "power",
but if rashly acted upon could be very dangerous. As I said
before, he liked to use the example of the atomic bomb. He
mentioned that one could feel the power and press the wrong
button, which could either be self-destructive, or, harmful to
great numbers of other people—possibly even change the course
of humanity. In Petsan's opinion, one of the most terrible examples of the taking of life would be fishing with underwater
detonators-because so many sentient creatures could be killed.
He liked to point out that before men fished with a string or a
net, fewer fish lost their lives, and hence there was not so much
bad karma for those who were doing the fishing. Dropping an
atomic bomb is a little like throwing a hand grenade into a fish
pond. A little knowledge can go a long way to destroy and

poison the world.

Those who sincerely engage in a spiritual practice, Petsan said, would probably taste siddhi. The difficult part is to be able to use the power in a way that would be beneficial for other creatures. In the context of Great-Time a continuous practice creates good karma. Time can also be measured in terms of rebirths. What is not attained in this life may be realized in the next. The word "now" refers to the "now" of the next moment which is the passing present. In order for the taste of siddhi to be put into the effective practice of medicine, there must be an offering of the senses.— "Now, immediately after the offering whatever is desired yet not attained will come to be realized."

One of the powers realized through sādhanā is Medicine Power (siddhaushadhi). Everyone who practices Tantric Buddhism believes in the healing efficacy of the practice. Every substance, being and thought has healing potential in the framework of sādhanā. But to just taste the "power" is only to feel the cure where it is not. In order for the malignancies to be transformed, the transformation process must parallel the forces of fire and earth that process the corpse into a new beginning.

The claims of the sixteen-handed sādhanā seem exaggerated, but understandable since they were conceived in Great-Time, a somewhat exaggerated yet philosophical concept in itself. The scale is unmeasurable. Hence, its verbal expression is to be taken in the same way as one might describe the results of a healthy meal: "The shrimp was not overdone; it was exquisite. The miso soup was exactly the right temperature; it made me feel like I would live a thousand years. The brown rice was cooked to exactly the right consistency. It was sweet and made my blood surge. I felt purified."

There is a thin line between taste and spiritual experience. Both have the potential of creating a rush that comes in the stream of natural experiences that sometimes erupt in artistic expression. A language with poetic sensibilities describing sensual pleasures develops proximity to spiritual modes of being. Yet, at the same time, it is also a distortion, for the bottom line is wordless and indescribable. The expletive is an eruption of inner experience which may come after the fact; or, after the taste: Oh, what a wonderful flavor! The mantra stirs the waters of the psyche, and channels this oceanic abyss into a world of telepathy and awareness. It is the realm of Great-Time— "Why is it said that the body becomes healthy for a thousand years, like Mahākāla's? Is it because this is the victorious offering mantra? When drinking water is blessed one hundred times with this wisdom mantra, it protects the pregnant woman, she will easily give birth".

The images of Mahākāla's ritual-meditations always have a destructive as well as a creative form. The weapons and tools of destruction and torture that the Great-Black-One carries in his hands are reminders of affliction, terror and life's overwhelming odds against fulfilling one's goals. The Mahākāla-mandālā is ringed by The Great-Black-One's various weapons. The image of the chopper, vajra, elephant hide, mallet, three pronged spear, sword and the staff of a vedic god of death has an outward conveyance of infliction, pain, suffering and death. Every sādhanā, ritual and meditation on the Great-Black-One is a means to remove denial as symbolized by the weapons used in this ritual meditative surgery, which functions on the psychic plane. Substance becomes sacred and is exchanged. The weapons of The-Great-Black-One point the way to the raw structures of our animal-like survival modes, as well as the pathological aspects of sadomasochism. The imagery of violence, terror, addiction and deception vary somewhat from person to person. The miasma of feelings, thoughts, substance and beings that plague us unconsciously and consciously are the targets of the Great-Black-One's sādhanā. As we enter the dark forest of our karma the weapons pierce, cut and bind the demons sailing on the clouds of our mind's eye. Our images become like flotsam moving in and out with the tide and eventually carried away by the waves and currents.

When I see the chopper, I think of the variety of shapes and textures in our kitchen table foods, and in existence itself. It reminds me of my grain of rice disappearing into the silver lining of my Tibetan tea bowl, and the kaleidoscope of nervous manifestations that disappear into the realization we call emptiness.

On the altar, in the hall, where the monks and lamas perform the rites, there are two silver skulls modeled on tripods with the

images of three severed human heads. The skull on the left represents a vessel containing a sea of blood; it has an oceanic feeling of flowing energy, the drainage of every single life that ever existed. My father used to say that money is blood; each cent represents some drops of blood that drained through the sieve of human endeavor. Empowered with the forces of karma blood (rakta) is the life, which the earth stores and transforms into new energy—the sap of flora and fauna. But the blood projected to be in our silver skull is in the process of (to appropriate a Christian term) transubstantiation: It is the blood of the goddess, the transpersonal female substance of procreation. On the right, is the male counterpart called in Sanskrit amrita which literally means "immortal." The Tibetan term is bdud-rtsi which emphasizes the neutralization of malicious· forces rather than immortality. This male procreative energy like the rakta or blood is also transubstantiated. The two together—referred to as rakta-bdud-rtsi—expresses the experiences called "equal-taste" (samarasa), or the perfection of experience that comes at peak moments in the process of sādhanā.

During the New Year's ceremony called "satisfaction and fulfillment"(bskang-gso), there is another altar placed directly in front of the constructed image of The-Great-Black-One, which has a human skull bowl filled with rice, on top of which, is placed a large vajra-knife. There are assortments of other offerings including a black bean called the fruit of Mahākāla. In front of this alter is conducted the "dagger ceremony" (phul-cho).

In the dagger ceremony, miniature weapons are used to hammer, burn, poison and decimate the inner enemy. Even a little success in quelling our inner demons will give us a taste of extraordinary power-just a taste of siddhi. The dagger ceremony casts a pervasive spell.

The iron gates to the monastery, where the ceremony is performed were slid shut and locked. The multitudes, the pilgrims, clamored to be let in and clawed at the iron gate. It was a holy time of the year and there were pilgrims from all over India. It was impossible to do this particular ceremony with so many people crowding and clamoring for a touch from the head lama. After one of the monks drew a green and blue curtain over the iron gate, most of the pilgrims who were trying to enter the monastery drifted away. New arrivals attempted to peek through the gate and curtain. Anyone who caught a glimpse of the hierophant performing the dagger ceremony was automatically blessed. But the pilgrims only saw the black face with the protruding white fangs of The Great-Black-One. He glared from the inside of the meditation hall through the iron gate, ready to act from his multicolored mansion ornamented with flayed skins and weapons of destruction.

The main assistant called the "offering master" (mchod-dpon), placed a chair in front of the image. He then brought a tray on which would be placed an assortment of miniature weapons. He made an offering of rice and tea. He lit a butter lamp and some incense. Afterwards, the "offering master" walked away for a moment and returned with a black flag. Another monk followed behind him with a brass plate on which is a bell, vajra; and a pointed red, black and yellow hat. The monks conducting the ceremony seemed unusually serious. Except for the whispering of mantras and the pilgrims milling around near the outside of the gate, it was very quiet.

The atmosphere was already charged when the chief lama strode to the front of the image. He sat in the chair and recited a mantra. He was a large man almost the size of a sumo wrestler. He blew his nose and donned a pointed hat that reminded me of a picture of a high priest in a book on Sycthian archaeology. The pointed hats seem to be reminiscent of the ancient Persian and Scythian priesthood. The offering master brought out the weapons and placed them on the tray. The lama nonchalantly sipped some tea, and then meditated on the ceremonial circle: He cast the thought that "the whole world is pure in its own nature." He had more tea and proceeded to generate and empower the ceremonial circle with Mahākāla and his consort. The circle then attained a fierce and dreadful ambience. In this instance, the lama was called The Great-Black-Protector in union with his consort. The Great-Black-One was literally sung and gestured into the body, speech and mind of the chief lama and the ceremonial circle. The cue that the fusion between The Great-Black-One and ceremonial circle took place are the mantric syllables dzāh-hūm-bām-hoh.

Dzāh is alluring the image. Hūm! is fusing with the image.

Bām! is locking the image into place (onto one's being). *Hoh*! is totally melting with the image. The lama breathes out with the *Hoh* evaporating the whole of one's personal ego. I think of the simile, like the sand which sucks in the last of the outgoing waves. The Tibetan word for the sound of the sucking is Sib-Sib. The female principle here is further identified with yaksavetali, the spirit of corpses.

Having covered their mouths with white gauze, the "offering master" and one other monk knelt beside the officiating lama and faced the gaping jaws and white fangs of Mahākāla while reciting the mantras. The image of the white gauze reminded me of a hospital and also of those conscientious individuals—like the Japanese—who protect themselves and others against flu epidemics by wearing gauze masks. The white gauze commits the mind to purity, and is hence an extension of that phase of the ritual when the circle and all things are rendered pure and empty. The fear of contagion was real; and at that time, in that place, the line between contagious spirits and bacteria was almost nonexistent. They continued their recitation with the other lamas lined up a few feet away who were sitting crossed legged with their ceremonial texts and musical instruments. There was a sudden curdling blast of horns; the recitation for the moment stops.

The light was scattered. The dark corners of the monastery rolled up into floating black blobs that danced above the altars and the singing monks and lamas. Off to the side rested three iron triangular boxes on top of one another. They were black. The chief lama was still sitting, facing the image of Mahākāla, holding an offering cup, vajra and black hat. The chanting began and then the music. Silence. The chanting and the music started again, this time in a fast mode; and then suddenly, it was again silent. The chief lama lifted his tea bowl. He paused, as if struck by a thought from outer space, and then put on the black, red and yellow hat. For a stunning moment there was no music. The silence becomes a sound. The offering master brought a human-like effigy into the ceremonial circle. He placed it in the top black metal box, and then purified the effigy.

The three black boxes with the human-like figure on top appear ominous. In order to have the appropriate perspective, I needed to focus on my own many demons amalgamated into the body of the effigy. The ritual was dangerous, but also exhilarating. The sacrifice of my distorted karma was about to culminate in the feeling of transformation.

There was a sudden blasting of horns. The lama, now possessed of The Great-Black-One rang the ritual bell as if to balance out the seeming harshness of the ceremony. Suddenly came the rapid beating of the cymbals. The lama waved the black flag. At the same time there were intermittent drawls of the horn that sounded like the grunting of a monstrous boar, blending a flatted fifth with the cymbals and chants. Silence. The silence was broken by the piercing Tibetan trumpets. The bell rang; there was the discordant clatter of cymbals, the flapping of the black flag and guttural short bursts of the long horns. Silence.

This was repeated eight times, and if one has not experienced it before, the heart beats a little faster with a strange uprising of terror, which is eventually realized as not just a dreadful atmosphere from the vortex of cremation and it's lingering souls, but a channel to life itself. With the waving of black flags and the rest, the power of the eight cremation grounds are beckoned. All the malicious remnants of the past year, month, day or moment are empowered in the effigy about to be subdued in the blackest of boxes.

For the participant, the box is a forbidding image. It calls to mind a place where there is no way out. In fact, there are no doors. For some, a place with no way out would be the epitome of suffering. It reminded me of more than a passing fear during the Asian wars: There was a rumor among the soldiers that the North Koreans put prisoners in a black iron box just barely large enough for a person to huddle and stoop—especially tall white persons like myself. I could not imagine being incarcerated in a box which would not allow me to stand upright for an entire month.

I had a dream once that Rudee helped me escape from a black box. Indeed the black box is a place of torture where the afflicted image reflected in oneself the anxiety, frustration and pain that constitutes the human condition. Yet, it is a space that can be entered by the invisible forces of the decaying, burning and transforming earth. Indeed, the demons and other malicious forces have been allured into the aura and body of the effigy. The effigy is called a reflection (pratibimba), i.e. it is like a mirror of our own minds.

Petsan said our minds are like a magnifying glass that burns the spirits into the effigy. But, then, there are the allies, the retinue of The Great-Black-One who are ordered by the lama to come and aid the officiants to cast the appropriate spells. The tormented image feeds back to the participant a vision of his or her demons. After the eight wavings of the flag with a sequence of music and bell ringing, there were a few moments of silence. The monks then started chanting and the weapons were given to the lama wearing the black hat. There was the hammer to burst the brains, the hook to pull out the heart, the noose that strangles and the iron chain to shackle the limbs. There was the bell that intoxicates the victim into a stupor with its sweet hypnotic sounds, and the whirlwind to twist and shred one into outer space.

As one of the chants depict: "There will come a darkness pervasive with the feeling of depression which clouds one's vision while a club smashes the victim from behind. There will be the sensation that one is being pressed from above by the great mountain of Meru, and that one will be cast into the burning conflagrations of the end of time. The protective gods will be of no help, one will meet the demons that drain life and contract all kinds of diseases. The weather will turn ferocious: Thunder and hail will harass the world like flares and bombs. In the great cities and realms of our world there will be vast earthquakes. And every thought that comes into one's mind will turn into the opposite thought; as if to prove for the last time, that the thought processes bring forth a series of unrealities."

The chief lama recites: "Bring the enemy here to the iron black box so that it cannot escape. Seize, bind and tie the apparition. Beat and torture the effigy until it is in total shock. As soon as it is under one's control, let it be destroyed and cut it up into pieces, and let the warm blood be drunk by The Great-Black-One and his consort and retinue."

The lama who projects the evils of the community, self and the world into the black box laid the miniature weapons on the effigy. Now, again, there was a sudden blast of horns, the black flag was raised and waved, the bell rang and the cymbals clattered and cracked. The weapons were returned to the tray. Again, there was a sudden blast of horns and so on. The music stops and the chief lama, exhausted by the drain of psychic energy, took his hat off and drank tea.

My lesson, in this ceremony and meditation was that doing sādhanā extended into more subtle and sophisticated forms of practice. Grandfather always said that one could extract hidden and invisible images in one's self; that new images would arise in the course of any serious work. He said that we can learn how to move them around at will, and to chose which one's would be the best allies. He always thought of the emotions as living entities which had somewhat of an independent existence, and that the soul was really a condensation of one's total existence at any one time. The social institutions that I have filtered through, for the most part regard these folk attitudes as superstitious and not useful. It was more than curious to me that my new friends and teachers were serious about the same phenomena in which grandfather had an interest. These days, I accept the idea that these hidden and invisible entities, higher and lower powers, are realities with which we can communicate and influence: With practice these entities can be moved about in space and time.

When I participated in the "satisfaction and fulfillment" rite and sat within the ceremonial circle, I realized the power of the rite. The lama separated his consciousness from his body, suspended all defilements and became The Great-Black-One. Now, on behalf of the community, he could coerce the consciousness of the enemy into the effigy within the iron box. The effigy, then, became alive with the essence of the enemy within, and vulnerable to the machinations of the man in the black, red and yellow pointed hat.

The offering master brought two offering cakes to the lama. He held them with his hands crossed, and purified them with water blessed by The Great-Black-One. He pondered that all those malicious forces, who might disturb the course of the ritual, be satisfied with the offering of the cakes and go away. That is, "you enemies with spoiled vows who reek with moral blemishes, who are not protectors, who desire to cause confusion, agitate and make trouble, come here and be satisfied with this offering cake. All you deities shake (out your bad energy), and settle yourselves. Give up completely the activities and motivations that will spoil your vows and go quickly to another place." Then, the offering master threw outside the two offering cakes that had trapped the bad spirits.

I have found the phrase "made in the image of God" a curious contrast to our man-imaged effigy that is decimated, and fed to The Great-Black-One. But then, in Buddhism the gods are empty and relative. The imagery of our dagger ritual is disturbing for we know that the borders of dangerous hidden dimensions could be crossed: that consciousness of sentient beings, including the spirits of the dead could be moved around, indeed, infused into a figure made of butter and powered barely. I used to give workshops where we would use pillows, and other objects as effigies. We would beat and curse them in various ways, and at some point visualized our enemies, not as our enemies, but as other human beings caught in the same negative grip of life as ourselves. We released our anger and guilt, and expressed our compassion as well. We talked, and occasionally came up with some ingenious alternatives to frustration, anxiety and violence. In the dagger ritual, at the bottom of the three iron boxes the lama placed a picture of a person with their limbs chained as is mentioned in the chant. The effigy rested in the smaller box on top.

As soon as the figure was purified and the unwanted spirits were dispersed, the figure itself was given the life or energy of the enemy. With the uttering of a mantra that includes the expression "*rūpa hūm phat*" the figure was brought to life. The term rupa affirmed that the spirit of the enemy is a perceivable entity. The head lama reidentified with The Two-Handed-Great-Black-One, and there was another purification of the circle. As soon as the lama felt comfortable that he was identified with The Great-Black-One, he uttered a mantra that designated his new transformation: "I am Mahākāla with consort Mahakali within the own nature of Vajra who has established the Vajradagger" This transformation was necessary for finishing the final touches of neutralizing the designated enemy.

The officiant was now called Vajrakilimahākāla with consort. He pondered his own nature as the nature of Vajra. He meditated on the dagger, which is compared to a dragon who carries winds from the heavens. I heard the story that the dagger used in this ritual was formed from a lightning flash striking and then melting some naturally formed mineral deposits and reshaping them into a vajra (a miraculous act of Mahākāla). The Vajramaster contemplated the top of the dagger which symbolized the gods from above. They are images that have evolved from the planetary forces. They are images that have been accommodated into the image system of the Buddhist Dharma. He contemplated the center of the vajra, and realized victory over the cannibalistic deities of the middle regions that are thought to live there. Then, there was the space of the water-demons; they crept there in an entangled manner. The vajra was victorious over all these creatures of space. When the Lama looked at the three pointed knife section he thought of it as illuminated and flaming with fire. By rolling the blade in his hand the three worlds shook, and when he lifted the blade, all the deities become terrified. When the dagger was plunged, the realms of existence were reduced to ashes. When it is hurled it takes the heart-life of the enemy who becomes rigid and dies.

The enemy, the figure in the iron box, was called the bad karmic body of hatred. Of course it was the enemy within ourselves. Every part of its body was pierced with the mantra: *"Oh Vajrakili kill the enemies and obstacles"* The offering master and the lama together picked up the large vajra-knife placed in the skull bowl, and profusely cut the figure in the triangular box. As they carved the image, there was a rapid beating of cymbals along with short bursts of the long horn. The offering master handed the decimated effigy to the lama, who then fed it to The Great-Black-One. As he put the effigy into the gaping jaws, again, there was a sudden blasting of the horns, the flapping of the black flag and the ringing bell.

CHAPTER VIII

The Arising Divinity
(Image/Im)

Images take on the character of their environment—natural and man made. They proliferate according to the likes of their surroundings. They are also functional. For example, the Goddess Vāsundharā bestows wealth and fertility, Hārītī causes as well as avoids diseases (especially smallpox); the serpent-water deities, the Nāgas, bring rain, and are called upon to cure any of the diseases associated with an imbalance of liquids. Mahākāla, The Great-Black-One is the chief protector of the Dharma and therefore can be summoned to correct and cure all ills which are obstacles to spiritual practice.

Like humans, images accommodate thoughts and more complex meanings in the process of their own evolution. Unlike humans, they are almost immortal. Many of them will last as long as humanity, and as they are preserved in stone, plastic, canvas, metal and computer chip—even longer. Images will be accommodated by the archaeologist of the future—from mind-sets and galaxies that are far away. Images find their way into museums only to become implanted and activated in the consciousness of the curious, and seekers of truth.

Even my dreams and images of Rudee, although emerging from my own unconscious, maintained an imagery that could have been associated with almost any culture. A friend asked me if I was positive that Rudee was not an incarnation of the devil. I told him that the devil had horns like on the bottle of tobasco sauce, from which he was about to douse a clam chowder. I was brought up to associate horns with the devil. Although our conversation was not very serious it did initiate some thoughts about images. There are images in the Buddhist pantheon and in other religions that are ornamented with horns, however they are not the devil.

The six images found associated with this chapter take the form of Tibetan religious paintings (thang-ka) which reflect iconographical descriptions in the Mahākāla-Tantra. If I were able to draw Rudee there would be some similarities in such features as the fangs, the dwarf-like countenance and the hair. The overall features, however, would be quite different. Mahākāla can appear in any form. In some cases he appears in human form: for example as in the appearance of the Brahmin Mahākāla (Bramze-mgon-po).

When I ponder the original form of an image, I am inspired to pass my thoughts on to a new discovery of self amd nature. An image will arise in the context of the wonders that enter my domain each day. The gods arose in the beatitude of nature: They are artifacts of substance, thought, being and process. They are found in the ground, in genealogy, in the oral tradition (stories), in the thought process and in dreams. I may not find the absolute origin of a thing, but its nature, its own being (as we can literally translate from the Sanskrit svabhāva) may be revealed.

In the beginning of my own search and travels, I entertained the idea of finding the original form of The Great-Black-One without realizing that my experiences with Rudee were bringing me close to that for which I was actually searching. Rudee was a blend of emotion, thought, forces of nature and varied imagery. At first I had no picture. It was an in-between space with the energy of Im—a space between feeling and image.

When I think about the evolution of image the idea of origin fascinates me, but I also know that origin is relative to what came before what I might think of as the origin. Then, there is the future image that I do not yet see, but feel with my deepest emotions. I can also personalize the origin. The origin for me lies in my boyhood experiences with grandfather, in and around the well, and in his Bavarian forest.

The similarities that the image of Rudee has with Rudra of the Rig Veda, when I first discovered it, seemed uncanny, but now I view the similarity as a natural merging of the historical and the personal—a discovery of a hybrid homunculus. Rudra (or Rudee) is an experience of time (Kāla), blackness (kāla), destruction and the bestial, but it is also touched with light, creativeness, good fortune, humaneness and healing qualities. In the Hindu scriptures Rudra is not only associated with destructive qualities, but has the characteristics of a healer. Even in the Rig Veda, Rudra is conceived as a healer: In Book 7, verse 46 Rudra is said to possess a thousand medicines, and is asked to come to the devotee's place of dwelling to heal all disease. The date of the Rig Veda is not really known, but most scholars will conservatively estimate the date anytime from 3000 to 1500 B.C.

By the time of the twelfth century, the time that we can accurately date the Mahākāla manuscript, Rudra's characteristics had been combined with those of other Vedic and Hindu deities-especially siva. In the epic the Mahābhārata, Siva is said to burn up the world. He is called sharp, severe, and flaming. He is said to eat flesh, blood and marrow and is therefore called Rudra (dreadful). Also in the Mahābhārata Siva is called time (kāla), who is the beginning of the world as well as it's destroyer. The image of Rudra, in a sense, became the shadow of Siva and finally part of Siva's very image.

A similar synthesis took place with the deity Prajāpati (the lord of creatures). Rudra who is considered a master of the hunt and archery, is said to have threatened Prajāpati with his arrow. Prajāpati promised to made him Lord of the Beasts (Pasupati) if he did not shoot. Rudra complied, hence his epithet Pasupati. There is a polarity between the epithets the Lord of Creatures (Prajāpati) and the Lord of Beasts (Pasupati). By the time of the Mahākāla-Tantra (the Ngor version), the peaceful lord of creatures and the wrathful lord of beasts had merged into the concept of two in one—indicative of the dark and bright sides of our consciousness. In Tibetan Buddhism, Mahākāla is an emanation of the peaceful deity Avalokitesvara, yet at the same time, like Rudra, he has a wrathful countenance.

From around the time of the fourth century the name Mahākāla replaced the names of other deities like Rudra, Kala, or Siva.

Sometimes Mahākāla is depicted as an assistant of śiva, with the face of Bhairava, and is often confused with a similar deity, Ksetrapāla, who is actually a member of Mahākāla's retinue. Ksetrapāla figures prominently in the rituals and meditations of the Buddhist Mahākāla. In Kathmandu Nepal every locality has a sacred spot set aside to make offering to Ksetrapāla (literally protector of the earth).

The seventh chapter of the Mahākāla-Tantra is not an original, but a prototype (in the sense of model): it describes six images. The chapter is also a prototype for the Tantric rituals and meditations that we learn in the practice. It appears to be the oldest preserved manuscript in the Buddhist tradition describing the images of the Great-Black-One.

The first paragraph of the ensuing translation reflects the check and balance that is explicit or implicit in every Buddhist practice (not just Tantra). This check and balance is the self recognition of our shortcomings and addictions—the awareness that we will go to extremes to deny our addictions and dependencies. Our shortcomings, addictions and attachments are like demons and ghosts that attack, haunt and sabotage our serenity, and hence our ability to help ourselves and others. If we focus and cultivate on the four keys of balance and harmony (compassion, friendliness, joy and equanimity) in the context of our general practice, these inner demons and ghosts will be neutralized and become a means rather than a hinderance. Without these four harmonizing influences it is quite likely the practitioner will go astray and flounder. In the preparation for the practice of Mahākāla (actually every Tantric practice) is the understanding of the mantra *"Om I have the nature of Vajra which has its origin in the experiential knowledge of sūnyatā"* With this mantra, our perception shifts into a space where everything within our consciousness loses its conditioned meaning, i.e. becomes detached from the reactive mind that automatically stimulates a conditioned response (either in thought or in action): That mechanical power is then handed over to a higher power.

I imagine this space as being empty; or, being in a state of emptiness. Yet empty is a kind of image, which may be difficult to abandon simply by making it an essence. An essence can still be an image, so even the essence must be in the nature of Vajra which has its experiential knowledge in the origin of Sūnyatā. Sūnyatā is a quality which gives the image a hidden dimension—it is sacred. It is an experience out of which the Im can provide the energy to generate what I experience as raw structure, which is indicated by the term Vajra (and by the symbol of the ritual item vajra). The vajra stands for the five elements, directions, colors, basic emotions, sounds and the five Buddha families—the five-fold raw nature of the universe.

The following is a translation of the seventh chapter of the Mahākāla—Tantra. It is a text about image, ritual and contemplation which appears to be the first preserved written formulation in the Buddhist tradition concerning the images of the Great-Black-One. The text goes back to at least the twelfth Century. The title of the chapter is "The Arising Of The Divinity," (i.e empowered image).

To begin with, having admitted one's errors, made offerings, cultivated the four keys to harmony and balance (compassion, friendliness, joy and equanimity), and having understood *"Om I have the nature of Vajra which has its origin in the experiential knowledge of Sūnyatā,"* one should purify everything for a long time.

The master of yoga should practice the divine stance of the eight-handed Mahākāla: the lord is embracing the Goddess and surrounded by four yoginis in the manner of conjugal union; he has three faces with a yellow beard and hair which raises upward (into the shape of a vajra). He has dreadful fang-like teeth. His first face is very terrible and black; his second face on the left is red and the right one is green. He wears a tiger skin and is adorned with a garland of human heads; he is dwarf like; a hanging belly is decorated with the ornaments of snakes. He has eight hands: The right and left hands are embracing the Goddess, the second right hand is holding a chopper, the third right hand holds a vajra, and in the fourth there is a drum. The second left hand holds a skull bowl filled with blood, the third left hand holds bell and the fourth a cudgel. He is riding a corpse with his left leg outstretched behind him (like a bow stance), and is surrounded by four yoginis. To the East is Chandesvarā. She is yellowish white; her hair is dishevelled, has dreadful fang-like teeth and holds a chopper and skull bowl. In the Southern direction is Carcikā. She is naked and black holding a chopper and skull bowl; she stands with her left leg outstretched, has dishevelled hair and dreadful fang-like teeth. In the West is Kālikā. She is blue-black with dishevelled hair, holds a three-pointed spear and so on. To the North is the Goddess Kulikesvarā. Her hands are stretching upward, in her left hand is a skull bowl and so on. All of the goddesses have three eyes. First, having generated the syllable *hūm*, one should allure the divinities, gurus, Buddhas and Bodhisattvas who reside in the three worlds: Contemplate the whole world through the (individual and collective atmospheres and channels created by the sounds, images and other invisible structures) of the mantra *"Om I have the nature of Vajra which has its origin in the experiential knowledge of Sūnyatā."*

After creating the seed syllable *hūm*, cultivate (the mind-body complex) as the vajra skeleton. Meditate continously on the four-faced Mahākāla whose presence (image) has its own nature in the highest bliss. He arises with the sound *"ha ha"* and the ominous *"phet"*, and takes the form of the syllables *kāli kālaya*. He is the protector in the manner of great bliss; and is—, this world, whose purpose is to pacify (the malicious forces in the universe).

According to the yoga of the garland of mantras, *hili kili*, the Great-Black-One is endowed with the Buddha's teachings. His first face is black, the right one is red, the left white; and on the backside, is the face of a boar. His (left) four feet are stretched outward. His color is black, he has a hanging belly, his hair is dishevelled; each head has three eyes, and on the first face there is a beard. He has twelve hands: The first left and right hands are embracing the goddess, and the Lord is biting her lower lip with his fang-like teeth. He holds a white yaktail in the second left hand, in the third a trident, in the fourth a skull bowl, in the fifth the hide of an elephant, and in the sixth the tusk of Ganesha (the deity with a elephant's head). In the second right hand he holds a chopper, in the third a vajra-trident, in the fourth a cudgel, in the fifth an elephant hide, and in the sixth a vajra. Standing on a buffalo, he stomps on all the demons. Having moved into conjugal union with the Goddess, his tongue rolls with flowing blood. He is surrounded by four Goddesses who have offerings and are singing.

For pacifying the obstacles, and for the purpose of gaining complete power, the Lord described the creation of the four-handed (Mahākāla). Cultivate one of his faces as black with dreadful fang-like teeth, a hanging belly, yellow rising hair and beard. He is ornamented with snakes and stands on a corpse. He arises from the syllable *hūm*, and has four hands. In the two left hands he holds a chopper and skull bowl; in his right hands are a trident and cudgel. He is flanked by two yoginis.

Then, there is the erection of the six-handed Mahākāla, whose purpose is to pacify all the obstacles. He is the best. He has the own nature of supreme bliss. He ameliorates sin; assists, and is beneficial to the teachings of the Buddha. The yogi who has equipped himself with the yoga of the vajra-skeleton becomes the chief divinity who stands on a lion. He has three faces, and arises from the seed syllable *hrāh*. His first face is blue like a rain cloud, the left one is green, and the right face is white. His limbs are

relaxed. He has fang-like teeth and yellow hair which
rises upward. He has three eyes and is ornamented
with snakes. His neck is embraced by the goddess.
He is surrounded by the four yoginis: Chandesvarā,
Kālikā, Kulikesvarī and Carcikā. Alluring all the goddesses with the yoga that stimulates conjugal union,
he arises. Their names encircle him. He is completely
enveloped by the five elements.

This is the erection of time.

The goddess asked: How are people empowered
by means of the image/Im of their own divinity?

The lord answered: The goddess Umā whose very
nature is creativity (yoga), is for the purpose of the
creations of Mahākāla. Any other thought (concerning the purpose of Umā) is incorrect. To begin with,
at the time of beginning meditation, whoever desires
the power, should make a space conducive to gaining
the best success. The singer of mantras, who is meditating in those power places, or in one's own large
house, should make sure that they are always practicing in a lonely place or an empty house. One should
completely cultivate the sixteen-handed (Mahākāla)
as being surrounded by Nārāyana and the other gods.
He should be with the eight yoginis. Dwelling with
the five sacred families partaking of the great flesh he
should, indeed, always create insight—thinking: "I
am the power." That is, the yogi should always take
the five ambrosias as well as the cow (go), dog (ku),
horse (da), elephant (ha) and man (na).

In this way the yogi who desires the power will achieve
this goal. When he dwells within the five families, he
should then eat the meat of the yellow cow. The yogi
should cultivate the sixteen-handed (Mahākāla) thinking, "I am Mahākāla." Whatever has already been
mentioned should always be practiced.

The two-handed Mahākāla should be cultivated for the purpose of achieving more power. Indeed, whoever with great energy realizes the power of mudrā, will afterwards easily and certainly achieve all the powers.

Whatever potential substance, thought and being that is brought into existence should eventually be cultivated into nonexistence; in that way, the power of understanding can always be realized. Therefore whenever a person feels a sense of power, that sense should be thought of in such a way (that one's sense of success and self-worth will not become an obstacle to understanding). Again, while making offerings of various scents, flowers, incense, garlands and whatever, realize the syllable *hūm* in the heart, and the ritual is continued. Having experienced Mahabhairva in front of the self, the errors of life should be admitted. Afterwards, one should cultivate the four keys of harmony and balance—the realms of Brahma (compassion, friendliness, joy and equanimity). Then one should do the touch ritual: that is, one should utter the sound *am* while touching the left hand with the right hand; for the consecration of one's place of sitting, one should utter *om thamu āh hūm* (touching oneself sometimes with a flower on the head, both shoulders and where one is sitting); one should touch the eyes uttering *ksam;* on the left ear *ah*, on the right one *am*, on the nose *trām*, on the tongue *hrīh*, on both feet *vam-vam* and on the genitalia *hūm*. Afterwards is the empowerment of body, speech and mind: *om phem hūm*, on the heart *hūm*, on the throat *om* and on the head *phem*.

Having completely cultivated the square palace with four doors and four arches respectively, with the throne in the center, one should focus on Sūnyatā uttering, *"om I have the nature of Vajra which has its origin in the experiential knowledge of Sūnyatā"*. Then, when the (mantra) is realized, one will hear the musical instruments: sitar, drum, flute and cymbals as well as dancing and singing. Contemplate using the syllable *hūm*, that Narayana with his entourage are singing these praises, and completely realize the vajra skeleton in its sundry parts (that is, the inner body of invisible channels).

The goddess asked: Oh Lord, please arise! Work for the benefit of sentient beings! They are sentient beings, who are playing in the world. Please give them the various powers.

The lord answered: Oh Goddess, look! Look at the great being, the Reverend Mahākāla (The Great-Black-One), who has four faces, who has the image/Im of sky, whose own-nature is the highest-bliss, and who arises from the syllable *hūm!* His first face is black. His second face to the left is green, his right one is red; and on the backside, is the face of a buffalo. All the faces have dreadful fang-like teeth and are very fearful. He is more terrible than terrible. Each face has three eyes and a beard. One face has yellow hair connected with rays that rise straight upward. He is wrapped with the snake taksaka, stands with all four feet on a buffalo, and has sixteen arms. The first right and left arms embrace the Goddess; and with his left legs outstretched stomps the four gods of death. In the second right hand he holds a chopper, and in the third a cudgel. In the fourth he holds a white yaktail, and the in the fifth the club of Yama (the Vedic god of death). In the sixth hand he holds a vajra, and in the seventh the tusk of Ganesha. In the eighth hand he holds the hide of an elephant. In the second left hand he holds a skull bowl filled with blood, in the third a trident, and in the fourth a small drum. In the fifth he holds a bell ornamented with a vajra, and in the sixth an ordinary bell. In the seventh he holds the head of a buffalo, and in the eighth the hide of an elephant.

He has a hanging belly, and around his waist there is a tiger skin tied with the clan's emblem. He is bedecked with a garland of (human) heads, and belts his waist with the serpent Ananda: Around his neck is Vasuki, and for an earring there is the serpent Sesena. Covering his arms are the embellished ornaments of all the serpents. Falling under his feet is Nārāyana and others. He is surrounded by the eight dakinis. Screaming the sound *kāli kāli* and resounding a great *phet*, he thunders a great noise, and arises, with the cry hāhā hāhā hāhi hehe hehe hoho.

In the eastern direction there is Chandesvarā whose seed syllable is *cam*. She holds a chopper and skull bowl, and is decorated with a garland of (human) heads. Her color is yellowish-white and she has dreadful fang-like teeth. In the southern direction is Carcikā. She is black and has the seed syllable *kam*. In the same way as Canādsevarā, she holds a chopper and skull bowl. In the western direction is Kālikā who has the seed syllable *lam*. She holds a trident and a skull bowl. As the goddess Chandesvarā the rest is the same. In the northern direction there is Kulikesvarī who has the seed syllable *ram*. Her hands are raised upwards, and the left one has a skull bowl. All the Goddesses have three eyes, and are bedecked with human heads. Decorated with eight serpents, they stand on corpses. They are standing with their left feet stretched outward. They are naked, dreadful and have dishevelled hair. In the outside direction is the black Cauri holding a yak tail. She has the seed syllable *cām*. In the southern direction, is the green Lanchanā holding incense sticks and has the seed syllable *cha*. In the western direction is Mahānandā arising from the seed syllable *mām*. She is red and holds a vajra and bell. In the northern direction, is Nandesvarā arising from the seed syllable *nam*. She is yellow. Umādeva is embraced by the Lord of the gods. She is yellowish-white, has four hands, and has

dreadful fang-like teeth. She has the ambiance of the
great goddess. She is poised in a very blissful stance
(mudrā).

The mantra of the Buddha mentioned before produces various great powers. The wise ones who respect holy beings and are composed in supreme bliss
should not be attached to one thing or its opposite
(that is, like ugly or beautiful; good or bad). They
practice their ritual-meditation on the eighth, tenth,
and fourteenth days of the lunar month. For example, the yogi who does his practice with wine, the
meat of cow (go), dog (ka), elephant (da), horse (ha),
and man (na) should drink blood with the five
ambrosias. The yogi who has even the slightest bit of
doubt will soon be destroyed, but when he practices
with great effort there will be success. If he inwardly
dwells among the five families, and practices in the
above manner, one's practice will not be broken. That
is, the secret will remain intact. If one practices in an
indiscreet manner one will lose clarity, and the momentum will be broken.

The goddess asked: "What is the meaning of twilight
language? I want to hear; please tell me the truth".

The Lord answered: "Twilight language has extended designations—it is metaphorical. For example,
the word `strength'- means `wine', it also refers to
`flesh'. The wise man teaches in such a manner, and
accordingly should be understood".

The female energy of the five families, whom we
shall briefly mention, is very important for the practice of realizing one's powers. That is, the sweeper
woman is related to the Vajra family, the dancing girl
is born in the lotus family, the brahman girl belongs
to the jewel family, the washerwoman is born in the

work family and the warrioress is in the body family. These mudras are said to produce one's own power. The practitioner of mantra, after worshiping the juices of these woman, should drink their semen, [in Sanskrit the orgasmic liquids of woman are also called semen (sukram)] which in turn is also called vajra.

Oh, kind goddess, you should follow very respectfully everything that I have mentioned. This other speech (the twilight language) is wonderful. In this way the initiated man should teach about The Great-Black-One. On the other hand, whoever is uninitiated, will die in seven days. If he is not dead, he will be sick. So, all the gods, yoginis and sky goers will be angry at those men who have no faith in the teacher; who are liars, uninitiated, and who, also, touch the holy books.

Oh, goddess, I will impart to you all that I have mentioned. The practices that I have mentioned so far, which are in all the Tantras, as well as the the eight Tantric powers, should be diligently pursued. Therefore, if the initiated man should read, write and cause to be written this Tantra, he will easily attain everything. He will draw an image of the Lord Mahākāla. It will be sixteen fingers high painted with red ink mixed with various scents. He will draw it on a birch bark with a pen made from a nimba tree. At that time, the image will be drawn on a cloth with menstrual blood; or, on a cloth found on the cremation grounds. Having completed the touch ritual, he will contemplate and enter into union with the goddess.

The goddess sung: 'Oh Lord, if you arise, you are inspired. Oh Mahākāla, great being, please listen! Oh, kind hearted Lord, please arise! I am the goddess who dances here. Oh, my husband, let me ask, how should I do my work"? Mahākāla immediately sat on the corpse (and answered): "I dance as a hero circumnambulating the three worlds. In your body are the Goddesses Kālī, Bhohī, Chandesvarī and Kulikī; they are kept in your navel, and spread in my heart. You who satisfies the world, again I say, what do you ask? There is no beginning or end. According to one sound you become the lover of sentient beings. If you are going to do the work, please enter my body'.

When the meditation on Mahākāla has reached a peak moment he will be allured, and will arise. At that moment, the consciousness of transformation is understood; this is the complete acceptance of the sixteen-handed Mahākāla.

The two-handed Mahākāla is described as the image by which the suffering of sentient beings is removed. Indeed, it is only through the birth of ordinary consciousness that all suffering is created. Oh God, one should contemplate on the skill-in-means (of the two-handed Mahākāla).

The Lord said: "To begin with, meditate on hūm. Since you desire the power of Tantra and have performed the religious observances including the offerings, cultivate the two-handed Mahākāla who has one face and two arms". He holds a skull bowl in the left hand, and in the right one a chopper. He is black and is standing on a corpse. His yellow hair raises upwards and is embellished with the ornaments of serpents. He is dwarf-like with a double hanging belly, and is in the intimate company and surroundings of two yoginis.

Oh, goddess, if what has been said has not been realized, when the protector of the conch is recalled by the thunderous sound of lightening and rain what other practice is mentioned.

Then, the goddess asked: "Oh, Lord, if the Lord of yogis is intimate with the five families, why should he be living in the ordinary world (samsāra)? Oh, great divine one, the completed flower is not hindered by its thousand parts; it grows into a whole flower. Likewise, one should practice with their four limbs (the whole body and mind) as one."

The Lord answered: "The yogi who has accommodated the three worlds as The Great-Black-One, for sure, will realize the Tantric powers."

CHAPTER IX

Birthing The Child Within

Mahākāla, The Great-Black-One, is birthed within us. If one is grounded in The Four Keys of Balance and Harmony, realizes the nature of Vajra, experiences the knowledge of sūnyatā and is truthful about one's transgressions, the procreative and birthing process will go with ease. The phrase "Four Keys of Balance and Harmony" though an accurate translation is not literal. A literal translation from the Sanskrit caturbrahmavihāra is the "four dwelling places of Brahma." If one took this phrase literally and added the question, where are these places and who is this Brahma? and then began looking around for such a place or being, one would eventually find them. Actually, one could start looking in a Buddhist temple, like one of the monasteries in which I stayed, or perhaps one of the Buddhist religious centers here in California. No matter where they are in the world, they are called vihāras. One might wonder about who Brahma is: Brahma is a deity, an image in the Indian pantheon, but the word Brahma is used in various ways. In the formation of Sanskrit words (compounds), the spelling of the words change. There-fore Brahma could come from Bráhman which means sacred sound or prayer. The "n" drops when used in the formation of compounds as in Brahmavihāra.

It is very common for the Tibetans to translate caturbrahmavihāra, the four immeasurables (tsad-med-bzhi), instead of Tsangs-pa-bzhi the more literal translation. Tsangs pa means Brahma. The phrase 'four immeasurables' is telling the reader and the practitioner that compassion, friendliness, joy and equanimity have an immeasurable and nondiscursive values. Although we use these concepts in our everyday activities, it is clear that in Buddhist parlance they are anything but ordinary ideas, and have "immeasurable" possibilities.

In the context of dialogue there is the tendency to lose oneself in abstraction. The abstractions and inventions are inexhaustible. The purpose of the rite, the contemplation and the sādhanā as they crisscross and blend, is to cultivate and experience the strength and depth of the previous experience in the ritual-meditation process—much in the same way that a body builder may notice and experience the strength of a developing muscle. We have many such muscles and ligaments that are little used, and many more unused channels of invisible thought patterns that can be brought together and realized. In a way, one does not understand an idea until it becomes like a muscle that one can feel and use. On the other hand, one can feel their muscle and still not be able to apply it to any good purpose. A professor of physiology, for example, may be able to tell us all about our muscles, but a gymnast will be able to demonstrate how they can be used. A baseball player will show us a particular function of using our muscles. Body builders sometimes speak of that inner spirit that needs to be cultivated as well as the outward image. Many of them see their practice as a spiritual dimension. In Buddhist meditation the goal is to experience the meaning in the body and mind i.e. the meaning becomes somatic. The Brahmavihāras are related to many images that relate to one's life, and to wherever one might be treading on the path. In Tibetan Buddhism, there is the idea that images must not be relied on, but be given respect for their possibilities of transformation. It is based on the process of empowerment.

In the rituals of Mahākāla, the Vajrabody is conceived as an outer and inner psychic structure. It is created through a special phase in the rite to ensure that the practitioner has an aura of protection which is the outer body of vajra and is sometimes called vajraskeleton, i.e. vajrapañjara: It also concieved as a net. The vajrabody as a protective device is built through one's vows, meditation and ritual performance for the sake of others. The network of Vajra gives one the confidence that what has been developed so far in one's practice, will be protected, which in turn will be an extension of the process. It is a stage of practice which builds upon the previous phases. The previous purification becomes enclosed in a protective shell. The Four Keys of Balance and Harmony (compassion, friendliness, joy and equanimity), on the other hand, gestate and mature within the inner vajrabody deep within one's being within the web of thousands of invisible channel. The body, speech and thought of the Buddha, which has been formed within the practitioner will have an arua of protection. When we are sure that the offering is made; when we have truly let go, the compassion, friendliness, joy and equanimity will unlock the hidden elements that will create the child within; it will include the dark side, but as an ally—maybe an image like Rudee.

There is a phase in the ritual-meditation called "the purification of the three doors." The three doors are body, speech and thought. When they are opened they lead to the five cakras; the five energy centers of ones invisible body. These are located in the regions of the head, neck, heart, navel and genitals. I like to imagine three wells that sink into an underground cavern with arteries going to five reservoirs. Each reservoir (or cakra) has the potential to generate a healing ambrosia, appropriate to where it is located in the body. Each cakra has a manifestation of Mahākāla represented by a different color. Starting with the region of the head the colors are: white (head region), red (neck region), very dark blue (heart region), yellow (around the navel), green (the genital region).

Another way of looking at this invisible potential structure of imagery is that the three doors and the five-fold inner realms are like tunnels into the body of the Great-Black-One, through which the ancestral spirits and the Great-White-Red-Blue-Yellow and Green ones are channeled in the tradition of spiritual transformation, and across minds, cultures and galaxies.

In the purification phase, the dominant image is The White-Great-Black-One—the white Mahākāla. The removal of obscuration, and purifying the inner being is here associated with the color white. In the actual meditation, the white seed syllable *Om*, in the thirty-two petaled lotus-like image in the

head region, sucks and absorbs the miasma of "confusion", and
is then burned by the heat of yogic breathing (generating inner
fire)—the result is the arising of the white Mahākāla in conjugal
union with his consort, i.e. the white female sky goer who carries
a skull bowl and chopper. Except for the change in the size of
the lotus-like image, its color, seed syllable and corresponding
emotion, the structures in the remaining chakras are the same.
The color red of the neck region is associated with uncontrolled
"lust", which is absorbed by the syllable Hrīh. The dark blue of
the heart is identified with "hatred", absorbed by the syllable
Hūm. Yellow corresponds to states of mind that are opinionated
and "egotistical", which is absorbed by Trām, and the green of
the genitals is symbolic of "jealousy" absorbed by Hām. The
corresponding Mahākāla and female sky goer in each cakra arise
and produce rippling waves of ambrosia—what we can think of
as psychic spermatozoa. The five cakras act as psychic strainers
and invisible alchemical furnaces. As one breathes and works
the bellows of each cakra, one cakra purifies the other, until they
coalesce and there is no color at all. There is a tremendous letting
go of emotional and cognitive accumulations. Yet, my experience of this phase is one of being filled with an uncommon
charge. Actually, one feels emptied and filled at the same time.
Petsan said this feeling was not unusual; and for most people,
pleasant. He assured me, however, that this experience was not
enlightenment. Maybe this is the origin of the phase "fulfillment
and satisfaction"—The fulfillment and satisfaction of emptiness,
i.e. the coming and going of images. As soon as one feels clean
and the unconscious impressions are purified, the inner channels are free to be filled by the rippling ambrosia. There is a calm
rush and a natural high. An image/Im of the father Akshobhya
is then formed in and on the very top of the head. The officiant
then utters the phrase, "Oh, Lord, please clean and purify all my
transgressions, obscuration, noxiousness and distorted feelings."
Akshobhya, the father, in the form of a bubbly mass of ambrosia
begins to leak and finally, in an orgasmic burst, flows downward
until this inner body is completely filled. There is a huge surge
and one feels like a ray of light. It is like a ray of light which
imparts a detectable aura. It is more than a healthy look; it is the
look of someone ready for both life and death. I saw this look in

both Petsan and my father.

Compassion, friendliness, joy, and equanimity are concepts. These concepts have power. They are real mindthings that affect the body, and everything around one. For the practitioner they are not just a morality that one is brought up with, but are concepts and feelings to be consciously created and enhanced. We need to think of them almost as physical properties that are reduced to their own state of natural gravitation, a state of raw structure—like a heartbeat.

In the ritual-meditation process, the actual muscle and chemistry of compassion, for example, is cultivated and used over and over again in a ritual context: The muscle of compassion is brought into being, it is exercised. When an image of Mahākāla is brought into being, compassion is also generated.

The examples given in Buddhist literature that demonstrate compassion portray an act of sacrifice: It is the spirit of sacrifice that ultimately brings the act of compassion into reality. The dynamics of sacrifice are hidden because it goes against our natural instincts of self- preservation and survival: It is not a pleasant topic to consider; we repress the thought of giving up something we desire. The Buddhist literature demonstrates this quite graphically which is the historical background for the reference to the offering of flesh in the Joy Luck Club by Amy Tan: There was the woman, Rūpāvatī who offered her breasts to a starving woman who was about to eat her own recently delivered child. Rūpāvatī was afraid to leave the woman alone for fear of her eating the child. She cut off her own breasts and then gave them to the starving woman for food. Then there was King Sibi who sliced off his flesh pound by pound to satisfy a hovering hungry vulture, or the former Buddha who threw himself into the tiger pit to satisfy a brood of hungry cubs. To have compassion in this sense means having the ability to offer up one's body. The intention of these examples is not to encourage people to go out and offer their flesh to the animals, but to implant the idea of self-sacrifice, and to indicate the spirit in which to contemplate. If we can do our practice with that same spirit, our compassion will grow. Sacrificing our confusion, lust, hatred, egotism and jealousy is creating space for the growth of the vajrabody.

Stories demonstrating bodily sacrifice as an act of compassion, also depict the principle of the "power of truth", as when the offered flesh is often miraculously replaced by the gods who are secretly watching the transaction. In the instance of Rūpāvatī the Hindu God Indra observed her compassion and allowed her to be reborn a man (in those days the desire of all woman). In the case of King Sibi who offered his flesh to the hovering vulture, his body was restored by the same deity through the power of truth. Regardless of the type of offering, if done in the spirit of self-sacrifice, we will have one of the keys to balance and harmony. In the twenty-second chapter of the <u>Lotus Sutra</u> the bodhisattva Sarvasattvapriyadarsana burns his arm for incense as an offering. He made the promise that he would regain his arm through the power of truth: A golden arm miracously grew in place of the sacrificed limb. Whether it is a golden arm or a wonderful change in life for the better, it happens out of the blue of personal practice. For the recovering addict, this means sacrificing all the distorted emotions and images that rob him or her of sobriety. The person in recovery does this one day at a time and promises to recover. Each day the miracle of new life unfolds.

Emptiness (sūnyatā) is the unknown that confronts one at every step in life. It is inherent in every event and phenomena. Emptiness is a hidden dimension which does not reach out to the practitioner but hides behind a curtain of substance, thought, being and process. The emptiness of a thing, then, is disclosed with not only the event or thing perceived but in the thought and insight of the perceiver. The subject and object both are empty, but the experience of emptiness evolves through their coming together. It is in this combined emptiness where the birthing of an empowered image can take place. In the birthing of an empowered image one's accumulating impressions and symbols are constantly maturing and moving through transformative stages—the blending or union of these constantly uprising pictures and thoughts are always immenent: This fusion may not happen exactly as it is written in the meditation-ritual manuals or in an orderly manner, but it will happen.

I once had a client who liked to practice log rolling, a popular sport in the logging towns of the Pacific Northwest. He was curious about the idea of emptiness (sūnyatā) and asked me to explain it. I told him, as I tell everyone, that it cannot be explained so easily and depended to some extent on the experience of the person. We dropped the subject and he began to explain to me the skill of log rolling which involves hoping from log to rolling log floating in a river or bay. An idea came to me about how he might approach an understanding of sūnyatā, and I asked him how he hops and rolls to get from one log to the other while trying, for example, to cover a fairly large distance with few logs? As he was explaining the process I asked him if he ever stepped backward to the log from which he just jumped? He said that the idea is to keep going as if the log behind him was not there-it might indeed not be there-one never knows. I told him that sūnyatā was a little like that-whatever support one might have (life itself) at some point might not be there. So, in Buddhism the experience of sūnyatā, as much as one is able, is practiced in everything one does—as if the log is not there. All things are sūnyatā (empty). As much as that is a dictum that all things are empty and in a sense not really there, so is the idea that all things are inconceivable. It is a conundrum because we think we can perceive accurately the world around us, but most of our judgements are determined through consensus. In Buddhism it is axiomatic that the world is never exactly the way we see it.

The next in line, after the emptiness of things (sūnyatā) for the most inconceivable is nature itself. Nature and sūnyatā are very close in the competition for inconceivability. In some inexplicable way these two are interlocked into a puzzle. Within the core of the puzzle are the raw elements. The elements of earth, air, water, wind, metal, wood and space, in whatever form they might be conceived, hold the emptiness of that form. Images are the result of fabricated substance, thought and being, all of which, also, are empty. The realization of its emptiness is an ongoing practice: It makes the empowerment of image a possibility.

There is no log in the river that is absolutely safe. An awareness of this insubstantial phenomena coupled with the confidence that one can survive on the logs changes the configurations of ones inner life. Then, an awareness of sūnyatā springs the lock on "the three doors" (Body-Speech-Mind and a fourth is added Vajra). The elements then begin to work in a new way, and gravitate to the light in each door. Each opening of a door reveals an element. Body reveals earth, Speech unveils water, Mind exposes fire and Vajra discloses wind—here we have the basis of the mechanics of the formation of the Vajra-body.

The practice is grounded in nature and grows through the elements. The images of nature become dominant. Everyone can identify with these images and corresponding feelings. One can smell the earth in the palm of one's hands, as I saw my father do many times; as I do myself. We feel the warmth of the hearth, and are poignantly aware of fire's destructive capacity. The wind fans the flames, sometimes to the extent that it cannot be extinguished easily. It is easy to identify with nature with our breath. We become aware of our inner wind, fire and earth. I am fond of running on the ocean beach with the wind blowing in my face and feeling the ocean salt spray. The mobility and power of water is awesome. These images too are empty, but they are very close to their own nature—to their Im. They are the basic chemistry of our spiritual muscles.

Petsan used to say, "you are what you think and perceive". What one thinks and perceives moves from inward to outward and then feeds back to the conscious mind. It is psychic cooking and eating. We design the menu, cook it and then eat. Our mental projection comes back to us in a transformed and hopefully tasty state. The images and thoughts mix and recycle in our environment, and then come back to us. We are what we eat. Our spiritual or enlightenment muscles develop through our practice and prayer.

In cultivating The Four Keys of Balance and Harmony, the muscles are flexed by means of the five hidden spirits—The Five Buddhas. In the practice of the Great-Black-One these Five Buddhas are concieved as Five Mahākāla and their consorts. The Four Keys of Balance and Harmony unlock the potential for inner growth, and initiates the generation of the fetus of the inner body: They unlock and open the channels and stimulate the chemistry that creates the original organs of the Vajra body-the transpersonal child within. It is a fetus that gestates in every meditation. The Four Keys of Balance and Harmony correspond to the four limbs (body, speech, mind and vajra) of this transpersonal-hidden child. Within each cell like part is an organ that matures in combination with one of the elements. The Body-Speech-Mind-Vajra structure is identified with four goddesses who gestate one of the four keys. Here is the way it works: If you want to accomplish compassion, observe and contemplate water. Watch and listen to the rain. Study and meditate on the ocean; become aware of the weather and feel the water nature of yourself. In meditation, occasionally contemplate on your speech chakra located in your neck region because that is where water energy predominates—the spot of the womb of the Goddess sabari. If it is friendliness that you are working on then consider the aspects of earth. Earth power that lies in the body chakra in the region of the head is thought to be in the womb of the Earth Goddess Pukkasi. When one focuses on Joy one should contemplate the nature of fire. Contemplate the heart chakra and the Fire Goddess Candali. For equanimity observe and meditate on wind and breath. Wind and breath are the most important because, wind controls fire and hence the temperature of the environment. Following one's breath as in insight (vipasyana) meditation, is cultivating equanimity—it is in the ring of Vajra with the womb of the Goddess Dombini. The inner body evolves as a child within and matures as a Buddha—as oneself.

It had never occurred to me that offering water might be building character, let alone have an intrinsic relationship that in turn is related to speech. Certainly, it might have seemed a little odd, at one point in my life, to associate water with speech—let alone as the context for the dwelling place of a goddess called Sabari. Whether things go together or not depends on the context of experience in which images, words and feelings are uniting. It does not have to be logical. On the other hand, if the context, for example, is sound, then speech and water go together very nicely. Anyone who has practiced mantra meditation realizes innumerable possibilities. Sometimes, the melody of a piece of music will linger on in one's consciousness—reoccuring in ripples and waves. And think about the emotions and feelings that are generated by different kinds of music. A sound that is associated with water will homologize with the basic energy of speech. It is outgoing and pervasive. In the

Tantric system of the Great-Black-One, it teaches compassion. Offering water is a common practice: It is an easy offering that one can take advantage of when watering the plants and so on. Water can be offered by uttering a sound that is a water sound. Here is a simple ritual action that has the power of conditioning one's behavior. Compassion will arise. Likewise, the offering of fire can create the possibility of extraordinary joy, i.e. of an actual place within one that can exude joy. An offering of earth, then, will generate friendliness; and to offer wind would produce equanimity. What I am translating "The Four Keys of Balance and Harmony" opens the windows to that person within our person, and turn on the energy that allows the muscles of compassion, joy, friendliness and equanimity to grow. Sometimes it's nice to catch a glimmering of just who that person might become.

CHAPTER X

Breath

I am on a mountain top overlooking patches of sky-piercing redwoods. Clusters of granite and wooden dwellings slice illogically into the mountainsides. I see an iron bridge with a curve that reminds me of a woman, church spires that aspire to the same heights as the redwoods, startling green meadows and winding creeks searching for the bay that separates me from an outlying metropolis. Except for the miasma of fumes rising from the metropolis, I am taken back to my stay at the monkey temple, where I shared a vision of an ancient civilization with the spirits and gods that manifested themselves in the natural surroundings, as well as in the ancient architecture. The Valley of the Moon, where I live now, seems more like the Valley of Kathmandu every day. I visualize the tops of pagodas emerging through the morning mist, and then, they disappear into California palms which dot the blacktop roads snaking their way into vineyards or abruptly stopping on another mountain top. There are rivers, lakes and, from a vantage point, a not-so-distant ocean. But I am not the only one seeing and experiencing. There is the circling hawk far above me, the frightened rabbit who darted into the earth, and an ominous looking, but harmless snake whose eyes meet mine in a moment of recognition. I imagine being under the scrutiny of an almost extinct puma. Once Pumas were found in great numbers in these rolling hills—the receptacles of an invisible potency. Even the rocks, oaks and distant redwoods have their own way of seeing.

The all-seeing eyes that are painted on the white domes of Kathmandu Valley remain in the memory of every person who has visited Kathmandu. The domes are Buddhist reliquaries. Many of them hold the relics of past Buddhist saints. Indeed the actual structure called in Sanskrit chaitya (a piling up) is treated by many of the faithful as holy flesh itself. Sometimes the obvious round part (kumbha) is called Dharmadhātu, which is also the name for the ashes of Sākyamuni Buddha: Dharmadhātu is described as formless (nirākāra, i.e. Im). Like the gurumandāla, mentioned in chapter six, it represents not only an ideal space and place, but an actual path as well. It is an image-space. Each section of the reliquary or chaitya, symbolizes an aspect of the Buddhist Dharma. As one circumambulates the chaitya the devotee and the charisma of the chaitya become one. Without their golden spires (actually a row of thirteen circular disks called canopies that represent the thirteen phases to pass through on the way to the highest stage of enlightenment), these spires would look like giant white marbles with little golden closets. When the thirteen golden-like circular canopies glisten in the sun they remind me of grandfather's descriptions of the some of the nature spirits in his Bavarian forest: They were described as round and full of light ready always to help one making an effort in the process of self-discovery. Actually, the first circle is called the universal light (samantaprabha), and the eleventh one is referred to as the light of insight (prajñāprabha). The top disk is called the knowledge of having known all forms (sarvākārajñātajñāna).

The chaitya is on the way to becoming a popular American symbol. Tourist agencies advertise their Asian travels with these eyes that scan our world. They are powerful images that seem to impel most people toward introspection. Sometimes I feel like I am seeing with these eyes, as the images of California blend and become one with the images of the Himalayas. As these eyes, now my eyes, cast their gaze on the Valley of the Moon, I see that nature is for itself, not solely for the eyes of man. Nature is for the sake of nature's own manifestation of those same spirits that seem to settle on the tops of these white domes. I know that the energy of the water, sun and earth of this valley is spread before me like a giant offering cake and will be shared by the whole world as I make it my own offering. And, as in the beginning of the above translation in chapter eight, and implied in the beginning of all Buddhist rituals, my infractions of others and nature cannot go without notice.

I must put these infractions into the cauldron that burns, cooks and purifies the senses. The rusty gears and pistons of my sensory machinery must become quiet. My body will become centered and alive with the energy of heaven and earth, like the great white spirit cocoons that dot this Himalayan Valley—like the rolling hills of the Valley of the Moon.

My iniquities and transgressions take on shape and image in my mind's eye and appear as an inventory of different beings that run and disappear into trees and under rocks like roaches, pincherbugs and what my friend calls L.A. black beetles; they crawl and work out their life cycles in the pipes of kitchen sinks, toilets and sewers. Friends and enemies alike appear dreamlike, curling in the technicolor and smoldering vapors from an oil refinery. I hold my breath, and the images materialize in odd and difficult-to-recognize shapes. I feel their blood and fluids draining from my cakras and I slowly exhale. The exhale seems, paradoxically, like an inhale, i.e. there is the sensation of incoming air in my innermost being. I am exhaling and those poisoned images flow out with my breath and disperse into the lifting mist before me. I hold my breath and the remnants of those sundry images are squeezed, compressed and then with a final exhaling breath they are liberated to the fertility around me. A silver dollar eucalyptus slides into view, then some pampas, a lonely sycamore, a distant olive orchard and an oleander. Off in the distance I see the skyline of San Francisco. I feel purified and make a final offering of all of this into the fire of the senses. Like watching a rock drop in the sky blue caribbean waters, I drop my consciousness. I briefly hold my breath and sense that same unity as when I meditated in the monkey temple. I repeat the breath cycle again and again; the material world deflates and inflates with all its imagined motion and play—much like a set of dances. Each set, each deflation and inflation, moves energy from the former set into a new choreography. Each cycle has a new appearance and a different quality of offering; a new experience of purity and emptiness. Each breath cycle brings me closer to Great-Time.

As I contemplate, my vision stretched across the Sonoma hills, I experience an extended natural euphoria—is it a feeling of enlightenment? It is a realization of the possibility of balance and harmony with mother earth? The elements have their demands. And the euphoria has its price—the admission of ego, and the willingness to let it go. There are many ways to turn the ego into an offering—a gift to nature. Before me lay a table of offerings. How can one conceive of admitting one's errors without the offerings? If it is easy to apologize there must be an offering. If it is not easy, the apology could be the offering. And, then, even an easy apology can be worth it's weight in gold. The errors must be let go and transformed. I have the sensation that everything within my sight is transformable; it must be so in order to conserve the raw structures of what lies outside my window.

A confession of errors can be a formality. But offering the very objects of desire, indeed my immediate surroundings of the world, makes the admission a reality. The land and mindscape represents the whole world and can be focused within the ceremonial circle—within the heart. For example, as I drive through the North Bay countryside in the early Spring, there is a sudden burst of rich metallic green grass. A rush of image in its totality. The whole world becomes a hologram of the senses. As I sit behind of the wheel of my son's vintage Chevy, I lose touch with the importance of ego, staring out the window into green rivers, and feeling the oneness with the hum of the engine: It is transformed beyond the four hundred and fifty-four horses compacted within that block of metal; beyond the chassis that I am driving to a destination in my mind's eye. I do not have to suppress the details of the various scapes that fall across my vision. The grass moves like a green ocean. A distant hilltop, appears as if it were flowing out of the sky. Soaring above me are two chicken hawks, their eyes pierce beneath the grass mask. Out of the unconscious comes the thought of being eaten alive and I remember the story of King Sibi who gave his flesh to the hovering hungry vulture. For a moment, I have the fear of being food for the birds. I slow down, and purr to a stop beneath a eucalyptus tree. I have lost my senses to the hologram and could easily, it seems, purr into oblivion. I just sit and look. Off to my left are two black rocks the size of humans; they jut from the green in a manner that suggests they are male and female engaged in conversation. I later learned the name of that particular place: Two Rock Gulch. The sun shone through a eucalyptus grove giving the rocks a crystalline look. A string of vans ambulated westward toward the Pacific. There was nothing but the grass, rocks, distant hills and sky. A Porsche containing a peroxide blond with ruby red lips at the wheel whizzed by; and then, what appears to be a hippie bus comes blundering down the blacktop. On a closer look, instead of flowers, chinese clouds, peace symbols and angelic beings painted on its side, there are creatures of the underworld with huge fangs and giant black wings, crooked bodies, swords dripping with blood, witches holding sawed off parts of human bodies and misplaced svastikas. These pictures reminded me of the depiction of the Buddhist world of demons and ghosts that are seen in the wheel of life—a veritable torture chamber for unfortunate souls. I remembered a newspaper article about a cult that performed an orgy of human sacrifices. Over the hill I saw a chicken farm, and slightly beyond, a pasture of breeding bulls. Closer, within sight, were grazing sheep. I thought I heard the crack of a rifle, and there were images of the Asian wars. My old friend Rudee danced in my minds eye. This was my ceremonial circle, on this balmy Northern California day; the keys to balance and harmony seem in place: "Om I am approaching an experience of Sūnyatā; I see the outline of Vajra." I will purify everything in my vision and beyond for a long time.

It was close to two years before Petsan taught me anything about yogic breathing. I had never really requested any yogic teachings, and possibly gave the impression that I did not want any instruction. I was self-conscious about asking for anything that smacked of my preconceived ideas about Tantric yoga. Petsan knew that I practiced a form of breath control in my tai-chi meditation. He approved, and never encouraged me to change my style or to be isolated for any long periods of time.

One morning, around tea time, a few days before the New Year's ceremony, Petsan discoursed about becoming one with the deity, i.e. "seizing the self of Mahākāla" (nga-rgyal-hdzin). He emphasized that The Great-Black-One's very substance would become the substance of the practitioner seeking union within. He discussed breath control, and how it was used to infuse spirits and atmosphere into other substances, beings and ideas. "Just because you blow on an object and say a mantra," he said, "does not mean that an object is empowered." He emphasized over and over that an object, idea or process could even be empowered in the wrong way by the infusion of a malicious spirit. In order for the mantra to work in the intended fashion, the practitioner must go through the process of cultivating the Four Keys of Balance and Harmony. These four qualities, compassion, friendliness, joy and equanimity, are four aspects of the nature of Buddha. Possessing these four qualities, in the immeasurable sense, is to possess the body, speech, heart and vajra of the Buddha, and the practitioner will also be in harmony with the four elements or earth, water, wind and fire. The primary use of breath, Petsan taught, was to contemplate in a way conducive to realizing the experience of Sūnyata within the blueprint of Vajra.

Petsan said that my tai-chi practice was a good practice for a moving awareness. He asked me to breathe in different ways. How did I use my breath when I did Tai-Chi?, he wanted to know. Actually, he already knew, but he wanted me to show him. I performed "grasp birds tail", the first few movements of the Tai chi exercise, which utilizes the shifting of inner energy (chi), transferring that same energy from one side of the body to the other, grasping the energy in the two hands, circling the center from one direction to the other and yogic breathing—all at the same time. In this way, I demonstrated several different methods of harmonizing thought, movement and breath. Petsan mimicked my movements in a humorous way. It was the side of him that was not totally accepting of Chinese culture, but he understood and appreciated the value of one Chinese interpretation of yoga. He also saw that this was a practice I would not give up. Petsan was a refugee from the Tibetan-Chinese conflict: It was his way of making fun of something Chinese. On the other hand, he had quite a lot of respect for Chinese ideas, materials and services. Petsan was trained in Chinese astrology,

which he preferred to the Indian version. The conflict was quite
fresh in his memory. He was making fun of me a little, too. The
outcome of our session on breath was this: I would do a little
more sitting and offering meditation—despite the fact that I
could never, nor, can I now, do a full lotus position. I was to
focus on my breath. I was, and still am fascinated by the healing and learning effects of structured and yogic breathing. Yogic
breathing assists in the realization of one's inner Vajra. The
development of breath control and equanimity go hand in hand.
The Sanskrit word for equanimity, upeksha, is usually translated
"detachment." Because of the connotations of detachment around
the idea of separation, and being cold hearted, it is not a very
good translation. The literal meaning of upeksha is to look
closely in the sense of being able to see the whole picture. The
phrases that I think of are "moving behind the phenomena" and
"in-between space". When the Tibetans translated "upeksha",
they must have thought a great deal about the term, because they
did not translate it literally. The Tibetan translation is bstang-
snom, which combines the sense of letting go (bstang) and equi-
librium (snom). Petsan described it as a balance: the attachments on one side, and one's practice on the other side of the
scale. "Without upeksha", he said, "the emotions would run
wild like intoxicated monkeys". Monkeys are often depicted as
the various uncontrolled emotions. There were several tribes of
monkeys around the temple, hence the name "monkey temple".
"The emotions make the mind and body toxic. "Yet", he continued, "if the emotions are too weak, the practitioner would not be
able to identify with the problems of humanity". He reminded
me that in the poisons is a healing strength, and that breath
control helped stimulate the chemistry that extracts the medicine
from the venom. The ideal, of course, for the Vajrayāna or
Mahayāna practitioner is the concept of the Bodhisattva. The
Bodhisattva is someone who experiences the emotions and problems of others, but because of equanimity, does not become
enmeshed in their web of difficulties. He or she is able to see the
traps from many angles, and some possible ways out.

    Petsan had me play with my breath. I watched myself as I
held my breath for varied lengths of time. Each change of
volume of breath created a different experience; it would change

depending on which nostril did the inhaling and exhaling. If there was a thought in the way, it would of course be different. The thought would carry the consciousness to an unknown area of my being—indeed of the universe. This is why the thought as an obstacle is so important. It could be the kind of thought that raises demons; or, it may fill one with waves of happiness and move the consciousness into a heavenly realm. To cling to either one of these for very long would throw the balance off to the side of co-dependency with the emotions—with pathological over-tones. Following the thought to its destination and purpose can determine its general character. Yet, at some point, it will be prudent to let the thought go—this is part of the purifying process. There are different subtle methods for letting go: One of them is "exhaling"; the other is "drinking your thought." "Drink-ing the thought" is a little more advanced: that is, the experience is one of transformation of image, whereas the former is one of feeling like the thought is disappearing into the atmosphere until there is the feeling of nothing. I think of the "drinking of thought" as the swallowing of breath—as if I might inadvertently swallow a thought or an image. We swallow thoughts and images all day, but when we swallow consciously, in meditation, we have the opportunity to become aware of the transformation of the image process. We watch the changes of transformation and develop clarity. A thought or image may also sneak into our invisible being without our awareness. Sometimes the thought or image takes root and multiplies. It may unexpectedly arise at a future time in an unhealthy and diseased form.

With experience, one can feel these images and their transfor-mations move around within—transformed in one's being. Un-der the right circumstances the images could be supercharged, and projected into the world onto other thoughts, being and substance. Breath energy can be pumped to different parts of the body: it is the thought that is pumping psychic energy. When holding one's bladder or bowels, one automatically sends the message not to urinate or defecate, indeed, to hold it so that no one will notice-a model for both repressive and conscious con-trol. One can notice numerous variations of retention in very young children and the elderly. For the average healthy male the biggest problem of retention is not with one's urine, but with the semen.

Some breathing techniques assist in semen retention—First follow the breath in a circle within the body. There are channels that go down the front part of the body and up the back. These channels are part of the Vajrabody—its image. As one practices, the Vajrabody manifests itself within as interlocking streams. Some people think that the semen is retained, and then transformed. Others think that it is not the semen that is retained and transformed, but, rather, the essence of the semen, which is not the visible substance but its inner energy. So, theoretically one can discharge their sperm and retain the essence—a novel slant on celibacy. As I practiced with Petsan, more and more I felt the connection between breath, thought and energy; learning how to regulate the emotions through my breath; and how to retain, at least for the moment, some bits of clarity. The quality of equanimity that came to me in very small increments opened up space for the development of compassion, friendliness and joy. Almost unwittingly as a by-product of my practice, I discovered that ideas and concepts were understood on a cellular level— they were transported by means of the image and realized as Im.

With Petsan I learned how to pump concepts. Sometimes I felt like a racing carburetor that sucks in the air with a whoosh; first mixing gas with air and then bursting into ignition. Even though meditation is a very quiet time, on several occasions I could hear the intake of the breath, like a great wind roaring through a canyon. At first I was frightened: it felt as though I would blow up like a balloon, and that every cell in my body might burst into smithereens. My fear soon left me. Becoming one with the universe seemed okay—a good way to go. Since that time I have come to realize that this is not an abnormal thought. A passing thought was: a wish to disappear blissfully into the expanse of the universe is not so far from the desire for complete nirvana, or I suppose, even heaven. But, then, whoosh, the body is filled with the breath of life, carrying an image or thought mixing with all those bodily fluids and hidden chemicals that surge into the formation of Vajra. And, sometimes one hears the purr of a perfectly tuned racing engine—the hum of an inner image. But the metaphor applies to the driver; it is the hūm of the inner Im within himself. "Equanimity", an idea, becomes a moving part.

Pumping ideas and concepts as a process can be moral, immoral or amoral or any of those combinations. It depends on the idea. Pumping ideas is the way I express my own experience of a niche in the system of yoga and Buddhist Tantra.

Throughout Asian spiritual traditions, a stage of the development of the inner-body is represented by a cauldron or pot in one's lower abdomen. It designates the place in the body where the invisible forming of the inner body takes place, where it is forged and seasoned. It is the center of the body's gravity. The image of the cauldron is a mind-body process as handed down by many traditions. Even grandfather talked about the furnace inside the body. Although there are descriptions of standard methods of meditation that refer to the cauldron within, its nature will take on an individual feeling. I developed a definite but hard-to-define feeling of equanimity through my exercises with breath. Detachment was part of the result, but not disconnection. Petsan talked sometimes of the movement between pictorial dreams and deep sleep, describing its balance and a flickering awareness indicated by that moment when the sun rises or sets.

As a way of describing how the practice felt to me, I recounted to Petsan my experiences as a scuba diver. My meditative and diving experiences were similar. There is a feeling of weightlessness as one glides through this magical atmosphere of undulating kelp, colonies of plankton that I liked to think of as sea spirits, schools of fish and abstract formations of sand and rock. There is that same weightless experience at certain moments in breath meditation. Often, there is a plethora of images that kaleidoscopically rush and surround the center of the mind; just like the surges and sudden arisings as one travels through the underwater scape. I gave up spear fishing, when I did not realize the expected challenge and excitement. I guess I did not see much purpose in the sport. I felt differently about this when I went on camping trips. We would catch the fish and bake them on the beach. It was not so much an image of sport, but the imagination of survival. These two images always conjure different experiences. I did have a feeling of compassion for the dying fish. There was not a fish speared whose spirit I did not attempt to address in a humble and respectful manner. It is really quite easy to spear most fish. They are helpless in the dark world of man's cunning, greed and thirst for the excitement of blood.

When I gave up spearfishing, I began to enjoy the solitude and rush of swimming deep under water. I made friends with the fish, and retrieved from the sea floor what I pretended were relics from the past. I explained to Petsan, that after I sank to the level where my body weight including equipment was displaced by an equal weight of water, I was literally in an almost weightless state. With a slight movement of the arms and feet, I could easily move at that level.

Moving deeper into the depths is intoxicating, and there is always the fascination of going deeper. We go as far as we can, until we reach a barrier; and then, when we fail to cross it, we retreat and try again- the second time, in a slightly different way. At times the automatic nervous system takes over. When one descends below fifty feet, without the aid of a tank, the sense of ordinary time is distorted, even lost. For a minute or more, depending on one's lung capacity, there is the perception of a magical universe. The underworld seems like an Alice in Wonderland. Then, suddenly, there is a tension, one might even say, a war between the conscious mind and the automatic need to survive. A psychically magnetic attraction occurs in the underwater atmosphere, a total feeling of comfort, bliss and detachment-except, there is the feeling that one has found a kind of nirvāna. There might be the thought not to return, but then, one finds oneself breaking the surface gasping for air. For a brief period Great-Time engulfs one's consciousness.

Petsan said that diving sounded like going to another planet. In Tibetan Buddhism the universe is perceived as myriads of worlds inhabited by an assortment of other beings. He was fascinated and said that it was quite natural for a person to want to stay in a place of wonder, excitement and exhilaration. And, it is true that most people who try meditation occasionally achieve states of mind that are attractive to the point of desiring to remain in that state—leaving the world. These pleasurable states of mind, whether under the water or performing sādhanā, are however, obstacles to complete equanimity. The balance may tip. That is, the high, or the enjoyment always has a limit. My

underwater experience unwittingly pumped the concept of ecological balance and stimulated my interest in environmentalist
concerns. Learning breath control with Petsan generated equanimity, which in turn pumped the concepts of compassion, friendliness and joy. These muscles are exercised every time I sit in
meditation, utter a mantra, do Tai-Chi or any extension of these
forms of practice into the world.

Petsan was fascinated by the miraculous function of the scuba
gear. He compared underwater swimming to the spirits and
ghosts that roamed about the atmosphere. He demonstrated the
comparison as he danced about smiling and waving his hands as
if he were swimming through the air. It was very funny, but
accurate. I explained to Petsan that scuba apparatus allowed one
to go to depths of 300 feet or more: for the most part only salvage,
sponge, pearl divers and treasure hunters dared to descend to
these depths. I have been only as deep as 100 feet. I described
the metallic sounds of the air bubbles popping out of my lungs
into the metal chamber of the regulator, and then, how they
expand like a balloon as they float up to burst on the surface. I
tried to describe the elation, and how this form of joy created the
ambience of balance and connection with the creatures of the
deep. I don't think I ever convinced Petsan but he liked my
description; and said jokingly, that it should be canonized, which
is one reason I am reiterating it here. An underwater experience
cannot help but impress on one the significance of breath, and its
relationship to thought and inner energies. Maybe skin and
scuba diving is a good way to begin learning about meditation
and images.

Petsan said that everything was infused with a hidden spirit
and on one occasion pointed to the great white dome just a few
feet away, indicating with gestures and words, that the world
itself was really a great white dome that contained the nature of
the Buddha. The inner dome or chaitya is like the inner body
with a myriad of channels and inner seas of energy that one can
access with the breath.

Meditation-ritual or sādhanā is like constructing a bridge:
There are many different tools, machines and parts. They all fit
together to form a bridge, across an abyss. Any flaw in one part
will show up in the another—like the effect of an earth- quake
and its aftershocks.

CHAPTER XI

The Sexuality Of Image

In 1989 during the course of the student rebellion in China, the students sculptured and erected an image the American press named "The Statue of Liberty". The Chinese students named the image "The Goddess of Freedom"—a similar idea. Soon after it was erected, The Goddess of Freedom was toppled by the opposition. In support of the Chinese students, people all over the world constructed similar images.

During the revolutionary conflict, television portrayed the image and its demise. I saw on the television images of a historical magnitude; I saw a social process almost at the moment it was taking place. I saw the erection and destruction of the image. The manifestation of the Goddess of Freedom in Tien-An-Mien (Heavenly City) Square corresponded to the feelings of progress, hope and happiness that charged the air among the peacefully demonstrating students. The image was a collective and individual effort to realize freedom of expression.

It is only a matter of time before suppressed individuals and groups reach a stage where they will initiate that hopefully gentle step out of the darkness of suppression into a world of possible freedom and light. Whether this is internal or external, as the step is being taken, the risk of losing one's mind and body always exist. There are moments when a serious search for freedom and bliss places one's very being in jeopardy. There is the risk that at some point, this gentle, yet focused expression will magnify the opposition into an explosion. Anticipating the heat of such an event, there is a willingness for the committed to at least consider the possibility of a conscious sacrifice. Even though few will actually believe that an ultra-violent event will happen, an awareness of this possibility contributes to the process of serenity, and then a sudden outburst of brutality is a little less surprising. As the image in Tien-An-Mien Square came down, the dark forces again took the initiative, and as we could see on television, the heavenly square was soon splattered and poisoned with mangled bodies.

The image of The Goddess of Freedom was empowered with an energy that seemed to become self-generating. More Goddesses arose all over the world. The Goddess in Tien-An-Mien Square was easily torn down, yet it served as a medium to transmit the Im—an underlying energy that caused others to recreate the Goddess in other parts of the world—the image, the Im, that television could not directly portray.

An after-effect of the Maoist revolution of the 1950's was that the new Chinese government was able to consolidate its power as far as Tibet, where thousands of icons/images were destroyed. The Chinese communists believed the religious activities of the Tibetans, i.e. the ritual-meditation processes, were supportive of the Tibetan social system which the communists characterized as being feudal, backward and repressive to the masses. Therefore the Chinese communists tried to remove the power of the individual to use the imagery, and the ritual meditative practices that the images symbolized. They could not however destroy the invisible structures—the underlying Im.

During the Maoist revolution and to this day, there has been a steady exodus from Tibet to other countries, especially Nepal and India. The very Im that the communist revolution sought to eradicate has now found a home, not only in South Asia but in Europe and America. Images migrate with their hosts like seeds, transplanted by migratory birds.

Today, images and ideas can be instantly transplanted in their total process into an electronic space. In a matter of hours the American public saw the creation, destruction and further creation of the Goddess of Freedom. Ideas and images scatter throughout the world, probably the universe, and then, like worms settle into new ground, they are broken, cut and played with. Their pieces grow into new beings. No sooner than the Goddess of Freedom was toppled, new ones sprung to life. Electronic beams became empowered with the Ims of The Goddess of Freedom.

Goddesses are invoked for causes of freedom, creativity and compassion. But in the wake of the forces of the politics of violence, these female images that represent wisdom unwittingly become a tool for bloodshed and self-aggrandizement. As the source of life and epitome of giving pleasure and nurturing, she is seduced and fought over. Her images, whether they be Kuan yin, Kāli or Madonna are destined to be misrepresented. In the competitive net of desire bodies, her symbol is constantly interpreted. The feminist movements of all ages and cultures are a reflection of the conflict between women and the false images that evolve and take shape in their name. Relationships and marriages are poisoned with these myriad of misrepresentations and mental fabrications.

In my counseling practice I developed a concept that works quite well for people trying to understand and work out relationships plagued by these karmic fabrications. It is the idea that the word relationship refers to all the images, thoughts and substance that have accumulated between individuals. To be involved in a relationship is to be involved in the ancestral, cultural and genetic predispositions of oneself and the other person—despite the intentions of one person or the other to forget or repress their own past and upbringing. Due to the interplay of thought constructs between two individuals, new images and behaviors will add to the content of the relationship. The content is complex and for the most part it is hidden in the atomic and electronic space between male and female.

I like to present this concept in an anthropomorphic sense. Sometimes the collage that make up a relationship is viewed as a demon, and other times as a goddess of love, mercy or compassion. Since relationships are a composite of images, thoughts and emotional uprisings, they can easily be viewed as higher or lower powers which control our lives. Anyone who ponders this thought will realize that their connective links with another person are partly self-created, and partly inherited from family histories and culture. Whatever the immediate problem, family and culture of origin are looming and edifying considerations.

In modern society there are many examples of cross-subcultural conflict. Inter-cultural marriage and the drug culture are more obvious models of hidden conflicts that arise in a relationship through the interaction of different image-systems vying for the same space. The truth of the matter is that most of us are being affected by a variety of image systems throughout the day. They generate conflicting desires and expectations. Individuals in impaired relationships need to agree on the nature of the impairment and to look for new kinds of relationships. This means finding new kinds of images.

New kinds of relationships can be found in traditional as well as non-traditional spiritualities and politics—it depends on one's background and situation, indeed, on the images that have evolved in one's life. These images will be hybrid; the result of a lifetime of images coming together and creating new images. We can understand the sexuality of image process through myths, personal stories, dreams, creativity and memories. Images arise through opposition and dialogue. When the image system is stripped of most of its pictorial content, it becomes a raw structure of the elements of nature and human emotion, and filters through our transpersonal and metaphysical plumbing.

For example, the dialogue between grandfather and the Protestant side of my family left me with some images and thoughts that have served as a vehicle for my own life work and exploration. Grandfather, father and Petsan imparted to me the concept that nature is more than dirt, water and a variety of flora and fauna to be taken for granted or used up indiscriminately. Indeed, nature is mother. In Sanskrit this is designated by the word prithivī conceived of as the Goddess of the earth. For Petsan every woman was a Goddess of the earth; and all substance had a female empowerment. Both grandfather and Petsan thought that the human endeavor to pour concrete, make oil products and use pesticides were activities that in the long run would be self destructive, inappropriate and distorted uses of our natural functions. Activities that would not be pleasing to the Goddess.

If we look to the Rig Veda for an understanding of the archetype of the Mother Goddess, we find that she is usually described and eulogized in the company of heaven (Dyaus). The couple earth-heaven are called in Sanskrit Dyava-prithivī. They are seldom mentioned in the Rig-veda as single entities. As one might expect, they are referred to as the parents of the gods, and described as Mom and Dad. That is, the Mom and Dad of the universe for they never grow old. Of course they produce food and wealth, and by definition, have wisdom and establish a working order of things. In that sense, they are the primordial protectors and the teachers of the Vedic rite—the core energy of the Vedic sacrifice. They are the Archetypes of Mom and Dad.

Grandfather used to say that we needed to sort out our images. He once told a crony that his paintings were not for the purpose of creating more images, but to capture and receive empowerment from those spirits most significant to his life. He created a plethora of pictures that empowered the life and environment around him. Both grandfather and Petsan were reductionists; they were always offering their thoughts, images, emotions and possessions; they were reducing their baggage to the minimum.

The world and creation is constantly stimulating the senses. An ensuing relationship with all its arising images comes from our senses and thoughts that constantly touch and manipulate the world. If we do not let go of the senses, sacrifice them for an appropriate inner work, they can turn into a great negation—a darkness with no meaning. When we let go and make our offering, this great darkness will stimulate the Im and transform into a kaleidoscope of manifest energies.

Without a taste of this Im, the pleasure and beauty of the world can quickly transform into pain and ugliness. For about a year I seriously considered becoming a Buddhist monk. My teachers discouraged me and said that I could pass on my lessons as a lay person. They told me that I was mistaken to think that one way was easier or more difficult that another. Both the lay and Monastic practitioners have to work through the shapes and colors of existence in order to become one with the invisible Im. To think that one path is easier to follow than the other is an illusion. There are many paths.

My path was tied to nature which served as a model for the fertility of existence in general. For me the joy of sādhanā was found in the company of earth, water, fire, wind and space. In my practice of Buddhism the elements took on the image of the goddess: This was the role of the goddess in her dialogue with Mahākāla. I am stunned by the erotic nature of the elements of nature, and amazed at the lack of respect our industrial and political leaders give to the wilderness.

Once when I took a solo hike into the Cascades, I meditated on water; not on its lack, but on its abundance and variety. I hiked through a wilderness area that had been set aside for ecological research; even camping was not allowed. These areas are truly pristine with first growth trees and unspoiled earth and water. At the end of the trail was a lake at an altitude of about 5,500 feet. The trail moved upward, against the parallel stream which came cascading down in a million waterfalls. The stream had its origin in the lake to which I was hiking. There were small patches of snow melting under the ancient firs. Spray and mist were from the stream gushing over and between the rocks and fallen dead trees. Every particle of space seemed laden with a green moisture. When I stopped and listened, I could hear the soft patter of water dripping from the firs. In the background came the rush of the stream boiling around the rocky outcrops. As I continued my hike upward, the sounds subtly transformed. I found that I could be still, and conjure the kind of silence that seemed to produce new delightful rhythms and passages of musicality. As I slid myself around boulders with spots of wet spongy moss, I noticed the magnitude of the giant cedars, one of them on which I found myself leaning. Waterways of various dimensions were funneling their way into accessible areas of the forest. When I heard the sound of falling water it hypnotized me for a brief moment. My breath momentarily stopped and I moved on.

The Cascades, as the name implies, have myriads of rivers, streams, waterfalls (big and small), trickles, drops and lakes. The lake at the top was still. Water can take any shape that the earth provides. It can heave, batter, crash, spray, trickle, drop and fall; and yet, it can be so utterly quiet and tranquil. Before I reached this stillness I counted 23 sounds of water that were distinguishable to my ears—twenty-three sounds of compassion, I thought.

On my hike I remembered my grandfather's well. It was like

the opening to a great shell. I used to lean over the well, hang my head in the opening and listen. Sometimes I would run into grandfather's house and tell all who would listen about the sounds and voices I heard from the inner depths of earth. This irked Grandmother and filled mother with great consternation. Grandfather would try to explain that my behavior was not only perfectly normal but healthy. He said that I had found a spiritual expression. But that only made the situation even more tense. My parents who looked down on mental health professionals, even threatened to take me to a psychiatrist.

Grandfather took me aside one day and gave me my first lesson in family politics: That is, how not to express myself in negatively charged situations. I promised not to go near the well. However, when my parents were not present I would accompany grandfather to a spot between the well and an oak tree, where he would set up his easel and paint.

Shortly after the episode about the well, and upset with the dictum that I should not go near that mysterious hole in the earth, at least, not by myself, grandfather had a spontaneous conversation with me which took place during one his painting sessions, when I was playing near the oak tree. Grandfather sat on the side of the well and called me over to talk. He asked me why I thought people reacted to the well with such superstition? Why did I think that Grandmother was so concerned-so emotionally upset? "It was funny," I thought, "that he called Grandmother superstitious", it was exactly what she thought of him. Yet, it was clear that she was the one who was emotionally distraught. Grandmother never went near the well.

Grandfather had me put one hand, and then the other, over the well; then both hands. He asked me if I felt anything? I felt something but I was not sure what. The more I focused on what he wanted me to do, the more I tried to feel. "What did I feel" he asked? But, then, I was not sure.

"Did I feel a force—a kind of pull"? Yes, I did. "Was it a strong force and was I afraid of it"? Now I felt a strange sensation within me. Suddenly it was as if there was a huge person standing behind me—even though the well was in front. I wanted to turn around, but I was afraid of both the well and the invisible being behind me. Yes, there was a pull from deep within the well. Grandfather asked why I felt the pull so strongly at that particular time? Before I could answer, he took me by the hand, led me over to the oak tree, and told me to bring the palm of my hand closer to the tree. Could I feel anything he asked? He told me to move my hands around the tree in a circle. I slowly rotated my hands in half circles a few inches to about a foot from the tree. At first I did not feel a similar force. But, yes, I did feel a pull from the tree. I mentioned to grandfather that it was a different feeling. It was not quite so strong.

Off to the other side of the well was a statue of Fredrick the great. He told me to go over and do the same thing to the statue. I also felt a kind of force field, but it was not very powerful. I did not have the same rapport with the eighteenth century German king as grandfather did. Then he had me do the same thing with a large boulder. There was a tremendous pull. I repeated the action with several other kinds of rocks. The force of each one of the rocks was very strong. I kept going from rock to rock. I became fascinated and walked around the garden for the next few minutes feeling the emanations of various rocks and trees.

After a few more minutes had passed grandfather called me back to the well. "Now do it again", he ordered. I put my hands over the well. The feeling was the same, but my fear of the well was not there. I leaned over the well as I had before, but not quite so far.

I still wondered why grandmother was afraid of the well, but I had learned something very valuable. I made a new friendship with nature and never lost that memory of the feelings of the rocks and the trees; and of course the well. It was just a beginning, I acquired a method of creating a relationship with any substance with which I came into contact.

The well became a sacred place. It was a place, for the most part, where only grandfather and I would go. He would paint and putter in the garden. Once in a while, we would talk about the sounds and feelings that came up from the depths, and what they could possibly mean.

Occasionally, the fear would reoccur; especially when I imagined I heard crying and sounds of pain issuing from the depths. But then I gradually learned to cope with and understand the nature of the well. I also heard ordinary gurgling, tinkling sounds that would sometimes change into voices: there would be the sounds of mirth and odd voices with low and high pitch. Grandfather taught me that wells absorbed all the sounds that they hear. I asked grandfather if the well could hear my mother and father, who at the time were several miles away. Grandfather told me again that the well hears everything and that if I talked to it requesting to eavesdrop on my parents, my wishes might be granted. Looking back on the event it was a curious extension of the imagination and natural forces.

The well seemed so dark. Grandfather spoke of the many manifestations of darkness. The voices had their shapes which came out of the well during the night. Except on occasion, I could only hear them during the daytime. He often used the phrase "The Great-Black-One" in connection with the well: The voices, shapes and myriads of other possibilities were becoming more familiar to me. Fear was translated into respect and caution.

While investigating the mysteries of grandfather's well as a young boy of seven or eight, I began to assimilate the hidden dimensions of the elements; and now, I realize, that I was inadvertently introduced to compassion, friendliness, joy and equanimity in the forms of water, earth, fire and wind. It was on grandfather's guinea hen farm where I absorbed an inkling of the power of darkness, it's hidden energies, and an underground world, which grandmother attributed to the terrible demons of Lucifer. I also learned about family politics. Grandfather's instruction about the well created a way to an unconscious association with the female spirits that grandfather enjoyed to illustrate—the feminine nature of the Great-Black-One. Deep from the well came a primordial female voice. As I peered down into the darkness, I often had the sensation of wanting to allow myself to fall into it's depths. Now, there was only a curiosity, but without that same quality of fear which arose in me around the images of Lucifer and company.

Grandfather helped me work through my relationship with Grandmother and the unconscious. Her concern was protective. She sensed a great danger from unknown spirits which was expressed from her very Protestant outlook on life. She knew that grandfather had taken me under his wing. For grandmother falling into the well was symbolic of falling from the Christian faith—from the possibilities of true paradise and everlasting life. Watching me learn the secrets of grandfather's Bavarian mysteries was painful for her. She might have felt better if I had toppled over one day and drowned in the quagmire of the spiritual darkness below. This was an important phase for me, because I was separated from the mother and bonded with the father. It was a kind of rite of passage, complete with an inoculation of darkness, that only grandfather could initiate.

I think that most of us like to think of relationships as a means to attain harmony, peace and happiness. The dark side is the power struggle that takes place between mothers and fathers, yet the battle for control between grandmother and grandfather led me to an archetypal space, a raw structure, where the Black Forest and the dark well revealed The Four Keys of Harmony and Balance. In my experience as a counselor, I have learned that there are few long-term relationships without a connection to a dimension of the spiritual world-a higher power.

It is very difficult for the sexes to make the transition from mutual seduction to spiritual union—co-dependency to co-responsibility. In my opinion, images that conjure feelings of momentary pleasure and security are also pathways for co-dependency. Pornography or blatant materialism such as we see in advertising, attracts us like flies to spoiled food—a simile often used by Petsan. We go for the image and sometimes never even have a sense of the Im. Just the idea of an ego-fulfilling and pleasurable event is enough to turn on the senses. We hang on to the image for fear of losing out on the pleasure and power of the next moment. With the fangs of desire and self appointed righteousness, we inject that next series of substances, thoughts and beings that appears on our path. Happiness found only in images is always elusive.

CHAPTER XII

Letting Go Of The Darkness

The path from image to <u>Im</u> is sometimes fraught with a confusion of callings and voices. One hangs on to the image, like the Zen story of the person clinging on to the branch on the side of the cliff. As long as our images satisfy the senses and ego, we hang on. On one hand, we make fun of the commercials, and on the other hand, almost desperately, and sometimes secretly, cling to our own personal images that foster addiction and attachment. We deny the influence of these powerful images, yet their creation is based on the assumption that people will respond to them by rushing to the store. I find that television is a good place to begin to practice critical reflection and letting go of images.

As one practices the letting go of images, the <u>Im</u> becomes more dominant, and begins to call us. The nature of our dreams change and we begin to find ourselves in a more peaceful place and more receptive to the images of nature. Grandfather would say that nature would be an aspect of the feminine. It is the transpersonal. Petsan would take it one step further: "Melt into nature", he would say. Again, it is like a dive to the bottom of the ocean. To a fish, the diver becomes another creature of the deep. Letting go of the subject-object dichotomy when one is influenced by the rush of nitrogen deep under the surface of the ocean takes no effort—the enviroment does it for you. The images are blurred and disappear into a larger order of things where the <u>Im</u> seems more detectable. When one practices the letting go of images, new images appear which also need to be let go. Letting go of images and uncovering the Im is a conceptual and contemplative approach to the sense of the old Hindu dictum neti neti "not this, not that". Letting go of images creates a profound sense of space, and the objects of attraction become more subtle, at which point, the procreative desires begin to be transformed. The calling to procreate the flesh is transformed into a calling that leads us into a realm of aesthetics without the usual attachments to the flesh. There is a more mellow and balanced ecstasy. This can be done with or without a partner. It is called in the Eight Chapter "The yoga of conjugality (yogasamputā).

Everything has a female or male energy and category—even pipefitings, nuts, bolts, plugs and sockets are described as male or female. But, male and female energies come together in many other different ways than screws, sockets and washers. Of course, this is just a convenient method of categorizing phenomena that is in the process of coming together, but the reason the category is convenient is its description of an obviously natural phenomena—at least on the level of normal everyday shared experience.

Changing attitude, for example, can be compared to replacing a mechanical fitting. A plumber who finds a faulty fitting must remove the old fitting before it can be replaced with the new one. If the old fitting can not be recycled, we have to store it; or, if it gets in our way, we must work around it. Maybe we can turn the old fitting into a useful tool. But, if it is one of the newer plastic products there is probably not much we can do with it.

I have a friend, a master mechanic, who built his own version of a Buccati motorcycle. Buccati motorcycles are Italian racing bikes revered by most motorcycle enthusiasts. As his workplace is behind my house, I have the opportunity to observe and speak intimately with this lover of motorcycles. When he works on his machine he is very gentle. Gentleness is not the stereotyped notion of a mechanic. When I have watched my own reaction to the repair of machinery, my calm and gentle manner has been replaced by a tug of war with the nuts and bolts, accompanied by war cries and frustration. Many times I have watched him work: He does so almost in a manner of seduction. His work area is not an ordinary garage. Everything is laid out as if to impress his Buccatti-a sort of seductive offering. The tools are clean and placed where he can easily find them. Some of his wrenches that come in sets are glistening and waiting to be presented to his mistress—the Buccati. The light fixtures are adjustable, and there is a set of flashlights ranging from tiny to very large. Sometimes I have inadvertently come across him fondly gazing at his bike in his near theatrical setting. When applying a tool he talks in various tones to his machine. I have heard him say, "I love you baby, come on now", at which time the Buccatti seemed to respond and allow my friend to work on or replace the part. But I had the sense that she was very fickle and everything had to be perfect. He once told me that the sensitivity and the purity inherent in the Buccati, determined his practice as a mechanic. But my friend is also a painter and very adept with women. His bike is like an oracle that determines the clarity of his life practice. His life becomes more simple as time goes on. His workplace becomes less like a theatre and more like a pure and simple home for his Buccati. He allures and fondles her almost daily; and she, in turn, works for him. I would venture to say that she changed his life.

Metaphors and similes are powerful tools of communication and one of the most workable is whatever equivalents and likenesses there are for the courtship and procreative processes. It seems as if the female principle of the universe has an edge on the male principle. Maybe this is because of the extent, primariness and rawness of the earth. Although I think of this edge as being rooted in nature, it is philosophical as well. I think my friend's motorcycle and the material world in general, demonstrate this edge-at least on the semantic level of image. My friend's motorcycle dominated a huge part of his life-maybe more than sleep. He called himself a tinkerer of machines. He told me that I was a tinkerer of a different sort. He called me a tinkerer of thought. He said that I did not do the material world justice. My friend is a good model for how to approach imagery. Images are a function of both the material and the psychological world—they can be allured, analyzed, cooked, hated, bought, thrown away, manipulated and more significantly they could be the initiators of all the above. Imagery constantly draws us in to its own cycle of creativity which is to make more images. If our imagery is empowered with the transpersonal we will be be more predisposed to the transformation processes.

Like the Great-Black-One allures the Goddess, with his conjugal overtures, we allure the world around us. We allure the goddesses in their many forms. The goddesses are the personification of not just the elements as we normally perceive them, but of the hidden energy that makes them hold existence together. To allure the elements, the essence of the material world, is to allure the female principle.

Time is established, says the Sanskrit text, when Mahākāla and the female elements evolve. There are five elements from which arise five yoginis: This is a way of expressing and describing the five elements, their female embodiments, and how their images are structured in the Buddhist Tantric context.

The Tantra, by virtue of its sacredness, is embraced by Great-Time. When as a meditator or reader of the practice we confront the question, "Where are the elements in this Great-Time?" Or, if we ask ourselves, "how are the goddesses (the elements) related to Great-Time?" we might start with our daily activity, which brings us back into the world as we are perceiving it at the moment—the here and now. Before we can initiate our practice for accessing Great-Time, we must open the doors to our worldly or ordinary time, and be aware of the potential therein, and as Petsan used to say, "I must begin with the way I am today, and who I am today—if I know".

How do we find out how and who we are? How do we open the doors of our twenty-four hour a day life so that we are not living through it in a totally mechanical and unconscious manner? One approach is to enter into a dialogue with the elements and animal life with whom we share the planet. It helps to think of the plants and rocks around us as beings, because how could you talk to a rock unless it is a being in some sense. I had an acquaintance once who said, "But William, the rocks do not look like us; they do not even look like any of the animals".

Grandfather's teachings at the well opened the door for me to the possibility of communicating with nature. I can ask the rocks and trees how things are going. They can tell me the nature of things and sometimes how a hidden aspect of myself is doing. Yes, they answer back in a number of ways and when I hear them I hear them through the insight within me—that part of me which develops through the process of meditation and ensuing self-reflection. Sometimes it is enough to smell the earth, to soak in the hot springs, gaze at the sunrise or commune with the life forms. The elements in nature have their own means of communication that inhabit the feelings and other hidden dimensions of the mind and body. Blissful experiences of nature touch a space within me that is close to the erotic. The experiences of nature are encoded with a knowledge that transcends dogma and philosophy. Although nature has the qualities of both female and male it is the female energy that seems to predominate. The women are reflective of the elements which have been spoiled and polluted in our earth. The various women's movements are giving us strong messages about the distortions and pollutions that men have created in the balance and harmony of nature. The dialogue between the sexes reflects a process of change.

In the Mahākāla-Tantra, though still playing the passive role, the goddess is also the teacher. The goddesses that surround the six-handed Mahākāla represent the elements. As sensual images, they stimulate the erection of Mahākāla. The pun is intentional. It is meant in a serious, but not unhumorous vein. At least this is the manner in which Petsan and other teachers took it. The phrase "erection of time" conjures the invisible feeling of "Great-Time" (image of Mahākāla). It is the six-handed Great-Black-One to whom is specifically being referred. Petsan assured me in an amusing fashion that the Tantric Masters understood the mechanics of the erection quite well. Then, a little on the hilarious side, we have the stories of Uncle Tompa (the ribald side of Tibetan culture) humorously written by my friend Rindzin-rdo-rje.

A man's erection can happen without any conscious thought or outward stimulation: it occurs in sleep, when doing nothing and sometimes just before death. Sometimes it happens just like a sudden gust of wind. The ritual-meditation process is to connect with this unconscious force, and to stimulate its flow to those parts of the consciousness that are beneficial to the health and to spiritual practice. So, when the practitioner becomes one with the Great-Black-One; and allures the goddess, there is a process of mutual seduction and dialogue.

The goddess asked: "How are people empowered with the

form of their own divinity?"

Mahākāla has a straight forward answer: "Indeed, the Goddess Umā (one's own divinity), whose nature is yoga (union) is momentarily for the sake of the creation (the birth) of the Great-Black-One". The image of the goddess and the ensuing erection of the practitioner is, then, for the creation (the birth) of the Four Keys of Balance and Harmony.

An erection is a primordial function. To be curious about the process is not just childlike, but peculiarly human. It means that to some extent, we have separated ourselves from the natural process; not just because we were endowed with curiosity, but, in the case of the Mahākāla practice, because we want to put the process to work for the benefit of others as well as ourselves, i.e. to generate the process of transformation for the manifestation of the Four Keys of Balance and Harmony.

When we are fantasizing about the sex act we are creating a relationship of empowerment. Like everything else we imagine, we are conditioning ourselves for the outer physical event. Imagination is natural, but will gravitate to the nearest and most stimulating image—the conditioned part of ourselves. Television is a catalyst for the imagination which becomes an inner T.V.—an electronic homunculus. I wonder to what degree avid T.V. viewers learn acts of intimacy from television. We learn from what we see and experience, and much of it is subliminal. Hence, it is quite understandable that people feel uneasy over pornography and certain types of advertizing. A recent controversy over whether or not famous athletes should be allowed to be seen in advertisements for alcoholic beverages is certainly a valid one. Here role models give us the message that it is great to get high on alcohol. This is a kind of sympathetic magic where the onlooker transfers his or her admiration from the sports hero to the image of the beer can or wine bottle. The image is fluid.

The viewer makes love with the image. He or she melts into the qualities of the object; into the object's beatitude or it's gloom and anxiety. Then, in enacting the drama of fulfilling one's desire, to consume the object of desire there is the notion that the image is no longer the object—that the object has become oneself. This is one of the signs of approaching the Im. It is also an opportunity to recognize oneself as the object of another's desire.

One may have the feeling of being an object to be devoured by another person or even by another empowered object which can generate fear and intimidation; or, it can produce the feeling of a blissful annihilation. There was a popular song a few years ago titled "Killing Me Softly". There is also the feeling of dying joyfully for a cause such as the Boddhisattva in the demonstration of compassion. These are feelings that can easily be distorted and misdirected, but they can also be utilized in meditation to help one slide into the experience of spiritual union. It can precipitate the possibility of a positive transpersonal experience. The image of the Goddess consorting with the God is focused on in various ways. In one well-known, but not common meditation, the meditator kills the God and joins with the goddess. The god in this case represents those very emotions that we generate for worldly power—jealousy, lust, hatred and so on. When these negatives are neutralized, the union with the goddess occurs as a transubstantiation experience, i.e. the erection of time and the procreation of Im. The process does not assume the total eradication of negative emotions forever, but only for as long as they actually remain transformed. New demons await with each person's hidden culture and personality.

The empowered consort is one's own divinity. We may think of her as an energy, but she can take the form of any traditional goddess. She can take any form or she may manifest as a ceremonial and mental image. She is Im. She can take the form grandmother, nurse, call girl, wife and even a totally unknown apparition.

If every substance, thought and being has both male and female energies, then why do the Tantras use the image of the female in union with the male. Why is there such an emphasis on what seems to be, at first appearance, the most familiar yet private of relationships, the kind that keeps the world of suffering turning over and over again (samsāra)? Why not just unite with the female principle in anything-in a rock, a tree or the self?

When I search out the feminine within myself, I can understand the feelings of a gay person as well as the thought that I might not choose a feminine deity for my own spirit guide or my own divinity. I would have to understand fully that the femi-

nine and the masculine were fluid within the same image regardless of the initial shape and gender—that one leads to the
other and, that the purpose of the practice is not solely for my
own pleasure, but for other beings. I understand and feel the
underlying resentment that one must do a spiritual practice in a
specific way and use imagery that might be distasteful to aesthetic preferences. But, then, in a permissive society this is
understandable: America is a place where almost any form of
thought will receive a hearing. Our culture has become a kind of
experimental medium for cross-cultural ideas and practices.
Anything is possible.

The purpose of the image, whether it be male, female, or,
male-female in union is to get to the Im, which generates Great-
Time, i.e. a healing time and space where substance, thought and
being become healing entities (medicines), either for oneself or
others. This is, to a great extent, the test of our practice. This can
also work for male homosexuals, who feel significantly female in
their attraction to other men. The simulacrum can be male or
female, it can be an icon or it can be oneself. It is the phase called
in the ritual-meditation "creation in front (mdun-skyed)". As
one's own divinity and the practitioner move closer to each
other, the excitement of contact becomes the spark between the
practitioner and the Im. The image or the simulacrum then
becomes a medium for the creation of the Great-Black-One. The
arising of the Great-Black-One, then will involve one's own divinity—a channel to a higher power.

The goddess in the Seventh Chapter of the Mahākāla-Tantra,
translated in the Eighth Chapter of this book, is putting Mahākāla
on the spot, and in essence, is asking him how to live with this
higher power. She is concerned over her image—over how she
is being presented to the world, and in what kind of language?

At one point she asks the question, "what is twilight language?".

Mahākāla offers the explanation that the female principle in
each of the five families produces one's own power—he is
pointing out that the images themselves are part of the language.
The text calls them mudrās. A mudrā is an empowered image,
like a syllable or word that elicits a definite psychobiological
response. It does not have to be an icon—unless the icon is a part

of the grammar—it may or may not be. In the larger more public
ceremonies, a mudrā is a hand gesture that represents the exchange of images in the flow of the ritual process—a semantic
dialogue where the units of gestures are intricate parts of the
ritual. The interplay of Ims is the underlying reality. There are
many hand gestures (mudrās) for the various offerings. For
example, one can offer the musical instruments, the teacher's
mandāla and the five senses with hand gestures. It is a sign
language of the transpersonal. It is part of the semantics of
twilight language.

Mahākāla becomes more descriptive in his explanation: "The
semen (the sanskrit sukra is used for both males and females) of
these woman is of the nature of vajra and after worshiping it, the
singer should drink it."

Now just how literally should we take such a statement? In a
semantic system where words and concepts are commonly appropriated for a desired affect; or, to set the stage for another
activity, another empowered idea, one does not always know
from reading, what the word implies. As one makes an offering,
goes through purification, develops the Four Keys of Balance
and Harmony and becomes closer to becoming one with the
divinity, the offered substance returns transformed into a healing elixir. I was taught that drinking means absorbing. Although
it can mean absorbing through the nose or any bodily opening, it
usually means the breath—as in most disciplines that are influenced by the discipline of yoga. It is a mistake to think that
drinking the semen of woman refers to a sexual act only, but it
could refer to a sexual act. Sexual acts are part of the offering
system; as such, part of the grammar of images and mudrās. The
term mudrā can refer to either image or Im, but when Mahā (an
honorific) is added, it always designates Im more that it does
image. Mahāmudra for example is the insight which one embraces. One's wife may be referred to as Mahāmudra not because she is just a sexual partner, but because she is sharing the
spiritual dimension of the relationship.

The energy of sexual and other sensual pleasures cross the
barriers created by our ordinary awareness. The experiences
reach new peaks and last longer because they are not restricted
to one kind of identification or relationship, such as a feeling of

euphoria while gazing on a sunset or field of flowing grass. In Tantra, there is a bridge between the orgasmic and the spiritually ecstatic; they reflect and shift into one another. The material world of flesh, blood, earth, water, fire, metal, wind and wood is all a potential mudra in the nature of Vajra. The Tantric does not avoid the world of materiality and image—it is accepted as a medium or even an oracle; it becomes a sign. These signs and images have been codified by the various traditions as how to realize the transpersonal and achieve salvation or enlightenment. Signs and images always seem to call for a ritual or meditation, if not for becoming one with the Godhead or generating the elixirs of immortality, for coping with the barbs and thorns along the path. The seduction and procreation processes are natural rites that can give rise to the inner dialogue between male and female.

Sometimes we hear of a very successful person who publicly attributes his success to an inspirational woman; the woman behind the man. Although this cliche has become a little out of date, the image of the inspirational female indicates an underlying dialogue and truth; and, of course, it can work the other way around. Getting in touch with the inner dialogue means to begin to flow with the Im of seduction and procreation, and it will not remain a static or formalized process. The male or yang energy seems to always be pushing and pulling. The male function of the Great-Black-One in our translation is for the purpose of passing on the appropriate teachings to the goddess. Yet, it is not as if she is learning something that she does not already know, but Mahākāla needs to be slightly more than assertive in his communication (typical male behavior?): "Oh, kind goddess, you should follow very respectively everything mentioned by me". But, then, the goddess asks more questions, and sings a song in the dialect of Apabhramsa (the most popular of the common languages spoken in India at that time). In a fashion, Mahākāla is being teased, but it sparks a truthful and direct confrontation between herself and The Great-Black-One:

"Oh, Lord, if you arise, you are inspired. Oh Mahākāla, Great Being, please listen! Oh, kind hearted Lord, please arise! I am the goddess who dances here. Oh, my husband, I ask, how should I do my work?" Mahākāla immediately sat on the corpse (and answered). "I dance as a hero circumambulating the three worlds. In your body are the Goddesses Kālī, Bholi, Chundesvarā and Kulikā; they are kept in your navel, and spread in my heart. You who satisfies the world, again, I say, what do you request? There is no beginning or end; according to one sound you become the lover of sentient beings. If you are going to do the work; please enter my body". The song is a peak moment in the spiritual loveplay. It is the time of becoming one with the divine—with Great-Time. At this moment the creative mind is understood. It is the complete acceptance of the sixteen-handed Mahākāla.

In the translation, Mahākāla continues his instruction. He briefly describes the image of the two-handed Mahākāla. And, then, he mentioned that Sankhapāla, "the conch-protector" is recalled by the thunderous sounds of lightning and rain. The passage always puzzled me. When I asked Petsan, he mimicked the sounds of numerous insects and birds. He especially liked the sound of the CooCoo bird which is quite common in Nepal, just before the rains come in the Spring. The Tibetans say coo-coo-char-bab "coo-coo the rain is coming". The Tibetan version of the conch-protector, passage is more explicit:"...the conch-protector, at the time of the existence of living creatures, should be recalled by hidden sweet sounds". Here we are close to Im, which came through in Petsan's look, that same countenance that grandfather had when strolling through his Bavarian forest after a rain. Sometimes he would pretend that he was a bird or some other creature. At any rate, I felt comfortable with this answer, and gave up looking for a more esoteric interpretation.

"The hidden sweet sounds of nature" are a pathway to the other hidden dimension of image and Im--a sign to the possibility of bliss and contentment—to the state of harmony and balance. The early Buddhist writers are fond of analyzing varieties and levels of meditational states of mind; the above passage reminds me of the meditations that ask the meditator to focus on aspects of nature such as ocean waves, raindrops, swaying trees, the beauty of living creatures and so on. A hidden sweet sound or vision of nature can be a key to a more profound and mystical experience, in the right state of mind; and when the sounds of nature blend with the devotional songs of the worshipers, a common experience in Kathmandu Valley where there is an uncanny feeling of the transcendental.

As Mahākāla is passing on teachings about the conch-protector he more or less abruptly interjects the rhetorical question: "Oh, goddess, if this (the hidden sweet sounds) is not realized, what practice is mentioned"?

The goddess, then somewhat chides Mahākāla for being so attracted to nature's charms as a means of spiritual practice. The goddess has sung her song and completely allured Mahākāla. But now, she is seemingly suspicious of the seduction process and says: "Oh, Lord, if the Lord of yogis dwells in the five families, then why should he live in Samsāra (the ordinary world and be so concerned with my seduction)? Oh Great Divine One, the perfectly completed flower is not afflicted by its thousand parts (or more in accordance with the Tibetan version: 'when there is a rain of flowers with a thousand petals, eventually it becomes one') In the same way, we should conduct ourselves towards a single purpose, and with all four limbs (with the whole being and not just the sensual world)"

The Sanskrit word for blooming flower, puspasampanna, can also mean falling flower. The Tibetan translators were inspired to write "raining flowers", i.e. me-tog-gi-char-hbab. Sampanna also has the sense of "turning into". One cannot help but think of the story that tells of how the weapons of Māra (the carrier of death) were turned into flowers by the force of the Buddha's meditation. The goddess wants to make sure, indeed, that the flowers, and not the weapons become the dominant symbols.

Mahākāla seems to be on the edge. The process of seduction could go any number of ways. In a sense, the goddess empties the mind of The Great-Black-One. But, then, Mahākāla brings the dialogue back to image, for it is image with balance and harmony that he is teaching. Mahākāla seems to get in the last word, but the teaching is clearly coming from both. The teaching of the goddess comes closer to the philosophy of emptiness (Sūnyatā), the doctrine that nothing is ever what it seems; nor absolute and in essence empty—like the rice grain I cut into a million pieces. However, Mahākāla moves us in the direction of the school of Vijñānamātra, the school of thought that teaches everything is consciousness-only; a near figment of the imagination—the other side of the coin from emptiness. Buddhist Tantra is a combination of both—a kind of philosophical and intellectual union, realized in the context of the practice itself.

In demonstrating the meaning of the passage from the Mahākāla-Tantra, Petsan put a nashpati (an asian pear) on the table, walked back a few feet and got down on all fours to return to take a bite from the fruit. He asked me to do the same, so I did. We then sat and stared at the nashpati for a few minutes. There it was, a slightly greenish apple-like fruit. Its two small concave cavities reminds me, even now, of the sour taste. It was green and did not taste very good. Was that the point? Or was the point made when Petsan gave the nashpati to a big monkey who was staring at us and the nashpati, who immediately took the nashpati behind a tree and devoured it.

Well, whatever the point, Petsan was enjoying himself in the teaching process. Unless he was mimicking, Petsan would always smile profusely when he was demonstrating a point of dharma.

Mahākāla ends the chapter and punctuates the dialogue with the idea that a practitioner who searches for power while embracing the three worlds will attain it for sure. Another way of putting it is, that he who desires to progress in the practice, should accommodate the world of image as a channel to the underlying Im.

I wonder where the images of the Goddess of Freedom are now, and how many more there are? The one that received the most publicity here in California was the Goddess of Democracy erected in Los Angeles by sculptor Tom Van Sant and set up at a Civic Center footbridge. The last I heard of its fate, to quote the Los Angeles Times July 4 1989:

> "...With the assistance of a dozen city workers, the monument was lifted onto its feet on the front steps of the Chinese Consolidated Benevolent Assn. headquarters on main place in Chinatown for at least the next two weeks. Said association president Jon G. Wong: 'We welcome the statue. We may try to put it in the Chinatown Plaza but otherwise it will remain here. We're not going to let anyone destroy it.'

The monument, built of plastic foam and wood by a Santa Monica artist, startled and fascinated onlookers in Chinatown.'The more the better', Bill Brophy, 39, a tourist from San Diego, Said of the 1,000-pound statue..."

The desire for image and for enlightenment move together in various shapes accompanied by some very complex emotions. Sometimes the arising of desire for substance and flesh fuses with the mind of enlightenment, and other times, a clear harmonious mind becomes entangled in a web of sensual intrigue. Regardless of which way it goes, the true mind of enlightenment is detached—not disconnected. The material world has a little edge in life. There are some things that cannot be changed. It is the world of image; a twenty-four hour a day phenomena. Images never sleep. The Great-Black-One never sleeps. Peace.

Bibliography

Ackerknecht, Erwin H. *Medicine and Ethnology*. Baltimore: The John Hopkins Press. 1971.

Arnold, Sir Edwin. Trans. *The Song Celestial (Bhagavad Gītā)*. Boston: Roberts.1885.

Avalon, Arthur (or Sir John Woodroffe). *Sākti and Sākta*. Madras: Ganeshan & Co. 1959.

_____ *Principles of Tantra*. Madras: Ganeshan & Co. 1955.

Bagchi, Prabodh Ch. *Studies in the Tantras*. Calcutta: University press. 1939.

Basham, A.L. *The Wonder That Was India*. New York: 1959.

Bendall, Cecil and Rouse, W.H.D. trans. *Sāntideva's Siksāsamuccaya*. Delhi: 1971.

Beyer, Stephen. *The Cult of Tara: Magic and Ritual in Tibet*. Berkeley: University of California Press. 1973.

Bhattacharyya, Benoytosh. *The Indian Buddhist Iconography*. Calcutta: 1968.

_____ *Sādhanāmāla*. *Gaekwood Oriental series xxvi & xli*. Baroda: 1925-28.

Bhārati, A. *The Tantric Tradition*. New York : Samuel Weiser. 1975.

_____ *The Ochre Robe*. Garden City : Doubleday & Co. 1970.

Birnbaum, Raoul. *The Healing Buddha*. Boulder: Shambhala Publ. 1979.

Blofeld, John. *The Way of Power: A Practical Guide to the Tantric Mysticism of Tibet*. London: George Allen & Unwin LTD. 1970.

226

Bose, D. N. & Haldar, H. L. *Tantras—Their Philosophy and Occult Secrets*. Calcutta: Oriental Publishing House. 1956.

Bridges, Hal. *American Mysticism from William James to Zen*. New York: Harper & Row. 1970.

Briggs, George Weston. *Goraknāth and the Kānphata Yogis*. Calcutta: 1938.

Brown, W. Norman. "Change of Sex as a Hindu Story Motif" *Journal of the American Oriental Society* 16 (1927). pp. 33-40.

Brunton, Paul. *A Search in Secret India*. New York: Samuel Wieser. 1970.

Campbell, Joseph. ed. *The Mystic Vision*. Princeton : University Press. 1968.

Candler, Edmund. *The Unveiling of Lhasa*. Berkeley-Hong Kong: Snow Lion Graphics/SLG Books reprint. 1986.

_____ ed. *Oriental Mythology. Vol. 3, The Masks of God*. New York: 1962.

Chang, Garma C.C. *Six Yogas of Naropa & Teachings on Mahamudra*. Ithaca, New York: Snowlion Publications. 1963.

Conze, E. *Buddhist Meditation*. New York: Harper Torchbooks. 1969.

_____ ed. *Buddhist Texts through the Ages*. Yew York: Harper Torchbooks. 1964.

_____ trans. *The Perfection of Wisdom in Eight Thousand Lines*. Bolinas, Ca: 1973.

Combe, G. A. *A Tibetan on Tibet*. Berkeley-Hong Kong: Snow Lion Graphics/SLG Books. reprint. 1989.

Csoma, S. *Tibetan Studies*. Baptist Mission Press. Calcutta: 1912.

Dasgupta, Surendranāth. *History of Indian Philosophy*. Vols. 1-5. Cambridge : University press. 1922-1955.

David-Neel, Alexandra. *Magic and Mystery in Tibet*. New York: University Books. 1958.

David-Neel, Alexander. *Initiations and Initiates in Tibet*. Trans.by Fred Rothwell. . New York: University Books. 1959.

Dayal, Har, *The Bodhisattva Doctrine in Buddhist Sanskrit Literature*. London: Kegan Paul. 1932.

Diehl, Carl Gustav. *Instrument and Purpose: Studies on Rites and Rituals in South India*. Lund: C. W. K. Gleerup. 1956.

Dorje, Rinjing. Illustrated by Addison Smith. *Tales Of Uncle Tompa*. San Rafael, California: Dorje Ling. 1975.

Douglas, Mary. *Natural Symbols: Explorations in Cosmology*. London: Barrie and Jenkins. 1973.

Dowman, Kieth. *Masters of Enchantment: The Lives and Legends of The Mahāsiddhas*. (illustrated by Robert Seer). Rochester, New York: Inner Traditions Internation. 1988.

Edgerton, Franklin. trans. *Bhagavadgītā*. Harper Torchbook. 1964.
_____ *Buddhist Hybrid Sanskrit Dictionary*. New Haven: 1953.

Ekvall, R. B. *Religious Observences in Tibet; Patterns and Functions*. Chicago: 1964.

Eliade, Mircea. *Yoga: Immortality and Freedom*. New York: Pantheon Books. 1958.

Evans-Wentz, W. Y. *The Tibetan Book of The Dead*. London: 1957.

Fields, Rick. *How the Swans came to the Lake: Narrative history of Buddhism in America*. Boston: Shambala. 1986.

Ford, Robert. *Wind between the Worlds*. Berkeley-Hong Kong: Snow Lion Graphics/SLG Books reprint. 1987.

Furer-Haimendorf, Christoph von. *Himalayan Traders*. New York: St. Martin's Press. 1975.

George, Christopher S. trans. and ed. "The Candamahāroshana Tantra". *American Oriental Series*. Vol. 56. New Haven : American Oriental Society. 1974

Gonda, J. "The Indian Mantra" *Oriens* 26. 1963.

Govinda, A. *Foundations of Tibetan Mysticism*. London : 1959.

Griffith R.T.H. Trans. *The Hymns from the Rig Veda*. Banaras: E.J. Lazarus. 1920.

Grunwedel, A. *Mythologie des Buddhismus in Tibet und der Mongolei*. Leipzig : 1900.

Guenther, H, V. *Treasures on the Middle Way*. Berkeley: 1971.
_____ *The Tantric View of Life*. Berkeley: Shambala, 1972
_____ *Matrix of Mystery: Scientific and Humanistic Aspects of rDzogs-chen Thought*. Boulder: Shambhala. 1984.
_____ *The Creative Vision*. Novato, Ca: Matrix Publication. 1987.

Hakeda, Yoshito. Trans. *Kukai: Major Works*. New York: Columbia University Press. 1972.

Hammer, Leon. *Dragon Rises, Red Bird Flies: Psychology & Chinese Medicine*. New York: Station Hill Press. 1980.

Hopkins, Jeffrey. Trans. *The Kalacakra Tantra Rite of Initiation*. Wisdom Publications. 1985

Hurvitz, Leon. Trans. *Scripture of the Lotus Blossom of the Fine Dharma.* New York: Columbia University Press. 1976.

Hastions, James. ed. *Encyclopedia of Religion and Ethics.* Edinburgh: 1908-26.

Hiedegger. Martin. *An Introduction to Metaphysics.* Translated by Ralph Manheim. Garden City: Doubleday & Company. 1961.

Hoffman, Helmut. *The Religions of Tibet.* New York: Macmillan. 1961.

Hume, Robert Ernest. Trans. *The thirteen principal Upanishads Translated from the Sanskrit with an outline of the philosophy of the Upanishads.* London: Oxford University press. 1975.

Jones, R. L. "Spirit Possession and Society in Nepal". *Spirit possession in the Nepal Himalayas.* Warminister: Aris & Philips. 1975.

Jung, Carl G. *Psychology and Alchemy.* London: Routledge and Kegan Paul. 1953.

Kern, H. Trans. "The lotus of the True Law (Sanskrit Saddharma-Pundarīka)". *The Sacred Books of the East,* Vol.xxl. New York: Dover Publ. (1963). (first Published in 1884 by Clarendon Press, Oxford).

Komito, David Ross. *Nāgārjuna's "Seventy Stanzas" A Buddhist Psychology of Emptiness. Commentary on Nāgārjuna's text by Geshe Sonam Rinchen Translation of Text and Commentary by Tenzin Dorjee and David Ross Komito.* Ithaca,New York: Snowlion Publications. 1987

Li An-che. "The Bkah-brgyud Sect of Lamaism". *Journal of the American Oriental Society.* lxix 1949

Lessing, Ferdinand. *Yung-Ho-Kung; An Iconography of The Lamaist Cathedral in Peking with notes on Lamaist Mythology and Cult. Vol.1.* (Sino-Swedish Expedition, vol. 8 part 1). Stockholm: 1942

Lessing, F. and Wayman, A. Trans. *mkhas grub rje's Fundamentals of the Buddhist Tantras.* Translated from the Tibetan. The Hague: 1968.

Liebenthal, Walter trans. *The Sūtra of the Lord of Healing.* Peking: 1976.

Marshall, Sir John. *Mohenjo-Daro and the Indus Civilization.* 3 vols. London: 1931.

Macdonell, A.A. "Vedic Mythology". *Grundriss der Indo Arischen Philologie und Altertumskunde,herausgegeben von G. Buhler, iii Band.* Strassburg: Verlag von Karl J. Trubner. (N.D.).

Mishra, Rammurti S. *Yoga Sūtras: Textbook of Yoga Psychology.* New York: Anchor-Doubleday. 1973.

Morreale, Don. ed. *Buddhist America Centers, Retreat, Practises.* Santa Fe, New Mexico: John Muir Publications. 1988.

Nebesky-Wojkowitz, Rene de. *Oracles and Demons of Tibet: The Cult and Iconography of the Tibetan Protective Deities.* Mouton: 'S-Gravenhage: 1956.

Nepali, Gopal Singh. *The Newars: An Ethno-Sociological Study of a Himalayan Community.* Bombay: United Asia Publications. 1965.

O'Flaherty, Wendy. Trans. *The Rig Veda.* New York: Penguin Books. 1981.

Pott. P.H. *Yoga and Yantra. "Their Interrelationship and their Significance for Indian Archeology".* Trans. Rodney Needham. Koninklijk Institut voor Taalland-en Volkenkunde, Translation Series No, 8. The Hague. 1966.

Reinhard, J. "Shamanism Among The Raji Of Southwest Nepal". *Spirit Possession in the Himalayas.* Edited by John Hitchcock and Rex Jones. Warminister, London: Aris & Philips. 1976

Richardson, Allen. *East comes West: Asian religions and cultures in North America.* New York: Pilgrim Press. 1985.

Ronaldshay, Lord. *Lands of the Thunderbolt.* Berkeley-Hong Kong: Snow Lion Graphics/SLG Books reprint. 1987.

Shane, John. ed. *The Crystal and the Way of light Sūtra, Tantra and Dzogchen The Teachings of Namkhai Norbu.* New York: Routledge & Kegan Paul. 1986.

Schmid, T. *The Eightyfive Siddhas.* Stockholm: University Publ. 1958.

Shahidullah, M. ed. and trans. *Les Chants Mystiques de Kanha et de Saraha; les Doha-kosa it les Carya.* Paris: 1928

Singer, Milton. ed. *Krishna: Myths, Rites and Attitudes.* Honolulu: 1966.

Sinha, Surajit. "A Note on the concept of sexual union for spiritual quest among the Vaisnava preachers in the Bhāmmij belt of Purulia and Singbhūm". *Eastern Anthropologist 14* (1961). pp. 194-6.

Snellgrove, D. L. *Buddhist Himalaya*. Oxford : 1957.

_____ ed. and trans. *Hevajra Tantra*. 2 vols. *London Oriental Series*. London: Oxford University Press. 1959.

Stacton, David. *Kāliyuga. A Quarrel with the Gods*. London, 1965.

Stablein, William. "A Medical-cultural System among the Tibetan and Newar Buddhists: Ceremonial Medicine". *Kailash 1*. 1974.

_____ "Mahākāla Neo-Shaman: Master of the Ritual". *Spirit Possession in the Nepal Himalayas*. Edited by John Hitchcock and Rex Jones. London: Aris & Phillips. 1975.

_____ "A Descriptive Analysis of the content of Nepalese Buddhist Pūjās as a Medical Cultural System with References to Tibetan Parallels". *The Realm of the Extrahuman: Ideas and Actions*. Edited by Agehānanda Bhārati. Mouton: The Hague. 1976.

_____ "Tantric Medicine and Ritual Blessings". *The Tibet Journal: Newark Museum Tibetan Symposium Papers*. Dharmasāla: Dalai Lama's Library of Tibetan Works and Archives. (1976) vol. 1 No. 3-4 pp. 55-69.

_____ "Textual Criticism and Tibetan Medicine". *The Tibet Society Bulletin*. Bloomington, Indiana: 1977.

_____ "The Medical Soteriology and Transsignification of Karma in the Buddhist Tantric Tradition". *Karma and Rebirth in Classical Indian Traditions*. edited by Wendy Doneger O'Flaherty. Berkeley: University of California Press. 1980.

Tart, Charles T. "Psychedelic Experiences Associated with a Novel Hypnotic Procedure, Mutual Hypnosis". *Altered States of Consciousness*. New York: John Wiley and Sons. 1969.

Tart, Charles T. ed. *Altered States of Consciousness*: New York: J.Wiley. 1969.

Tucci, G. *Tibetan Painted Scrolls*. 3 Vols. Rome : 1949.

_____ *The Theory and Practice of the Mandala*. London : 1961.

Turner, Victor. *The Drums of Affliction: A Study Of Religious Processes Among the Ndembu of Zambia*. London: International African institute. 1968.

_____ *The Forest of Symbols: Aspects of Ndembu Ritual*. New York: Cornell University Press. 1967.

_____ "The ritual process: Structure and Anti-Structure". *Symbol Myth, And Ritual Series*. Ithaca: Cornell University Press. 1969.

Trungpa, Chogyam. *Cutting Through Spiritual Materialism*. Boston and London: 1987.

Wayman, A. "Female energy and symbolism in the Buddhist Tantras". *History of Religions* vol. 2 pp. 73-111.

_____ *The Buddhist Tantras: Light on Indo-Tibetan Esotericism*. New York: Weiser 1973.

_____ "Buddhist Tantric Medicine Theory on Behalf of Oneself and Others". *Kailash 1* (1973).

_____ "Notes on the Three Myrobalans". *Phi Theta Annual 5* (1954-1955)

_____ "The Significance of Mantras, from the Veda down to Buddhist Tantric Practice". *Adyar Library Bulletin*. 1975.

_____ "The Concept of Poison in Buddhism". *Oriens 10*. 1957.

Waddell, L. A. *Lamaism or the Buddhism of Tibet*. Cambridge, England: 1967.

Wallace, Anthony F.C. *Religion: An Anthropological View*. New York: Random House. 1966.

Watts, Alan W. ed. *Patterns of Myth*. New York: G. Braziller. 1963.

Wheelwright, Philip. *Metaphor and Reality*. Bloomington. Indiana: University Press. 1962.

Williams, George M. *The Quest for Meaning of Swami Vivekānanda:* Chico, Ca: New Horizons Press. 1974.

Willis, J. D. *The Diamond Light of the Eastern Dawn: Collection of Tibetan Buddhist Meditation*. New York: Simon and Schuster. 1972.

Yongden, Lama. Illustrated by Roger Williams. *Mipam*. Berkelely-Hong Kong: Snow Lion Graphics/SLG Books reprint. 1986.

Zaehner, Robert Charles. *Mysticism: Sacred and Profane:* Oxford & New York: Oxford Univ. Press. 1967.

Zimmer, Heinrich. *Myths and Symbols in Indian Art and Civilization*. Bollingen Series No.6. New York: 1946.

Zurcher, Erik. *The Buddhist Conquest of China*. 2 vols. Leiden: 1970.

Index

ཁ། །འཕྲིན་ལས་མགོན་པོ་མ་ནིང་ལ་ནམོ། །

Mahākāla - Gombo Maning

**Amitābha
Buddha of Endless Light**

Maitreya
The Coming Buddha

Plate 1: The first page and translation of the Makākāla-Tantra.

Photograph by William Stablein Jr.

Translation of the first folio of the Mahākālatantra

Om our respects to the illustrious Mahākāla: I heard that at one time the Lord was dwelling in the womb of the Goddess in a desireless state.

The goddess asked: What method will the Lord use for those beings who have fallen into phenomenal existence? Oh Divine One, you are the manifestation of reality through which they will be happy.

The Lord replied: I will tell you about the yoga of creation and completion through which realities exist. Oh Goddess, listen carefully! Creation is maintained relative to dissolution. Such a path, i.e. the yoga of creation and completion has the potential to be harmoniously performed which bears fruits like a female giving birth. Therefore the initiation should be perfromed and the yogi should practice according to the teaching of yogic practice. When meditating according to that discipline, after one is in a state of conjugal union such a path arises – the path of creation.

Plate 2. The head lama Sa-bcu-rin-po-che with the pointed hat and right front my teacher Padma-rgyal-mtschan in ceremony.

Plate 3. Portrait of Sa-bcu-rin-po-che.

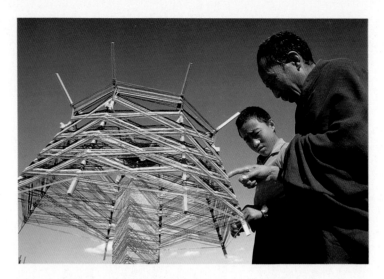

Plate 4. Petsan and student weaving five-colored mansion of Mahākāla called "sky" (nam-mkhah) and "The immeasurable dwelling" (gzhal-yas-khang).

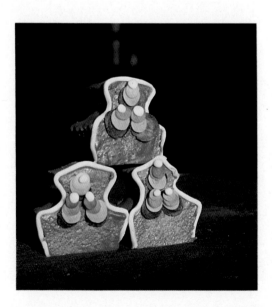

Plate 5: Bali offering as substitute for flesh and blood transformed into the five-fold Buddha-nature through the five colors. Bali is the sanskrit term also used in the Tibetan cultural context for food offerings.

Plate 6. Young lama constructing the sacred offering cakes of Mahākāla with the five colors of fire that burn away mental obstacles to enlightenment.

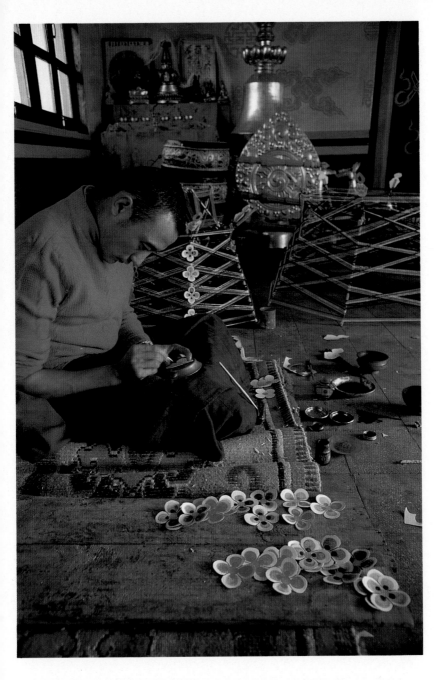

Plate 6A: Lama constructing five-colored paper flowers to adorn "sky" symbol.

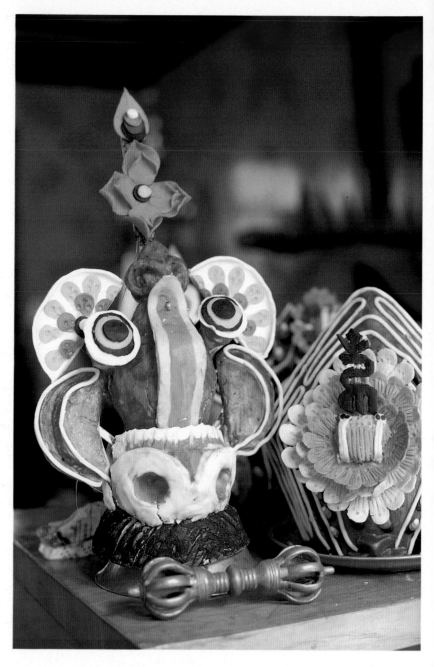

Plate 7. An offering cake representing the five senses called the five powers (dbang-po-lnga), also in five colors.

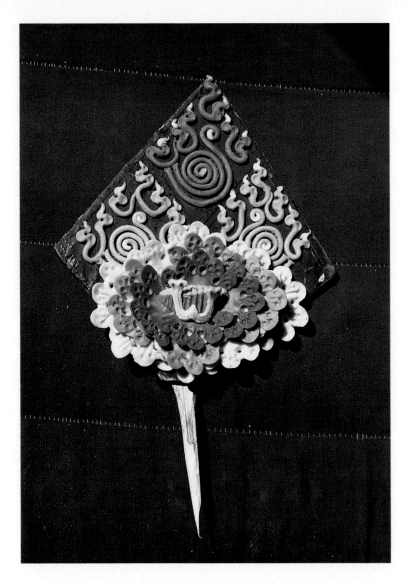

Plate 7A: Adornment of fire and flower for offering cake.

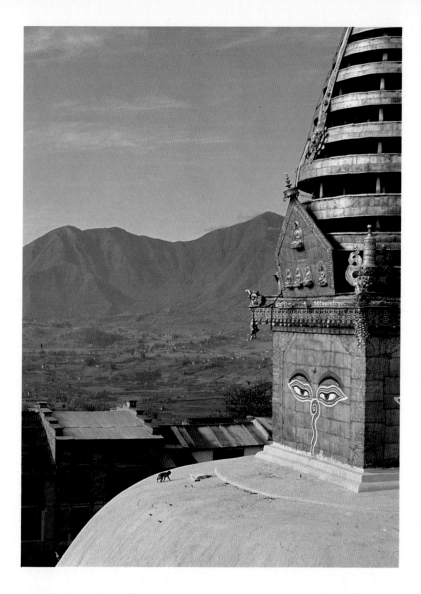

Plate 8. The divine eyes on the great reliquary (caitya) of
Svāyambhūnāth. The four cornered pillar from which the eyes are
staring represent the four keys of balance and harmony, i.e.
literally, the four domains of Brahma (Brahmavihāra) which gives
us an idea of how the eyes are seeing (with friendliness, compassion, joy and equanimity).

Plate 11. Priest making offerings.

Plate 9. Nepalese twohanded Mahākāla.

Plate 10. The Brahmin Mahākāla.

Plate 12. Sonam

Plate 13. The spire rising above the eyes. The golden spire (chantrabali) with its thirteen circular canopies (chatra) representing the thirteen realms that a person might pass through on the way to enlightenment and the sacred knowledge of all forms (sarvakarajnatajnana).

Photograph by Roger Williams

Plate 14. Ratnabirsingh.

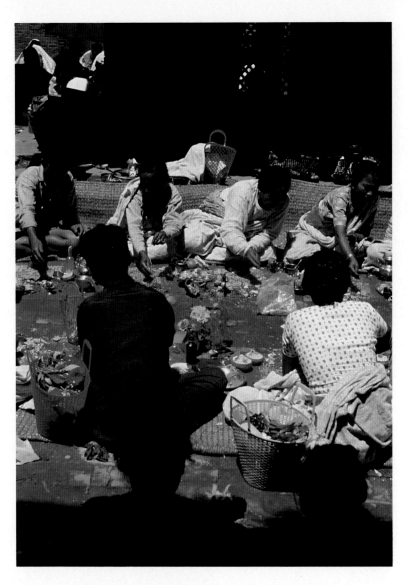

Plate 15. Outdoor ceremony during Gunla.

Plate 16. Tibetan sacred music at the monkey temple.

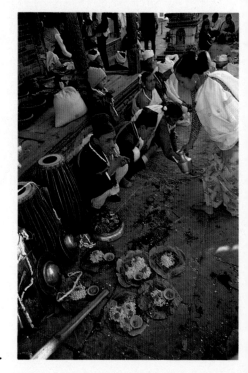

Plate 17. Nepalese musicians
playing sacred music in the
morning time at Svāyambhūnāth.

Plate 18. Mahākāla with the crown of five skullheads representing the five Buddhas.

Plate 19. Mahākāla with his five-colored mansion.

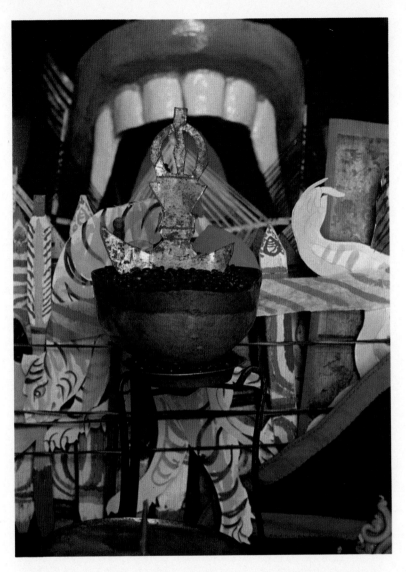

Plate 20. Another perspective of the skull that is filled with black
beans indicating the conglomerated and congealed darkness within
ourselves about to be fed to The Great-Black-One.

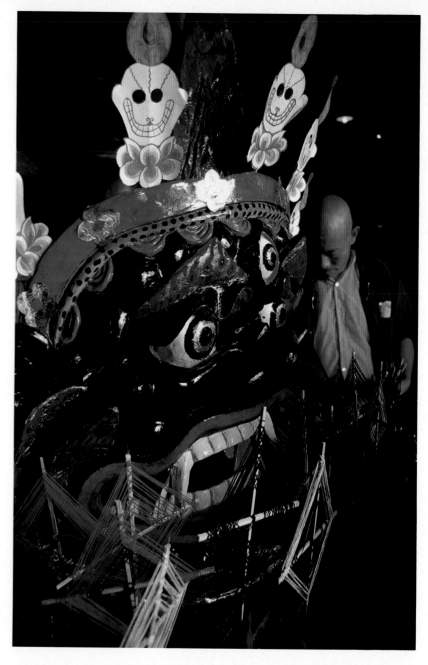

Plate 21. The image staring through the iron gates at the pilgrims.

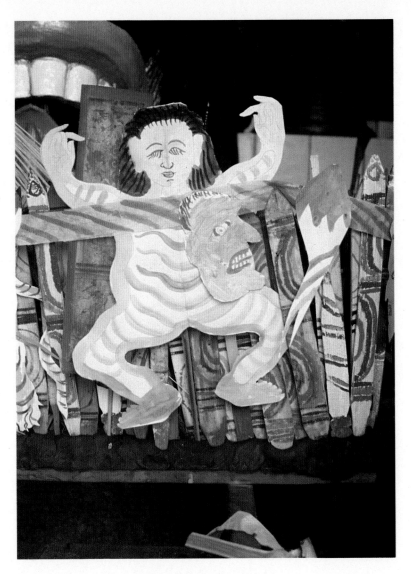

Plate 22. Image of flayed
human skin.

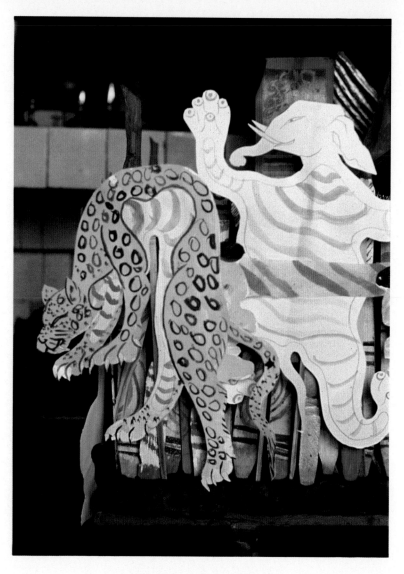

Plage 23. Image of flayed
tiger and elephant skin.

Plate 24. Weapons
used for torture.

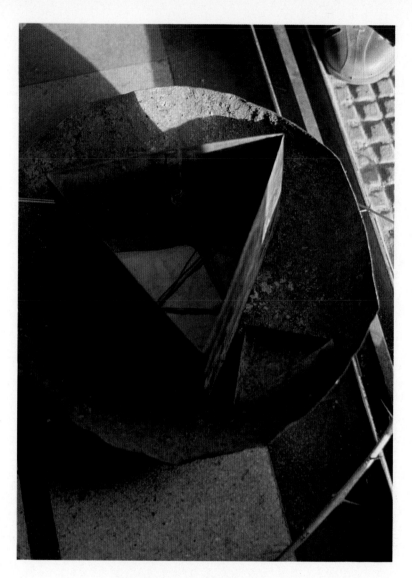

Plate 25. One of the black boxes
that contains the effigy.

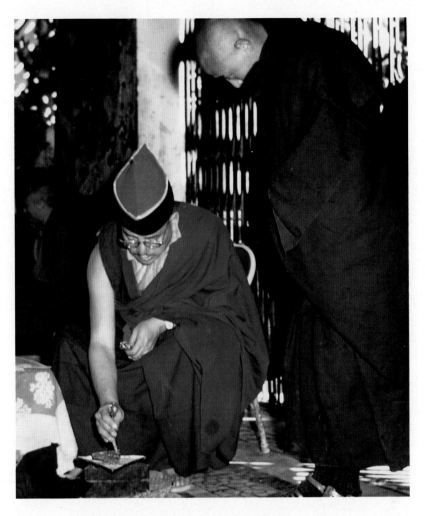

Plate 26. The priest becomes Mahākāla in order to
quell the dark forces with his vajra-dagger.

Plate 27. Eight-handed Mahākāla.

Plate 28. Four-faced twelve-handed Mahākāla.

Plate 29. Karma bkah-rgyud-pa four handed Mahākāla
with consort Sri Devi and retinue.

Plate 30. Four-handed Mahākāla.

Plate 31. Six-handed Mahākāla.

Plate 32. Sixteen-handed Mahākāla.

Plate 33. Two-handed Mahākāla.

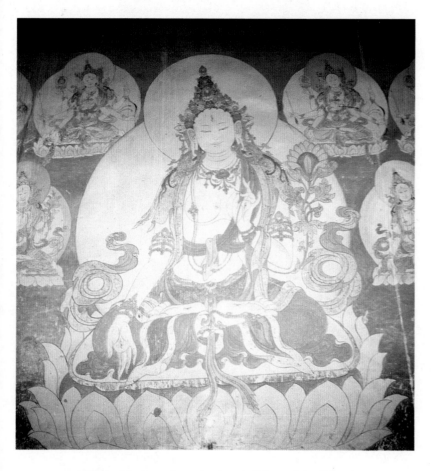

Plate 34. A compassionate goddess, the other side of Mahākāla.

Photograph by Roger Williams

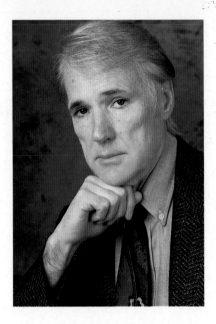

Plate 35: The author.

At the time of Woodstock, Dr. Stablein was searching on the Asian Subcontinent for a lost Tibetan Tantric Buddhist manuscript about The Great-Black-One (Mahākāla). He was also exploring the Philosophy and practice of the transformation of darkness – a plethora of images and symbols related to the dynamics of relationships and addictions.

His study and practice led to the translation of ancient written texts and practical spiritual modalities of ritual and meditation that contain solutions to life's addictions. He has been working for over a decade translating these solutions and parallel experiences into his practice as a mentor-counselor in the field of addiction and recovery. William's goal is to convey his experiences in terms of his own quest for the wisdom of the East as it has evolved in the milieu of his own family of origin and American culture.

Although there are many books on Eastern meditation and practice there are few if any books on the details of the writer's own experiences and personal history of the quest itself – the core of any authentic tradition (not unlike the Tibetan tradition of spiritual biography called Rnam Thar).

William accurately describes, maybe mythologizing, the significant details of his life that led him to the quest of The Great-Black-One. William's journey as a Fulbright Scholar led him into his own past, where he rediscovered not only his grandfather who had started him on this path, but his own proclivity for the healing arts.

This book is about the flow of images in his own life that led to his search, study and practice. William works as a consultant in the area of addiction and co-dependency in Northern California.